A Guide to Evidence-Based Group Work

A Guide to Evidence-Based Group Work

MARK J. MACGOWAN

OXFORD
UNIVERSITY PRESS

2008

Oxford University Press, Inc., publishes works that further
Oxford University's objective of excellence
in research, scholarship, and education.

Oxford   New York
Auckland   Cape Town   Dar es Salaam   Hong Kong   Karachi
Kuala Lumpur   Madrid   Melbourne   Mexico City   Nairobi
New Delhi   Shanghai   Taipei   Toronto

With offices in
Argentina   Austria   Brazil   Chile   Czech Republic   France   Greece
Guatemala   Hungary   Italy   Japan   Poland   Portugal   Singapore
South Korea   Switzerland   Thailand   Turkey   Ukraine   Vietnam

Published by Oxford University Press, Inc.
198 Madison Avenue, New York, New York 10016

www.oup.com

Library of Congress Cataloging-in-Publication Data
Macgowan, Mark J.
   A guide to evidence-based group work / Mark J. Macgowan. — 1st ed.
   p. cm.
Includes bibliographical references and index.
ISBN 978-0-19-518345-0 (pbk.: alk. paper)   1. Social group work.
2. Evidence-based social work.   I. Title.   II. Title: Evidence-based group work.
   HV45.M24 2008
   361'.4—dc22   2007023858

9   8   7   6   5   4   3   2   1

Printed in the United States of America
on acid-free paper

This book is dedicated to the memory
of my mother, Rosemary F. Macgowan,
1927–2007.

Preface

The purpose of this book is to educate and assist readers interested in conducting evidence-based group work (EBGW). The intention is to help group workers more effectively achieve their desired processes and outcomes. Building on developments in evidence-based practice (EBP) in the health disciplines, psychology, and social work, the book outlines a four-stage process for increasing the effectiveness and helpfulness of group work. Although utilizing a common framework for EBP (i.e., a stage process), this book includes resources specifically for group work. It is distinguished from other group work texts by its emphasis on describing the process of EBGW, as opposed to serving as a compendium of evidence-based group interventions. It offers a unique and compelling perspective for advancing best practices for group work.

This book will help group workers build on their competencies to learn basic knowledge and skills that will allow them to become evidence-based group workers. The steps needed to achieve this objective are detailed, and practical learning activities to facilitate skill acquisition are included. Readers will learn the stages of EBGW: (a) formulate a practice question, (b) search for evidence, (c) critically appraise the evidence, and (d) apply the best available evidence and evaluate its effects on the outcomes of the groups and well-being of the group members. The following are features keyed to respective chapters:

1. Step-by-step guidelines for implementing EBGW in practice (Chapter 1 and throughout the book)
2. Guidelines for formulating **M**ember-relevant, **A**nswerable, and **P**ractical (MAP) questions (Chapter 2)

3. Instructions on how to search for answers to "MAP" questions using the "COMPASS" search strategy (Chapter 3)
4. Extensive sources of evidence related to group work, both in print and online, available both for purchase and for no charge (Chapter 3)
5. Guidelines for completing an efficient and effective critical review of group-based research, such as randomized clinical trials involving groups, literature reviews (systematic and nonsystematic), and group-related measures (Chapter 4)
6. Presentation and selective review of practice-relevant group instruments, such as measures of group leadership and group processes (e.g., cohesion, therapeutic factors, engagement, interaction) (Chapter 4)
7. A discussion of the importance of paying attention to group members' cultures, values, and needs in selecting interventions/techniques (Chapters 4 and 5)
8. Examples of simple but effective research designs for assessing individual and group outcomes (Chapter 5)
9. Steps for advancing EBGW in research, practice, and higher and continuing education (Chapter 6)
10. Case examples, tables, and figures to facilitate learning (throughout the book)

This book is designed to supplement existing texts on group work. It does not include theoretical models and concepts, the historical development of group work, extended discussions of the value and ethical principles of group work, or presentations of the developmental stages of group work and worker actions within those stages. Thus, readers who would like to apply the principles and practices in this book should have sufficient foundation group theory and knowledge, values, skills, and clinical expertise (or supervision) to know when evidence is appropriate for a client or group situation and when evidence or practices are outside of their competence (principles that are delineated in the first chapter). In addition, some of the material in the book requires a foundation of research knowledge, such as that taught in introductory research-methods courses.

This book is suitable for graduate-level group work courses in social work, education, counseling, psychology, nursing, and psychiatry. The content may be taught over four to six sessions in a semester-long group work course, with the principles infused throughout. More discussion about educational approaches can be found in the last chapter. This text is intended primarily for group work students and practitioners. However, it may be useful for administrators, program evaluators, and researchers as a guide for implementing EBGW in their organizations, and as a resource for locating group-based instruments and research.

Acknowledgments

This book would not have been possible without the support of individuals who discussed and reviewed drafts of the manuscript. First, the students in my graduate course in group work helped refine the material and provided sources for some of the case examples in the book. Specifically, Karyll Scott, Inge Sengelmann, and Brett Engle provided comments on early drafts, and Cynthia Fraga reviewed later drafts. Thanks to colleagues at Florida International University: Stephen Wong for his substantial comments on the sections on single-subject design, and Frederick Newman and Andrés Gil for reviewing parts of the manuscript. Deep appreciation to Maeda Galinsky, Charles Garvin, and David Fike, who served as sounding boards in the preparation of chapters; the advice and support of these mentors were invaluable. Beulah Rothman was my first group work mentor; she died long before this book was conceived but had indirect influence on its development. Any balance achieved between preserving research integrity and the group process can be credited to her influence. I am also indebted to my anonymous reviewers, whose suggestions for improvement reminded me how important peer review is! Although this book has been strengthened by the assistance of these colleagues and reviewers, I bear full responsibility for its limitations.

Tangible resources and support came from Dean Ray Thomlison and former Executive Dean Ronald Berkman during the writing. Appreciation must be extended to Editor Maura Roessner at Oxford for her patience in listening to stories of hurricanes and other crises.

Most important, I would like to thank *mi familia*—Rosemary, Elizabeth, and Jessica—for their sacrifice, support, and understanding during the writing of this book—*con mucho amor.*

Contents

PART I

FOUNDATIONS

1

Introduction to Evidence-Based Group Work

Evidence-based group work (EBGW) is defined as *a process of the judicious and skillful application in group work of the best evidence, based on research merit, impact, and applicability, using evaluation to ensure that desired results are achieved.*[1] This definition is consistent with the literature on evidence-based practice (EBP) and evidence-based medicine (EBM), from which EBP evolved (Cournoyer, 2004; Gibbs, 2003; Haynes, Sackett, Gray, Cook, & Guyatt, 1996; Institute of Medicine, 2001; Proctor & Rosen, 2004; Straus, Richardson, Glasziou, & Haynes, 2005). EBGW is relevant to both treatment and task groups. The principles and practices of EBGW can be applied to groups whose primary purpose is to meet the socioemotional needs of its members (e.g., group therapy, group counseling) or to accomplish a goal that is not linked to the needs of the members of the group (e.g., committees, teams, task forces) (Toseland & Rivas, 2005, p. 14). Most of the examples in this book relate to treatment groups. The term "group work" means "goal-directed activity with small treatment and task groups aimed at meeting socioemotional needs and accomplishing tasks. This activity is directed to individual members of a group and to the group as a whole within a system of service delivery" (Toseland & Rivas, 2005, p. 12). Group work may function in many settings in both independent and organization-based practice, such as in hospitals, clinics, counseling centers, churches, and schools.

Assumptions of Evidence-Based Group Work

EBGW includes a number of elements and assumptions that also characterize EBM and EBP. First, EBGW incorporates critical thinking, which involves "the careful appraisal of beliefs and actions to arrive at well-reasoned ones that maximize the likelihood of helping clients and avoiding harm" (Gambrill, 2004, p. 3). It involves not only using knowledge and skills in practice but also questioning what is taken for granted (Gambrill, 2004). It helps practitioners to spot and avoid errors and fallacies in thinking and in practice such as inaccurate observation, selective observation, and overgeneralization (Rubin & Babbie, 2005). Emotional reactions can lead to errors in judgment and motivated reasoning (Ditto, Munro, Apanovitch, Scepansky, & Lockhart, 2003; Kunda, 1990). EBGW requires a willingness to participate in critical inquiry of cherished beliefs and practices. It requires an attitude of falsification, defined as "a willingness to seek information that challenges our own understandings and an openness to contradictory evidence" (Gilgun, 2005, p. 52). Thus, even "strong" evidence should be considered tentative or provisional, subject to change as new evidence emerges.

Second, EBGW is a *process* and not just a *product*. EBGW requires workers to *systematically* collect and appraise evidence, as this yields the best available evidence. Evidence-based group workers do not rely only on their own experience or on evidence that is conveniently available, such as assembled lists of "evidence-based" products; instead they engage in a systematic process that expands research to include additional sources that might yield more rigorous and applicable evidence (Corcoran, 2003; Rosenthal, 2004).

Third, EBGW assumes that science and practice are interrelated and should not be viewed or practiced as polar opposites. An evidence-based group worker considers both research factors and practice considerations. Practice judgment alone is not sufficient, and neither is research evidence that may be inappropriate to apply because, for example, the group worker is not trained to use it (in the case of a group intervention). Group work must be congruent with both practice and research in order to be helpful to the people it serves.

Fourth, EBGW assumes that variables in group life are measurable. For example, problems, goals, or tasks must be specified and assessed in order to assess the outcomes of group members. To assess group processes or group dynamics, dimensions of group life such as cohesion must be measured.

Relatedly, the emphasis of EBGW is on outcomes, which may be problem- or group-related and proximal or distal depending on when they are measured in group. The group worker, group member(s), and/or group determine what the *desired* outcomes may be. Table 1.1 gives examples of different outcomes in groups. The rows indicate subjects of outcomes (problem-related or group-related). Problem-related outcomes are the concerns or challenges that group members bring to the group, and are likely the reason they joined the group. Examples include depression, alcohol and other drug use, and anxiety. These outcomes could also be strength-oriented. For example, a desired outcome could be to achieve abstinence, to attain a new level of self-confidence, or to establish a new social network. Group-related outcomes emerge as a result of group formation and are not directly related to the problems that brought members to the group (although they may be indirectly related). These out-

Table 1.1.   Examples of Outcomes in Groups

	Timing of Outcomes	
Subject of Outcomes	*Proximal Outcomes (during life of group)*	*Distal Outcomes (end of group or beyond)*
Problem-Related Outcomes	*Problem-Related Proximal Outcomes*	*Problem-Related Distal Outcomes* [a]
	Reduced level of depression by third group session (compared with level at pretest)	Reduce depression to subclinical level by end of group
	Reduced level of marijuana use by the midpoint of group sessions	Marijuana abstinence by the end of group and at three months after
	Two new persons added to a member's support network by session five	Increase a group member's social support network by 50%
Group-Related Outcomes	*Group-Related Proximal Outcomes ("Process" Outcomes)*[a]	*Group-Related Distal Outcomes*[a]
	Rating of "good" or better on member rating of group satisfaction (at end of each session)	Average of "good" or better on member rating of group satisfaction by the end of group (averaged from all sessional ratings)
	Improved level of cohesion by sixth session (compared with fourth session)	
	All members verbally contribute in the next two sessions	

[a] These three items include the types of outcomes discussed in this book, with an emphasis on group-related proximal outcomes (process outcomes).

comes relate to group factors, such as interaction, cohesion, leadership, and group satisfaction. Examples include achievement of a certain level of cohesion, verbal contribution by the member, and member's satisfaction with the group.

The columns relate to the timing of outcomes, with the reference being the life of the group. Proximal outcomes are those that occur during the life of the group, with the end of the group being the marker for distal outcomes. Distal outcomes, if they are measured, may extend beyond the life of the group. For example, a group member's abstinence might be tracked and documented beyond the life of a group. Group workers may be concerned with any of the cells represented in the table. However, this book focuses on the three cells that are noted, with a particular emphasis on group-related proximal outcomes.

Sixth, EBGW builds on group worker knowledge and skills gained from introductory coursework in research methods and group work. Some of the discussions related to the guidelines for assessing group-based research presented in this book, for example, require some knowledge of research methods.

Similarly, weighing evidence and applying it in practice require knowledge and skills beyond what is offered in this book; these skills are gained from coursework and fieldwork in introductory research methods and group work. For example, an understanding of group dynamics, leadership, values and ethics, and methods in the various stages of group work is an essential foundation for EBGW. Thus, some of the materials presented in this book assume that group workers have a foundation in group work and research methods. This guide is not a cookbook for essential group work practice.

Historical Context of Evidence-Based Group Work

EBGW builds on developments within the evidence-based-practice movement and in the historical tradition of group work. EBP is rooted in EBM, which was "a term for the clinical learning strategy developed at McMaster Medical School in Canada in the 1970s" (Rosenthal, 2004, p. 20).[2] The term "evidence-based medicine" was coined in 1992 by the Evidence-Based Medicine Working Group at McMaster, led by Gordon Guyatt (Evidence-Based Medicine Working Group, 1992). Allied health professions, psychology, and social work followed.

Some of the elements of EBGW can be traced to the early years, when group workers functioned on the basis of their notions of what would help people: "[t]heir experiences, based on ideas they dared to try out, were their 'theories' " (Wilson, 1976, p. 2). The blending of practice with theories and techniques from other disciplines such as sociology and psychology developed during the early part of the 20th century, and the development of schools of social welfare (particularly Western Reserve University) stimulated the growth of science-based practice (Wilson, 1976). It is clear from the writings of this time, such as Grace Coyle's address to the American Association of Group Workers in 1946 titled "On Becoming Professional" (Coyle, 1948, pp. 81–97), that an important concern for early social group workers was to develop and use a body of knowledge, or evidence, in practice. Other social group work theorists over the decades, such as Wilbur Newstetter, Margaret Hartford, Helen Northen, Robert Vinter, and William Schwartz, advanced an understanding of how groups can be helpful to clients (Hartford, 1976).

Evidence for the benefits and potential pitfalls of group work accumulated early in social work and in other disciplines (e.g., Lewin, Lippitt, & White, 1939; Newstetter & Feldstein, 1930; Pratt, 1922). By mid-century this research had become sufficient to result in reviews of the accumulated evidence (Burchard, Michaels, & Kotkov, 1948; Thomas, 1943). The research evidence for group work has since been enriched by additional empirical studies. With the development of meta-analytic methodology (Glass, McGaw, & Smith, 1981), systematic reviews of the literature have documented the substantial evidence for the efficacy of group work (Ang & Hughes, 2002; Burlingame, Fuhriman, & Mosier, 2003; Hoag & Burlingame, 1997; Kösters, Burlingame,

Nachtigall, & Strauss, 2006; Tillitski, 1990). Much of this evidence is related to theoretical models that readily lend themselves to measurement. As a result, behavioral group work has been the change theory most often reported in the empirical literature since the late 1960s (Rose, 1969, 2004; Tolman & Molidor, 1994). Although they are relatively few in number, empirical studies of mutual-aid processes have recently appeared in the literature (Gitterman, 2004).

Despite the history of use of elements of EBGW, there has been little discussion of EBGW as a complete practice in the literature. Even so, there have been discussions about how group workers can evaluate practice; most group work texts include assessment and evaluation, and there have been important efforts to help group workers engage in empirical group work (e.g., Rose, 1980). In addition, there are strategies for promoting research utilization to improve group work (e.g., Macgowan, 2003; Rose, 1984, 1992). Specifically, Rose (1984) outlined a systematic process for solving particular group problems involving a partnership between the group leader and group members, but it lacked steps for systematically incorporating the best research evidence into the model. Macgowan (2003) outlined a process of using a measure of group process and the literature for increasing engagement in groups.

Although these efforts and models provided examples of elements and foundations of EBGW, it is only recently that the process and content of evidence-based practice for group work began to be described in publications. In the first publication about EBGW, Pollio defined evidence-based group work as "the conscientious and judicious use of evidence in current best practice" (Pollio, 2002, p. 57). More specifically, the evidence-based group worker is one who

> [a]ppraises critically systematically-collected evidence from all sources; Acquires knowledge through reading professional journals, attending conferences and presentations relevant to specific populations of practice, and writing/presenting knowledge that he/she develops; Evaluates the outcomes of practice, using consistent methods; Implements models (either existing or developed by the practitioner) consistently and rationally; Attends to the impact of individual differences in making evidence-based practice decisions; and Incorporates evidence in understanding group process, leadership, and development. (Pollio, 2002, pp. 65–66)

Pollio's contribution was an important foundation in the development of EBGW. Macgowan (2006a) subsequently built on this foundation by defining EBGW as "the judicious and skillful application in group work of the best evidence, based on research merit and practice relevance and appropriateness, using evaluation to ensure desired results are achieved" (p. 2). In that publication, Macgowan (2006a) identified the types of research evidence relevant for group work, provided direction on finding sources of group-based evidence and tools to examine evidence, and offered leads for evaluating the application of evidence in group work. However, as a journal article, the publication was limited in the resources it could provide within its pages. Indeed, both Pollio's

(2002) and Macgowan's (2006a) publications remain more conceptual than practical. This book builds on the definitions of EBP and EBGW by detailing a systematic process and extensive set of resources for undertaking EBGW.

In summary, the integration of science and practice has a long history in group work, and some of these elements are in EBGW. However, as based on EBP and EBM with their emphasis on ethical, evidentiary, and application issues representing a paradigm shift from previous practice approaches (Gambrill, 2006a, p. 339), EBGW offers much more. Unlike with the growing fields of EBP and EBM, there has been little discussion and advancement of an evidence-based framework for group work. In addition, there has not been an articulation of the critical steps that are at the core of EBGW.

Essentials of Evidence-Based Group Work

Although there are many varying definitions of EBP in the literature, there are common themes. Across definitions, EBP is a process that requires practitioners to (a) use findings based on best available evidence that demonstrates predictable and effective results; (b) use clinical expertise and professional ethics; (c) collaborate with clients with their best interests in mind, considering the values and judgments of clients; and (d) evaluate outcomes to see whether predicted results for clients were achieved (Cournoyer & Powers, 2002; Gambrill, 1999; Gibbs, 2003; Haynes et al., 1996; Rosenthal, 2004; Vandiver, 2002). EBGW includes these themes in three essential elements: best evidence, application in practice, and evaluation.

Best Evidence

The term *evidence* refers to "unobserved as well as observed phenomena if the former reflects signs or indications that support, substantiate, or prove their existence, accuracy, or truth" (Cournoyer, 2004, p. 3). However, phenomena that are unexamined or unobserved are considered less credible than evidence derived from observation, experience, or experimentation (Cournoyer, 2004). Items subject to observation include personal experience, results from one's own practice evaluation, expert opinion, case studies, randomized clinical trials, and meta-analyses (Cournoyer, 2004; Pollio, 2002). Thus, the term *evidence* is broad and is not limited to information derived only through observation or experience (i.e., empirical evidence).

There are differences in the literature as to what is considered the "best" evidence. Some consider the best evidence to be solely research based (Gibbs, 2003; Institute of Medicine, 2001; Rosenthal, 2004; Sackett, Rosenberg, Gray, Haynes, & Richardson, 1996). Others suggest a broader conceptualization including all knowledge, such as that acquired from both quantitative and qualitative research studies, expert opinion, and the results of personal practice evaluations (Cournoyer, 2004; Pollio, 2002, 2006), as long as the evidence "yields documentary support for the conclusion that a practice or service has a reasonable probability of effectiveness" (Cournoyer, 2004, p. 14). Many of the definitions overlap on the point that evidence must be (a) the most rigorous available and (b) relevant and appropriate for the client's situation, preferences, values, and needs (Cournoyer, 2004; Gibbs, 2003; Gray, 1997; Haynes et al., 1996; Institute of Medicine, 2001; Klein & Bloom, 1995; McKibbon, 1998). Thus, the quality of the evidence is determined by an assessment of its research merit, impact, and applicability to the group situation, which are described in full next.

Research Merit (Rigor)

The first area to be evaluated is the rigor of the evidence, or its efficacy in achieving a desired outcome. The most desirable evidence "links a particular intervention with a desired outcome" (Hyde, Falls, Morris, & Schoenwald, 2003, p. 4). The degree of confidence that an intervention will produce a desired outcome may be assessed using a " 'hierarchy of evidence,' with each level yielding a higher comfort level of certainty, from the most basic level of anecdotal or word-of-mouth testimonials to the highest level of scientific study, the controlled clinical trial with random assignment of subjects" (Hyde et al., 2003, p. 5). Such hierarchies of evidence or rankings of methodological rigor are commonly used in reporting the evidence base for interventions (e.g., Center for Evidence-Based Medicine at Oxford University, 2001; Chambless et al., 1998; Chambless & Hollon, 1998; Corcoran, 2003; Guyatt et al., 1995; Rosenthal, 2004) and are the best for determining treatment effects in group work (Gant, 2004). The preference is for research evidence and theories that have been tested for accuracy (see Box 1.1) and that increase the confidence that the intervention was specifically responsible for beneficial effects (American Psychological Association, 2002), as opposed to evidence that is authority based, such as "the opinions of others, pronouncements of 'authorities,' unchecked intuition, anecdotal experience, and popularity (the authority of the crowd)" (Gambrill, 1999, p. 7). The pitfalls of relying *only* on clinical judgment have been well documented (Dawes, Faust, & Meehl, 2002; Grove & Meehl, 1996; Grove, Zald, Lebow, Snitz, & Nelson, 2000; Westen & Weinberger, 2004). Although the preference is for research evidence and theories tested for accuracy, not all evidence has been tested in research. However, the rigor of all evidence, whether research based or authority based, must be critically appraised. A more detailed discussion of rigor and how it is determined is offered in Chapters 3 and 4.

Impact

The second area to be evaluated is the strength and direction of the research findings—that is, the impact of the intervention or technique.[3] Such

---

Box 1.1.   The Role of Theory in EBGW

A theory may be defined as "a set of interrelated constructs (concepts), definitions, and propositions that present a systematic view of phenomena by specifying relations among variables, with the purpose of explaining and predicting the phenomena" (Kerlinger, 1986, p. 9). Examples of traditional theories in group work include field theory (Lewin, 1951, 1975), social exchange (Thibaut & Kelley, 1959), social systems (Parsons & Shils, 1951), and psychodynamic theory applied to groups (Freud, 1922; Redl, 1942, 1944). Often drawing from these traditional theories are particular intervention theories or models, such as group cognitive-behavior therapy (Petrocelli, 2002; Rose, 2004). Their ability to predict and explain makes theories and models helpful in guiding practice. After all, it was Kurt Lewin, a father of group dynamics, who said, "There is nothing so practical as a good theory" (Lewin, 1951, p. 169). So how can theory fit in EBGW? In the absence of specific research evidence, respected theories can help guide practice. However, theories in themselves are not necessarily beneficial for groups and group members, nor are they, by virtue of being theories, supported by research evidence. Theories may be untested, and particular theoretical approaches can be harmful.

Thus, the preference is for theories that have been tested in research and shown to be accurate. However, theories with research support need to be evaluated for their applicability; they may not be suitable for the group situation. Untested theories may be considered evidence based on authority. Although this book does not provide a guide specifically for evaluating the rigor of theories, a guide for evaluating evidence based on authority (presented in Chapter 4) may be used. If the group worker intends to apply the theory to a practice situation, then he or she is responsible for determining whether group members benefit from the theory, using such evaluation (Stage 4 of EBGW).

---

evaluation determines whether there was meaningful change among group members. Rigorous studies should report both statistical and clinical significance. Group workers must evaluate the magnitude of the effects of the intervention or technique. Are the findings sufficiently clear and powerful to change practice? Findings are usually either positive or neutral, but any findings of negative or damaging effects require that group workers closely examine the circumstances of those findings and avoid such interventions/techniques.

Applicability

Determining the best evidence is an iterative process between weighing the merit and impact of external research findings and applying practice considerations. EBGW is not an exercise in building knowledge for its own sake but rather in gaining research findings that will help clients (Gambrill, 1999), an "integration of practice methods and knowledge with research methods and knowledge" (Blythe, 1992, p. 3). Thus, as the evidence is assessed for its research rigor and impact, it is also assessed for its clinical relevance, appropriateness, or applicability, often called "clinical utility" or "clinical applicability" (American Psychological Association, 2002, p. 1053; Rosenthal, 2004,

p. 21). To evaluate the clinical utility of evidence, the worker considers the service delivery system (i.e., agency setting, if relevant, worker values and competence, and costs and benefits) and the group's values and needs. Thus, applicability is essentially an assessment of how relevant, suitable, and supportable an intervention/technique is for a particular practice situation. The process of weighing practice relevance and appropriateness and the methods for doing so are more fully discussed in Chapter 4.

Thus, determining best evidence involves considering research rigor, impact, and clinical applicability of the evidence. The process is not "the mindless application of rules and guidelines" (Haynes et al., 1996, p. A-15) but rather is guided by the worker's thoughtful consideration of the research evidence; worker values, ethics, knowledge, skills, and experience; and client and group situation. Figure 1.1 shows that clinical expertise, as developed for evidence-based clinical decision making in medicine, consists of weighing the practice context and circumstances (e.g., group situation and context), client preferences and actions, and research evidence. This dynamic and iterative

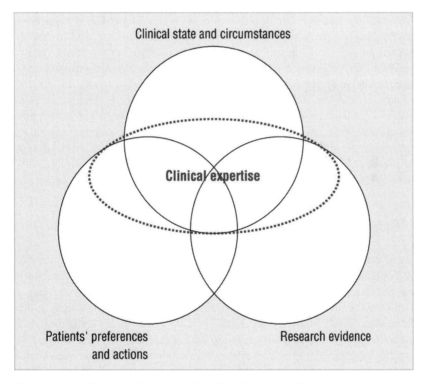

Figure 1.1. Model of evidence-based clinical decisions: Clinical expertise. *Source*: Haynes, R. B., Devereaux, P. J., & Guyatt, G. H. (2002). Clinical expertise in the era of evidence-based medicine and patient choice. *ACP Journal Club, 136*(2), A11–A14. Used with permission.

process is at the heart of EBP (American Psychological Association, 2005c; Cournoyer, 2004; Institute of Medicine, 2001; Levant, 2004; Straus et al., 2005).

Application in Practice

In the same way that the evidence is thoughtfully considered, it must be *judiciously and skillfully* applied and evaluated. In some cases, based on the critical review noted above, the evidence may need to be adapted to the particular group situation, drawing on worker knowledge, skills, and experience. Because of the possible misfit between the evidence and the situation, the intervention, technique, or strategy may need to be adapted. Worker competence consists of knowledge, judgment, and skill in determining best evidence and applying it to practice situations.

Evaluation

In their policy statement on EBP in psychology, the American Psychological Association stated that "the application of research evidence to a given patient always involves probabilistic inferences. Therefore, ongoing monitoring of patient progress and adjustment of treatment as needed are essential to EBPP [evidence-based practice in psychology]" (American Psychological Association, 2005c, p. 3). It is essential that actions be evaluated to ensure that desired results are achieved. Moving empirically supported treatments from one context to another does not invariably improve outcomes over what is currently being done (Weisz, Chu, & Polo, 2004). The evaluation of actions is needed to determine the effectiveness of the strategies/interventions within the context of practice. Evaluation must be conducted to assess whether desired results were achieved.

Four Stages of Evidence-Based Group Work

These three elements—determination of best evidence, application in practice, and evaluation—are essential to EBGW and provide the conceptual framework for this book. These elements are operationalized in the following stages outlining the process of EBGW. As adapted from other sources (Berg, 2000; Rosenthal, 2004; Straus et al., 2005), EBGW is operationalized through a sequence of four stages in which group workers (1) formulate an answerable practice question; (2) search for evidence; (3) undertake a critical review of the evidence (with respect to research merit, impact, and applicability), which yields the best available evidence; and (4) apply the evidence with judgment, skill, and concern for relevance and appropriateness for the group, utilizing evaluation to determine whether desired outcomes are achieved. Figure 1.2 includes the four stages keyed to their respective chapters. The figure depicts

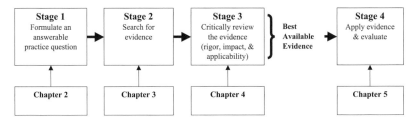

Figure 1.2. The four stages of evidence-based group work, keyed to the chapters in the book.

the process and flow of EBGW, with each chapter providing a full discussion and resources on undertaking that stage in the process.

Why Is Evidence-Based Group Work Important?

EBGW is important for the advancement of group work for a number of reasons. First, group practitioners are increasingly being held accountable for what they do in practice. EBGW provides tools to assess, evaluate, monitor, and improve practice.

Second, the elements of EBGW are part of the values and ethics of the helping professions. For example, increasing knowledge and skills by using the best evidence available is part of social work's values and code of ethics:

> Social workers should critically examine and keep current with emerging knowledge relevant to social work. Social workers should routinely review the professional literature and participate in continuing education relevant to social work practice and social work ethics. Social workers should base practice on recognized knowledge, including empirically based knowledge, relevant to social work and social work ethics. (National Association of Social Workers, 1999, standard 4.01)

It is also part of standards for the practice of group work across professional groups. For example, many of the Association for Specialists in Group Work's (ASGW) standards for the training of group workers include knowledge and skills related to assessment, evaluation, and incorporation of the research literature of group work (Association for Specialists in Group Work, 2000). According to *Standards for Social Work Practice with Groups*, group workers should include in their practice "monitoring and evaluation of success of [the] group in accomplishing its objectives through personal observation, as well as collecting information in order to assess outcomes and processes" (Association for the Advancement of Social Work with Groups, 2006, section 1F).

Third, the empirical basis for group work is growing and should be accessed, understood, and applied in practice. An EBGW framework for practice helps to classify and rank the accumulation of evidence and includes guides for finding and reviewing group-related research.

Fourth, although the dominant proportion of evidence clearly supports the effectiveness and helpfulness of group work (Ang & Hughes, 2002; Burlingame et al., 2003; Burlingame, MacKenzie, & Strauss, 2004; Hoag & Burlingame, 1997; Kösters et al., 2006; Petrocelli, 2002), there is evidence that group work can be harmful in certain circumstances (Dies & Teleska, 1985; Galinsky & Schopler, 1977, 1994; Schopler & Galinsky, 1981; Smokowski, Rose, & Bacallao, 2001). An EBGW perspective requires group workers to be aware of these findings, and to incorporate practices that are beneficial and avoid practices that might cause harm.

An appreciation of EBGW is also deepened when some clarification is made as to what it is *not*. Many common objections to EBP have been reviewed and dispelled (Gibbs & Gambrill, 2002). The following are only a few such concerns: (a) it ignores clinical expertise; (b) it ignores client values and preferences; (c) it is a cookbook approach; (d) it is an ivory-tower concept and can not be accomplished; (e) no clear evidence is available regarding questions posed; and (f) agency personnel don't have the time, resources, or inclination to implement EBP.

In general, these concerns about the use of EBP or EBGW can be dispelled through a careful review and application of the steps described in this book. Regarding the first two concerns, clinical expertise and client values and preferences are certainly incorporated in the steps of EBGW. Next, the use of reasoning and judgment based on knowledge, skills, and values clearly indicate that EBGW is not a cookbook approach. In terms of the ivory-tower concern, surveys of medical practitioners suggest that EBGW is applied in practice (Gibbs & Gambrill, 2002), and the codes of ethics noted above demonstrate that the principles of EBGW are required in the real world of practice. With respect to the fifth concern, there is mounting evidence that may answer the questions posed by group workers. Books and articles dedicated to accumulating the evidence are available (cited above), and more and more evidence is available online.

There are a couple of parts to the sixth concern. One part relates to the time needed for EBP or EBGW. This concern is being reduced by the ready access of information through the Internet and by efficient and effective search strategies. Great strides have been made toward quicker searches and evaluation in medicine; for example, see "Patient-Oriented Evidence that Matters" (Slawson & Shaughnessy, 2000), as well as Shaughnessy, Slawson, and Bennett (1994). Such developments are further presented in Chapter 3, and ideas for advancing EBGW in the face of agency obstacles are discussed in the final chapter of this book. Gibbs and Gambrill answer the resource concern with the question, "Shouldn't we prepare students to take advantage of developments that may benefit their clients?" (Gibbs & Gambrill, 2002, p. 468).

The alternative to using research evidence is to use reasoning and data that are considerably more fallible and vulnerable to harmful outcomes. Examples of common practices include clinicians basing decisions on deferral to expert authority, personal experience, rationality (i.e., "seems to make sense"), and "everyone else is doing it" (Berg, 2000). Underlying these practices are common errors and fallacies including inaccurate observation, overgeneralization, selective observation, ex post facto hypothesizing, and ego involvement in understanding (Rubin & Babbie, 2005, pp. 24–29). Gibbs and Gambrill have compiled and described a list of 34 practice fallacies and pitfalls (Gibbs & Gambrill, 1999, p. 151). These processes have been widely discredited because of the substantially larger biases and subjectivity involved. Critical thinking, an essential component of EBGW, offers advantages that can help achieve the best outcomes, such as the ability to evaluate the accuracy of claims, evaluate arguments, recognize informal fallacies, recognize pseudoscience or fraud, and avoid cognitive biases (Gibbs & Gambrill, 1999).

In summary, EBGW is a necessary part of contemporary group work. Many of the objections to EBP or EBGW have little merit, and some are based on an incomplete understanding of the process of EBP. EBGW involves incorporating the best available evidence in order to make the work most helpful to the group or group member(s). The process of EBGW is helped by a utilization of critical thinking skills.

Introduction to the Case Examples

To provide examples of how EBGW is used in practice, illustrations will be used throughout this book. The examples are drawn from experiences of students and other practitioners. To preserve confidentiality, the identities have been changed, and the examples represent an aggregation of experiences and not necessarily one application in a group. Three cases are used that will offer many examples to illustrate the principles described in the book. A brief introduction to each case, along with the practice question for each case, is provided next.

Keisha Smith: Refreshing an Existing Group Intervention

Keisha is a 32-year-old African American graduate student in a counseling psychology program. She has no previous group experience and is in her first practicum in a family service agency. As part of her practicum experience, Keisha was assigned to work with parents having problems managing the behavior of their young children (4 to 5 years of age). Keisha participated as a co-worker in a four-session parenting group with an emphasis on teaching knowledge about parenting practices. As she met with parents at intake, Keisha learned that many parents were facing challenges in managing the behavior of their children at home. However, she observed that the group sessions did not include content aimed at helping parents manage their children's behavior. It seemed that adding such content would meet a need.

In conversations with her supervisor, Keisha learned that the groups had been designed informally and were not based on any particular research, and that the supervisor had intended to redesign the group to be more in line with current research on effective parenting. They concluded that as part of a term assignment, Keisha would search for a research-based parenting program that would be relatively brief (to prevent attrition), was affordable, and could be used to possibly replace the current group program. Thus, Keisha's primary question was, "What relatively brief group intervention could help parents effectively manage their children's behavior?"

Roselia Gomez: Increasing Verbal Contributions

Roselia is a 22-year-old Mexican American graduate student in social work. Her practicum is in a middle school where, as part of her experience, she is leading a small group for eighth-grade adolescents at risk of dropping out of school. Roselia is concerned that two of the participants have said little since the group began. Thus, her question is, "How do I increase the verbal contributions of the silent group members?"

James Herrera: Increasing Attendance

James is a 24-year-old graduate student in social work. He has experience as a group leader, having worked as a cabin counselor in a summer camp and as a co-worker, with his supervisor, leading a group for adolescents in a secure treatment facility in his first practicum. This semester James was assigned to a county alcohol and other drug (AOD) abuse treatment facility to work with an outpatient group for older adolescents (16- to 17-year-olds) who were referred by high school counselors for AOD problems. The group consisted of six adolescents, all boys, with problems related to binge drinking of alcohol and regular use of marijuana. The group comprised three Caucasians (non-Latinos), two African Americans, and one Latino. The group convened twice a week for six weeks and included an established curriculum that James was required to use. The purpose of the group was to help group members achieve abstinence from AOD use. James was initially assigned to observe the group while a senior group worker led, and he was instructed to contribute when appropriate. The plan was that once that first group ended, James would lead his own group (which would be composed of adolescents, similar to the current group).

James observed that the youths attended infrequently, which created concerns about their missing important content and processes; at one session only two group members attended. After discussing his concerns with the primary group worker, James learned that this was typical and that as long as a couple of individuals showed up, the group continued. He also learned that the group worker had not made a concerted effort to deal with the lack of consistent attendance. Because he thought that the purpose of the group and the material were important, James expected that group members should attend as many sessions as possible. Thus, in working with his own group, James wanted to implement procedures to maximize attendance. So, James's question was, "What strategy can help achieve good attendance in this group for adolescents with AOD problems?" James's question might need further adjustments before it is finalized (e.g., what is "good"?), but it is a starting point.

Conclusion

This chapter provided an introduction to EBGW. The assumptions and historical context were reviewed, followed by a discussion of the essential elements that consist of best available evidence (determined by an evaluation of rigor, impact, and clinical applicability), application in practice, and evaluation. The three essential elements are operationalized in four stages: formulate an answerable practice question; search for evidence; undertake a critical review of the evidence (with respect to rigor, impact, and applicability); and apply the evidence with judgment, skill, and concern for relevance and appropriateness for the group, using evaluation to determine whether desired outcomes are achieved. The importance of EBGW for the advancement of group work was discussed. An introduction to the three core case examples used throughout the book concluded the chapter. The next chapter describes the first stage of EBGW: formulating an answerable practice question.

PART II

STAGES OF EVIDENCE-BASED GROUP WORK

2

Formulate an Answerable Practice Question

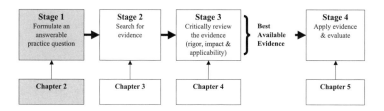

An important requirement of questions is that they are, indeed, questions and do not seek particular answers. Sincere questions are objective and impartial; they "inquire" and do not "advocate" (Ebell, 2000, p. 161). They should not be "questions of value" or ones that "imply an answer" (Gibbs, 2003, p. 68). Formulating sincere, impartial questions is a requirement of critical group-work practice. Workers must be prepared for results that may call for a change in practice.

The first step in evidence-based group work (EBGW) is formulating answerable practice questions that serve the needs of the group members. Adapted from other sources on evidence-based medicine (EBM) and evidence-based practice (EBP) (Gibbs, 2003 [Client-Oriented, Practical, Evidence Search—COPES]; Slawson & Shaughnessy, 2000; Slawson et al., 1994 [Patient Oriented Evidence that Matters—POEMS]), this guide requires that answerable practice questions be **M**ember-relevant, **A**nswerable, and **P**ractical (MAP). First, it is important to describe the substantive areas in which group-related questions may arise.

Categories of Questions in Group Work

Group work is a complex modality. A classification scheme helps to highlight the potential areas in which group-work questions may emerge. Empirical research has identified five areas related to therapeutic outcomes for groups (Burlingame, MacKenzie, & Strauss, 2004): change theory, the individual group member, group structural factors, group processes, and leadership.

The first area is change theory. Questions in this area ask which theoretical orientation or model is effective. An example of a question is, "Is interactional group therapy or cognitive-behavioral group therapy more effective in reducing depression among adolescents?"

The second area relates to the individual group member. This has to do with who improves or does not improve with group work. Questions in this area include the following: "Can an adult with a dual diagnosis (e.g., alcohol abuse and major depression) benefit from group?" "Can a child with attention-deficit/hyperactivity disorder benefit from group work?" "What is the evidence for group work with adolescents with bulimia nervosa?"

Group structural factors include the size, timing, composition, and setting of the group (Burlingame, MacKenzie, et al., 2004).[1] Questions about group structures essentially ask the question, "What group structural elements can help improve outcomes?" Specific examples include "Can groups consisting of four sessions make a difference in the problems that my group members have?" and "What is the most effective group size for treatment groups with children?"

Small-group processes reflect the unique properties of the group modality and are "a potent and independent source of patient change" (Burlingame, Fuhriman, & Johnson, 2004a, p. 649). Examples include group development, norms, roles, status, communication, degree and timing of group structure, and interpersonal feedback. The essential question here is, "What small-group processes lead to better outcomes?" Specific questions may include, "How do I build cohesion in my group?," "How can I move this group from the beginning stage to the work stage?," and "How can I establish positive group norms?" Questions may also be related to the measurement of processes, such as "How can I measure how well group members relate with each other?" and "How can I assess group interaction?"

The fifth area concerns leadership. Questions in this area ask, "What personal and technical aspects of leadership lead to better outcomes?" Specific questions may include "What is the best leadership style for treatment groups?" and "How can I relate better to group members who are not of my race?"

These five areas typically interact. Table 2.1 provides examples of interacting questions. For example, in work with adolescents in groups, a question related to leadership and the individual group member might be, "What is the most effective leadership style when working with adolescents with substance abuse problems?"

The organizational schema is valuable because it identifies *multiple* areas that are responsible for client or group change in groups, rather than only the formal change theory or intervention that researchers tend to consider in most outcome research. In addition to encompassing empirically supported interventions, the schema recognizes the different domains that contribute to effective groups, such as empirically supported therapy relationships (e.g., cohesion and the working alliance) (Burlingame, Fuhriman, & Johnson, 2001; Horvath & Bedi, 2004; Martin, Garske, & Davis, 2000; Steering Committee, 2002). Research over the years has documented the significant impact on

Table 2.1. Examples of Group Leader Questions Across and Within Elements of Groups

Elements of Group	Elements of Group				
	Change Theory	Individual	Group Structures	Group Processes	Leadership
Change theory	Which change theory is the most effective?	—	—	—	—
Individual	What change theory is most effective in reducing depression?	Can youths with conduct problems get better in group?	—	—	—
Group structures	How many sessions are required for cognitive-behavioral group therapy to be effective?	How big should my group be to be helpful to my clients with depression?	Are single-session groups effective for reducing alcohol use?	—	—
Group processes	Do mutual aid groups foster more communication among members than cognitive-behavioral groups?	How can involuntary clients become more involved in group?	What group size is too big to allow interaction among members?	How can I measure cohesion?	—
Leadership	What leadership style is needed for effective cognitive-behavioral group therapy?	What leadership style is most effective with children in treatment groups?	What leadership style is most effective with large groups?	Does leader gender make a difference in the level of cohesion in gender-homogeneous groups?	What leadership style leads to best group outcomes?

outcomes of these nonspecific or common factors in counseling (Lambert & Barley, 2002; Lambert & Ogles, 2004).

The schema is also important for highlighting the areas that group workers should consider in determining what might be related to or causing the concern that generated their practice question. For example, "background" knowledge (see Box 2.1) of individual psychopathology and group theory and research are important in generating an effective question related to individual or group process questions. Without this knowledge, one might engage in searches for answers to the wrong questions. Thus, it is helpful to generate hunches about what might be behind or related to the problem. For an individual within the group, a group worker may need additional diagnostic information or an awareness of how the individual's gender, race, ethnicity, or acculturation might relate to the concern. For example, is a group member's lack of participation due to a language barrier or communication problem? Does the group member

---

Box 2.1.   Background and Foreground Questions

The knowledge and skills that the group worker brings to EBGW provide an important foundation. The types of questions that group workers pose may be distinguished as background or foreground questions, and their relevance is determined by one's experience with the problem or challenge (Straus et al., 2005). When knowledge or experience is limited (such as with students or with those new to group work), questions are often background. Background questions ask for general knowledge about a concern or issue. This knowledge is often learned in foundation courses in helping methods (i.e., individual and group work) or in human behavior in the social environment. This is the background knowledge from which the group worker draws. Such questions typically consist of two components (adapted from Straus et al., 2005): a question root and a verb; and a treatment, strategy, behavior, or aspect related to group work. Examples of background knowledge questions include "Is group work effective?," "What is the most effective theoretical approach in group work?," "What behavior should I expect from group members over stages of group development?," and "What is the optimal group size?" Background questions may be tied in to a specific concern of the group at that time, but they do not necessarily directly press on the group situation at the moment. However, information drawn from background questions may be important in answering foreground or pressing clinical questions.

With knowledge, experience, and skill—and utilizing the EBGW approach—background knowledge makes possible a reliance on foreground knowledge (Straus et al., 2005). Foreground questions ask for specific knowledge about managing particular clients with a problem or, in group work, particular group or group member challenges. These are member- or group-oriented questions that include components for maximizing the efficiency and effectiveness of evidence gathering. More fully discussed in the next chapter, these components are (a) group member or group challenge; (b) intervention, technique, or strategy; and (c) outcome (what you want to accomplish or have accomplished).

This book is concerned primarily with posing and answering foreground questions, but it includes examples of background questions. Also, the skills involved in acquiring foreground knowledge are similar to those involved in acquiring background knowledge.

have a social phobia? Is the member's race/ethnicity or gender contributing to the perceived concern?

To get a better idea of a group-related concern, Rose (1984) has described an approach in which the leader involved the group in helping to understand the nature of a group problem, such as a lack of participation (a group process question). This might be particularly effective when a group worker's generational status, gender, culture, race, or ethnicity is different from that of the group, which may create a "blind spot" in which the worker may not accurately interpret or understand behaviors observed in the group. Thus, it is important that group workers form hunches or hypotheses about the origins of problems within groups, considering the different areas in which group questions may relate, to have the most effective question formulated.

Questions may fall in any of the above areas, but each question should be member-relevant, answerable, and practical (MAP).

Member-Relevant

Questions must help group members. Even if the target of change is the group or group worker, group members must benefit. Will group members be better off? Will incorporating this evidence help the functioning of the group to the benefit of group members? To determine whether a question is relevant for the group, the leader may preface the question with the statement, "To help this group or group member . . ." The question must fulfill the purpose of helping group members.

Answerable

Group workers should structure questions so that they can be answered effectively and efficiently. Questions must be clear, specific, parsimonious, and answered quickly. Each of these criteria is expanded upon below.

Questions should be *clear*. To make the question clear, the group worker might ask, "What is the core of my question?" or "What do I really want to learn?" The group worker should make sure that the essential elements of the question are clear. For example, for the questions "What leader strategy will help increase treatment effects in groups?" and "In groups for physically abused women, will perpetrator involvement help to reduce the abuse in the relationship?," the group worker might ask, "What is meant by 'treatment effects' or 'involvement'?" This often helps to identify whether another word or variable would sharpen the question or get at the true intent of the question. It can be helpful to give the question to another person, posing the same questions as above, to see whether the question and core words are clear.

Questions should be *specific*. This book deals primarily with foreground questions relating to particular practice circumstances. Foreground questions come out of real practice situations, which should offer sufficient detail to allow answerable questions to be constructed. Specific questions need to include the elements that relate to a *particular* group, so that an effective, relevant search can be done. Broad questions would yield too many irrelevant results in a search. In addition, questions related to active practice problems that arise once the group is convened require evidence that is as close to the current situation as possible. For example, there may be cultural reasons for a group member not to participate in a group composed of members from other ethnic or racial groups. A question that includes salient variables related to the current group would, in a subsequent search of the literature, yield material specific to the current situation—if such literature exists. It is important to be specific first and then broaden the approach if there is no available evidence dealing with a particular practice situation.

Although answerable questions must be specific and complete, they should be *parsimonious*. If a question includes too many variables or elements, it is less likely to be answerable, and such phrasing may suggest that more than one question is being asked (see Box 2.2 for prioritizing questions). Excessive length (questions of 25 or more words) or the presence of "or" or "and" are possible indicators that a question might be too complex to be effectively and efficiently answered.

Questions should also be *answered quickly* (or at least as quickly as possible). The length of time needed to answer a question depends on the nature of the question and the context. In medical settings where physicians need to make quick decisions due to the nature of the problem and the volume of patients, answers need to be obtained within minutes. In the case of group work, which typically does not deal with crises (group work is not an efficient modality for helping people make urgent and immediate decisions), a desirable period between asking a question and getting an answer is a few hours. However, with weekly group sessions, group workers may have a few days or a week to acquire and evaluate evidence. With the growing availability of accessible and affordable databases, the time needed to acquire and evaluate evidence should

---

Box 2.2.   I have too many questions! Which do I pick?

Group workers might have many potential questions. Because of time constraints, it is often necessary to prioritize the questions. The following are some suggestions for choosing the best questions (adapted and expanded from Straus et al., 2005, p. 21):

1. Which question is most important to the group or a group member's well-being?
2. Which question might affect the largest number of group members or groups?
3. Which question is most likely to recur in practice?
4. Which question is most relevant to your learning needs?
5. Which question can most feasibly be answered within the time available?
6. Which question is most interesting to you or your group member(s)?

decrease over time. However, an increase in the number of databases will also mean more irrelevant databases and the need for more effective search strategies. At this time, the goal should be questions that can be answered within the next day or two.

Practical

Questions must also be practical, defined as "concerned with practice rather than theory" (Soanes, 2003). Practical questions help answer questions of real concern to the group leader or group members. Such questions may come from group workers or from group members. For example, general questions from group members might include the following:

1. Do I really need to say something to get anything out of this group?
2. Will I get better if I attend this group?
3. Do we really need a leader to help us?
4. Can this group help me feel better about myself?
5. As a member of this team, how can I make this task group work harder?

Questions that group leaders might have include the following:

1. How can I manage disruptive behavior in the group?
2. How do I know if group members are getting anything out of this group?
3. Can an intern be effective in helping this group?
4. Are groups effective for clients in crisis?
5. As team leader, how can I motivate my team?

Constructing MAP Questions for Group Work

Effective questions should be complete and well constructed and should include three elements (adapted from Straus et al., 2005, pp. 16–17): (1) group situation, problem, or challenge; (2) intervention, technique, or strategy; and (3) outcome (what you want to accomplish) (Table 2.2).

The group situation is the issue that needs help or resolution. This provides the context of the question and describes the group or group member situation. For example, the group worker might have a question related to a group with depressed adult males, an adolescent who does not speak in group, or a need for a group screening instrument for adults with bipolar disorder.

The intervention, strategy, or measure is what would help or address the issue. Examples of intervention-related questions are "Can computer-assisted group work reduce symptoms related to social phobia among adults?" and "Is group cognitive-behavioral therapy more effective than individual therapy in reducing post-traumatic stress disorder among women who were victims of sexual violence?" An example of a question related to a strategy or technique is, "How can I increase the verbal participation of the adolescents in my group for

Table 2.2. Examples Of Well-Constructed Questions Using Criteria Adapted from Straus and Colleagues and Applied To Group Work

	Questions Arranged According to Criteria Adapted from Straus et al. (2005)	
Group Situation or Challenge: "In the case of . . ."	Intervention/Technique/Strategy	Outcome
. . . groups with depressed adults . . .	. . . will cognitive-behavioral therapy or interactional group therapy . . .	. . . best reduce depression by the end of group?
. . . groups with adolescents who use alcohol and other drugs (AOD) . . .	. . . what brief (4 to 8 sessions) group intervention . . .	. . . will significantly reduce their AOD use by the end of group?
. . . an adoloescent who is not speaking in group . . .	. . . what worker strategy/technique . . .	. . . will increase verbal contributions by the fifth session?
. . . a mixed-gender psychoeducational group with foster care adolescents . . .	. . . what worker strategy . . .	. . . will increase the participation of female members by the eighth session?
. . . establishing a group for Latino adolescents with conduct problems . . .	. . . what group size . . .	. . . results in the most reductions in problem behavior by the end of group?
. . . a group of mixed-race high school students at risk for dropout . . .	. . . what leader strategy . . .	. . . will improve cohesion within two sessions?
. . . a group consisting of adult victims of sexual trauma . . .	. . . what leader actions . . .	. . . will help establish a climate of mutual support by the middle group sessions?
. . . a group of single mothers seeking help for parenting skills . . .	. . . are female leaders more effective than males . . .	. . . in improving parenting skills by the end of group?

substance abuse problems?" An example of an assessment or measure-related question is, "What is a brief [i.e., completed in 5 minutes] but reliable and valid measure of cohesion?"

The outcome is what the group worker or the group member would like to see changed or improved, and both individuals play a key role in selecting and monitoring outcomes. As mentioned in the previous chapter, questions can be conceptualized as problem- or group-related and proximal or distal. An example of a problem-related distal-outcome question can be found in the first row of Table 2.2, related to what change theory is most effective in reducing depression. In this example, the group worker would measure depression before and at the end of group (or later) to see whether the group made an impact (another example of a problem-related distal-outcome question is in the second row of the table). A group-related distal-outcome question could be asked if the group worker wanted to know if a group intervention would result in member satisfaction with the group service. In this case, the group worker would utilize a "satisfaction with group" measure at the conclusion of group.

Group-related proximal outcomes occur during the life of the group and relate to the improvement of within-group factors such as interaction or cohesion. They are expected to help improve problem-related outcomes. For example, a group worker might want to know how to increase group members' engagement, with the expectation that this will increase the likelihood of achieving favorable, problem-related outcomes for the group members. The group worker would assess the engagement of the members in one group session, implement a strategy to increase it, and then re-measure engagement in a later session to see whether the strategy led to an increase in engagement. The worker could assess both proximal and distal outcomes to establish important markers of progress both within the group and at the end of group. Group-related proximal outcomes may include an individual in the group, a dyad, or the entire group. An example is, "At least half of the group members verbally participate within two group sessions" (a couple of other examples of group-based proximal outcomes are in the third and fourth rows of Table 2.2).

Table 2.2 illustrates the elements needed for effective questions, but the order of the elements is not important. Thus, the first example could also read, "Will cognitive therapy or interactional group therapy best reduce depression among depressed adults?"

Example of MAP Question Construction:
Keisha Smith

The last chapter introduced the essential ingredients of Keisha's question, which was, "What relatively brief group intervention could help parents effectively manage their children's behavior?" The question contains most of the MAP elements, but it needs some adjustment. For illustrative purposes, let us go over the steps outlined above.

Keisha's question is member-relevant and practical. The question is member-relevant in that it clearly relates to an issue of concern to the group members. It is practical in that it clearly addresses a concern of group members—how to manage the behavior of their children. It seemed to Keisha that adding this content would appeal to participants.

Keisha needed to modify the question to better meet the "answerable" criteria. The question, as worded, did not include enough information about the group and the specific outcome that Keisha wanted. For example, Keisha needed to clarify that "brief" meant no more than four sessions. As for outcomes, Keisha stated that she wanted changes to occur by the time the group ended and that the behavior changes needed to be seen at home. Putting the question into the syntax above, Keisha reworded the question as, "In the case of group work for parents and their children with behavior problems, what brief group intervention (2 to 4 sessions) could improve their child's behavior at home?"

Example of MAP Question Construction: James Herrera

Recall that James is a graduate intern assigned to work with an outpatient group of older teens referred by school counselors for alcohol and other drug (AOD) problems. James's group had noted attendance problems, and his working question was, "What strategy can help achieve good attendance in this group for adolescents with AOD problems?" James's question is member-relevant and practical. However, it needs modification to be made answerable. For example, the outcome is not clear ("good" is a vague descriptor). James clarified "good attendance" to mean that more than half (i.e., at least four) of the group members were in attendance. James reworded his question to read, "What strategy can increase attendance to a majority of members in a group for adolescents with AOD problems?"

Conclusion

EBGW begins with a clinical concern that must then be developed into a well-constructed question. These questions must be member-relevant, answerable, and practical (MAP). They should include important components: specific member or group challenge; intervention, strategy, or technique; and an outcome. MAP questions should be parsimonious but should include enough information to produce a manageable amount of evidence in the first search, which is the subject of the next chapter. Examples involving Keisha Smith and James Herrera illustrated the principles in action. The next chapter describes how to search for the best available evidence.

3

Search for Best Available Evidence

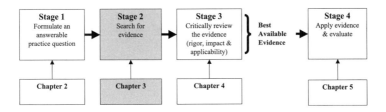

An important part of evidence-based group work (EBGW) is that it requires one to expand beyond convenient evidence (e.g., one's own experience) and to engage in a systematic collection and appraisal of best available evidence (Corcoran, 2003; Macgowan, 2006a; Rosenthal, 2004, p. 20). One's experience, knowledge, values, and skills provide an important basis for evaluating new evidence, but relying only on what one knows and has experienced limits the potential sources of new evidence that may help improve practice. A group worker's existing clinical expertise will help in evaluating the new evidence for its practice relevance and appropriateness.

After formulating a good question that meets the MAP (member-relevant, answerable, and practical) criteria described in the last chapter, the second step of EBGW is to undertake a search for evidence. Given that there are millions of articles published annually (Miser, 2000b), searches must be effective and efficient—effective in finding the right evidence and efficient in doing so as quickly as possible. Group workers must sift through the enormous literature to find the appropriate group-based studies. This can create " 'information anxiety'—the frustration that occurs when there is a great deal of information, but it does not tell us what we need to know" (Slawson et al., 1994, p. 2). This chapter intends to reduce such anxiety by explaining how to find the right group-work-related evidence as quickly as possible. Described in the following sections are principles of effective and efficient searches, specific techniques for searching for evidence, and two case examples that show the process of searching for evidence.

General Principles of Effective and Efficient Searches

In conducting an effective and efficient search for available evidence, it is important to know (a) where to look and (b) how to look. Specific applications of these principles appear later in the chapter, but it is helpful to first consider a general orientation to searching for evidence.

Know Where to Look

It is important to look in the right places. There are two elements to this principle. First, group workers should look for evidence with the highest research merit. Second, they should determine whether the search is for an intervention/technique or a measurement tool that assesses the impact of the leader's intervention/technique. These two elements are described next.

Hierarchy of Research Merit

The reader will recall that the first criterion of best evidence is that it should have research merit. Research merit, more fully discussed in the next chapter, has to do with evidence being the most rigorous available; that is, evidence that supports the belief that an intervention or practice is linked to a desired outcome (Cournoyer, 2004; Hyde et al., 2003). To maximize efficiency, group workers should first search in sources that are most likely to have the most rigorous evidence available. Figure 3.1 presents a hierarchy of levels of evidence, with the strongest research sources at the top of the figure (research-based syntheses of high-quality research) and the weakest sources at the bottom (authority-based). For example, rigorous experimental studies published in reputable, peer-reviewed sources are the strongest research studies. Because group workers typically have little time to search and evaluate evidence, the best sources of research evidence are meta-analyses; systematic reviews of high-quality research published in reputable, peer-reviewed journals; and expert panel opinions based on such reviews.[1] These preappraised sources are written by experts who have already critically weighed the research merit of the evidence using rigorous methodology, and the findings are published in reputable, peer-reviewed outlets (although group workers must still critically review these sources as well, and this is fully discussed in Chapter 4). These publications are often summaries of what are variously described as empirically based treatments, empirically supported treatments, or empirically validated treatments related to a range of problems or populations. They may also be publications or statements of best practices or practice guidelines, defined as "a set of systematically compiled and organized knowledge statements designed to enable practitioners to find, select, and use appropriately the interventions that are most effective for a given task" (Proctor & Rosen, 2003, p. 108). Theories that researchers have tested empirically would also have

Hierarchy of Research Merit
"What is the likelihood of an action achieving a desired outcome?"

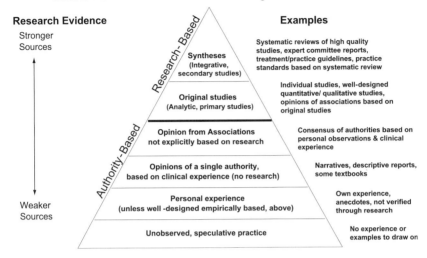

Figure 3.1. Hierarchy of research merit. Based on Hyde, Falls, Morris, & Schoenwald (2003, p. 5). There is a general principle in the presentation of this figure, which ranks, in ascending order, the quality of the research source. Thus, studies published in sources that are subject to rigorous peer review and are reputable are the most rigorous research studies. However, it is recognized that some sources that are lower in the figure may include rigorous studies, such as meta-analyses in certain edited books. Thus the figure should be used as a general guide.

high research rigor, but theories without research support should be considered authority based until supported through rigorous research.[2]

In general, there is less evidence available the higher up one moves in the figure. This is particularly true with foreground problems (i.e., those that require timely practice action). Thus group workers will likely not find a meta-analysis related to strategies for managing disruptive behavior of adolescents in groups. However, there are meta-analyses about the efficacy of group cognitive-behavioral therapy for adolescents. Thus group workers should first do searches for available evidence in locations cited in the top of the figure, and then move down. More details on specific sources to search are available later in the chapter.

Intervention or Measure of Change?

It is also important to know whether one is looking for an intervention (technique or strategy) or for an instrument related to an aspect of group work that a group worker would like to assess or see changed. EBGW involves both leader action and assessment of its effectiveness, so it is important to know where to locate both interventions and measures.

With respect to interventions or techniques, or to worker actions, the reader will recall from the previous chapter that there are five general areas contributing to outcomes in group treatment: formal change theory, client characteristics, group structural factors, small group processes, and the group leader. Worker actions would fall into one of these areas. For example, in the area of formal change theory, the group worker may want to know what model of group work to use in order to best reduce depression among adolescents.

In the area of client characteristics, a group worker may want to know what the research says about who benefits most from groups, or if there are client characteristics that contraindicate group work. Worker actions in this area might involve screening members for particular characteristics or behaviors or adapting group conditions to best serve a client profile. The research would dictate which approach, if any, is advisable.

In the area of group structure, a group worker might have questions about group size, the number and timing of sessions (if not dictated by formal change theory), or composition. Group worker intervention in this area would involve manipulating these conditions to optimize outcomes. In the area of small-group processes, group workers might be interested in making changes in the group to promote more attraction of members to each other, heighten interaction, or increase member verbalizations. In the area of leadership, a leader might want to adopt behaviors or a leadership style that has been associated with effective groups.

Thus, group workers may take action or intervene in a number of areas to maximize the benefits of group work. Group workers should appreciate the range of factors contributing to outcomes in group and become familiar with the literature—and how to search it—in each of these areas. Recent critical reviews of the literature in these areas are a good starting point (Burlingame, Fuhriman, et al., 2004a). Identified below are additional resources and tools for finding such resources effectively and efficiently.

In addition to looking for interventions, evidence-based group workers would also need to know where to locate measures of change. As noted in the previous chapter, there are problem- and group-related outcomes. Measures of problem-related outcomes have to do with the concern or challenge that brought the client to the group, such as substance use, depression, or anxiety. A number of general books include measures of change (American Psychiatric Association, 2000; Fischer & Corcoran, 2007; Hudson, 1982), and there are many compendia of instruments dedicated to specific problems and populations (Allen & Wilson, 2003; Dahlberg, Toal, & Behrens, 1998; Eliopoulos, 1990; Jones, 1996a; Kelley, Noell, & Reitman, 2003; Manusov, 2005; McDowell & Newell, 1996; Mezey, Rauckhorst, & Stokes, 1993; Naar-King, Ellis, & Frey, 2004; Nezu, 2000; Perkinson, 2002; Tzeng, 1993; Waltz, Jenkins, & Strickland, 2001). Readers may find further descriptions of some of these and other outcome measures in the excellent online resource developed by librarian Helen Hugh and her team at the University of Texas (Hugh, 2006).[3]

Measures of group-related outcomes assess the presence of or change in group conditions such as group cohesion, interaction, and group leadership. As an integral part of EBGW, group workers need to be able to locate psychometrically rigorous (i.e., reliable and valid) and practice-appropriate (i.e., relatively easily administered and scored) instruments. Reviews of promising instruments should be part of a group worker's library (recent examples include Beck & Lewis, 2000; DeLucia & Bridbord, 2004; DeLucia-Waack, 1997; and Toseland, Jones, & Gellis, 2004). Unfortunately, there is no "one-stop" source of measures of factors related to groups as there is for measures of problem-related outcomes, noted above. Table 3.1 includes a selection of instruments across areas of group work that are suitable for practice, empirically tested, and available for preview either in the article or by contacting the respective author. For additional reference, Table 3.2 includes an expanded list of group instruments, including some well-known but complex instruments (e.g., SYMLOG) that are suitable in contexts where group workers are trained to use them and have administrative support (i.e., time and resources) to complete them. Some of the instruments in Table 3.2 are comprehensive and multidimensional, which means that their subscales may be used. For example, the Therapeutic Factors Inventory (Lese & MacNair-Semands, 2000), consisting of 99 items, may be used in its entirety or in part; the cohesion subscale has only nine items. Similarly, the Curative Climate Instrument (Fuhriman, Drescher, Hanson, Henrie, & Rybicki, 1986) includes a cohesion scale. The Group Environment Scale (GES, Moos, 1996) consists of 90 items, but one could use the leader-support and leader-control subscales of the GES to measure aspects of leadership. If Tables 3.1 or 3.2 do not include a desired instrument, Table 3.3 includes a list of online sources that may be searched for specific instruments related to group work. Group workers would need to mount a specific search for a particular measure or instrument. More details on searching for instruments are provided below. In assessing an instrument, the group worker should weigh several variables to ensure it is rigorous and compatible with the situation. The next chapter contains a guide on evaluating the rigor and applicability of instruments.

In summary, evidence-based group workers seek and use interventions/techniques to maximize the benefits of groups, but they must also seek and use measures to assess changes in group conditions.

Know How to Look

A second component of effective and efficient searches is knowing how to look. Searches for evidence should be both active and passive. Most of the remaining discussion in this chapter describes how to conduct active searches for group material, but group workers should enroll in free services that alert them to new research in areas relevant to them (passive searches). Many publishers of group

Table 3.1. Selected Group-Based Measures For Practice

Aspect of Group Work	Instrument (source)	Description	Reliability & Validity
Cohesion	Group Attitude Scale (GAS, Evans, 1982, 1984; Evans & Jarvis, 1986)	20 items, self-report.	Reliability: Several studies (reviewed in Evans & Jarvis, 1986) have supported the internal consistency of the GAS, yielding α coefficients ranging from 0.90 to 0.97. Validity: GAS correlated (0.33 to 0.72) with the cohesion subscale of the Group Environment Scale and with observer's evaluations of the level of group members' attraction to group (0.66) (Evans & Jarvis, 1986). Evans and Jarvis also reported hypothesized relationships between GAS scores and interpersonal attraction, attendance, and termination anxiety. Other reports of construct validity.
Engagement	Group Engagement Measure (GEM) (Macgowan, 1997, 2000; Macgowan & Levenson, 2003; Macgowan & Newman, 2005)	Multidimensional measure of a member's engagement to group, completed by worker or observer about each member. Three versions: 37, 27, and 21 items.	Reliability (across studies, adults): α mean: 0.97; Test-retest: 0.66; "Interrater:" 0.28 to 0.47; Standard Error of Measurement (SEM): 4.48 to 4.83 (Macgowan, 1997, 2000; Macgowan & Levenson, 2003). Unpublished study involving adolescent sample: α: 0.95; Test-retest 0.68; SEM: 5.06 to 5.22. Validity: Adult groups, including clinical groups with AOD users: Construct (convergent, divergent, factor analysis) and criterion (concurrent and predictive) indicated favorable results (Macgowan, 1997, 2000; Macgowan & Levenson, 2003). Factor analysis confirmed the dimensionality of the original GEM for clinical groups and produced two shorter versions: A 7-factor, 27-item version for clinical groups, and a 5-factor, 21-item version suitable for clinical or nonclinical groups (Macgowan & Newman, 2005).

36

Group Climate	Group Climate Questionnaire (MacKenzie, 1981, 1983)	Climate is a property of the group that facilitates or impedes the work of an individual to reach a goal. Self-report rating about the group. Two versions: Long Form (32 items, 8 subscales) and Short Form (12 items).	Reliability: Alphas for adolescent sample: 0.92 and 0.90 for two subscales (Kivlighan & Tarrant, 2001). Validity: For adult sample: factor analysis yielded 3 subscales: engagement, avoidance, and conflict (MacKenzie, 1983). For adolescent sample: two-factor structure: Active Engagement (AE), Conflict-Distance (CD) (Kivlighan & Tarrant, 2001); as hypothesized, AE increased over time in group, CD decreased; AE positively related to leader engagement (perception of leader) and negatively related to leader disengagement (Kivlighan & Tarrant, 2001).
Leadership	Group Leader Self-Efficacy Instrument (Page, Pietrzak, & Lewis, 2001)	36 items, self-report. Measures group work trainees' self-efficacy for group work skills.	Reliability: internal consistency, 0.95; test–retest (2 weeks), 0.72. Validity: construct validity supported by no significant correlations with conceptually unrelated instruments (e.g., anxiety measure)
	Group Counselor Behavior Rating Form (Corey & Corey, 1987, pp. 36–38; DeLucia & Bowman, 1991)	30-item scale that assesses group leadership behavior and skills.	Reliability (DeLucia & Bowman, 1991): internal consistency, 0.96; Guttman split-half was 0.97 and the equal length Spearman-Brown reliability coefficient was 0.97. Validity (DeLucia & Bowman, 1991): Factor analysis indicated four factors: Interventions, Facilitative Conditions, Applications of Theory, and Professionalism.
Screening	Group Therapy Survey-Revised (Carter, Mitchell, & Krautheim, 2001)	20 self-report items concerning attitudes about group counseling.	Reliability: Internal consistency, overall scale: 0.88; subscales: Efficacy, 0.78, Myths, 0.77, Vulnerability, 0.75. Test-retest, 2 weeks: overall scale: 0.79; Efficacy, 0.65; Myths, 0.76; Vulnerability, 0.80 Validity, factor analysis with 25 items yielded three factors: Efficacy, Myths, and Vulnerability, with five items not loading on any factor.

(continued)

Table 3.1. *(continued)*

Aspect of Group Work	Instrument (source)	Description	Reliability & Validity
Therapeutic Alliance	Group Therapy Alliance Scale (Marziali, Munroe-Blum, & McCleary, 1999)	Alliance defined as "Perceptions of the therapists' attitudes, feelings, and behaviors toward the respondent as well as toward other group members" (Marziali, Munroe-Blum, & McCleary, 1999, p. 430). 36 items, self-report. Based on Integrative Psychotherapy Alliance Scales (Pinsof & Catherall, 1986), adapted for groups.	Reliability: Split half: 0.82. Inter-item correlations ranged from 0.66 to 0.83 for 30 items, and for the remaining 6 items r values were less than 0.20. Alpha for the 36-item scale was 0.88, and for the 30-item scale it was 0.91. Validity: Previous factor analysis of the Couples Alliance Scale (Pinsof & Catherall) revealed a unidimensional measure. No other validation reported.
Therapeutic Factors	Therapeutic Factors Inventory (Lese & MacNair-Semands, 2000)	Self-report measure to assess group member's perceptions of the degree to which the therapeutic factors described by Yalom (1995) are present. 11 therapeutic factors, 99 items.	Reliability: High internal consistency among subscales (0.83 to 0.93); Strong test–retest reliability, 1 week (most between 0.64 and 0.93; one subscale = 0.28 [corrective reenactment]). Validity: Preliminary support for construct validity of instrument (MacNair-Semands & Lese, 2000).

AOD: Alcohol and other drug

Table 3.2. Expanded List of Group-Based Measures

Domain	Instrument (source)
Cohesion	Cohesion Scale (Yalom, 1995, p. 54)
	Group Atmosphere Scale (Silbergeld, Koenig, Manderscheid, Meeker, & Hornung, 1975)
	Group Attitude Scale (Evans, 1982, 1984; Evans & Jarvis, 1986)
	Group Bond Questionnaire (Piper, Marrache, Lacroix, Richardsen, & Jones, 1983)
	Group Cohesion Questionnaire (van Andel, Erdman, Karsdorp, Appels, & Trijsburg, 2003)
	Group Cohesion Scale (Wood, Kumar, Treadwell, & Leach, 1998) & Group Cohesion Scale-Revised (Treadwell, Lavertue, Kumar, & Veeraraghavan, 2001)
	Group Cohesiveness Scale / Harvard Community Health Plan Group Cohesion Scale (Budman et al., 1987; Budman & Gurman, 1988)
	Group Environment Questionnaire (task groups) (Carless & De Paola, 2000)
	Group Identification Scale (Henry, Arrow, & Carini, 1999)
	Perceived Cohesion Scale (task groups) (Bollen & Hoyle, 1990; Chin, Salisbury, Pearson, & Stollak, 1999)
Climate, Environment	Group Environment Scale (Moos, 1974, 1996)
	Group Climate Questionnaire (MacKenzie, 1981, 1983)
Group Development	Group Development Observation Form (Wheelan, Verdi, & McKeage, 1994; Bordia, DiFonzo, & Chang, 1999)
	Group Development Questionnaire (Wheelan, Buzaglo, & Tsumura, 1998; Wheelan & Hochberger, 1996)
	Group Development Process Analysis Measures (Beck, Dugo, Eng, & Lewis, 1986; Lewis, Beck, Dugo, & Eng, 2000)
Engagement	Group Engagement Measure (Macgowan, 1997, 2000; Macgowan & Levenson, 2003; Macgowan & Newman, 2005)
Goals of Members	Session Agenda Questionnaire (Kivlighan & Jauquet, 1990; Kivlighan, Jauquet, Hardie, & Francis, 1993)
Interaction (with members, with leaders)	A Method for Quantifying Interaction in Counseling Groups (Noble, Ohlsen, & Proff, 1961)
	Behavior Scores System (Borgatta, 1963; Borgatta & Crowther, 1965)
	Experiencing Scale (Klein, Mathieu, Gendlin, & Kiesler, 1969; Klein, Mathieu-Coughlan, & Kiesler, 1986)
	Factor Analysis of Process Variables (Heckel, Holmes, & Salzberg, 1967; Heckel, Holmes, & Rosecrans, 1971)
	Group Emotionality Rating System (Karterud & Foss, 1989; Karterud, 2000)

(continued)

Table 3.2. *(continued)*

Domain	Instrument (source)
	Group Therapy Interaction Chronogram (Cox, 1973; Reder, 1978)
	Hill Interaction Matrix (Hill, 1965, 1971, 1977; Hill, 1986) Hostility/Support Scale (Beck, 1983)
	Individual Group Member Interpersonal Process Scale (Soldz, Budman, Davis, & Demby, 1993; Davis, Budman, & Soldz, 2000)
	Interaction Process Analysis (Bales, 1950, developed into SYMLOG, below)
	Member-to-Leader Scoring System (Mann, Gibbard, & Hartman, 1967; Gibbard & Hartman, 1973b)
	Process Analysis Scoring System (Gibbard & Hartman, 1973a, 1973b)
	System of Multiple Levels Observation of Groups (SYMLOG, Bales, Cohen, & Williamson, 1979; Polley, Hare, & Stone, 1988)
Leadership	Corrective Feedback Instrument–Revised (Hulse-Killacky, Orr, & Paradise, 2006)
	Corrective Feedback Self-Efficacy Instrument (Page & Hulse-Killacky, 1999)
	Directives Scale (Stinchfield & Burlingame, 1991)
	Effective Group Leadership (Tinsley, Roth, & Lease, 1989)
	Group Leader Self-Efficacy Instrument (Page, Pietrzak, & Lewis, 2001)
	Group Leader Intervention System (Nuijens, Teglasi, Simcox, Kivlighan, & Rothman, 2006)
	Group Counselor Behavior Rating Form (Corey & Corey, 1987, pp. 36–38; DeLucia & Bowman, 1991)
	Leader Adjective Measure (MacKenzie, Dies, Coche, Rutan, & Stone, 1987)
	Leader Behavior (Lieberman, Yalom, & Miles, 1973, pp. 470–474)
	Skilled Group Counseling Scale (Smaby, Maddux, Torres-Rivera, & Zimmick, 1999)
	Therapist Session Intentions (Stiles et al., 1996)
	Trainer Behavior Scale (Bolman, 1971)
Post-Session Ratings	Evaluation of Today's Group Session (Reid, 1997, p. 283) & modified version (Patterson & Basham, 2002)
	Post-Session Questionnaire (Rose, 1984, pp. 34–36)
	Session Evaluation Questionnaire (Rose, 1977, pp. 60–61)
Screening	Elements (update and expansion of the FIRO, Schutz, 1992)
	Group Assessment Form (Lynn, 1994)

	Group Selection Questionnaire (Burlingame et al., 2006)
	Group Therapy Questionnaire (MacNair-Semands, 2002, 2004)
	Group Therapy Survey (Slocum, 1987) / Group Therapy Survey-Revised (Carter, Mitchell, & Krautheim, 2001)
Self-Disclosure	Self-Disclosure and Feedback Behaviors (McGuire, Taylor, Broome, Blau, & Abbott, 1986)
	Self-Reference Content Analysis (Pino & Cohen, 1971)
Therapeutic Alliance	Group Therapy Alliance Scale (Marziali, Munroe-Blum, & McCleary, 1999)
Therapeutic Content of Group	Group Sessions Rating Scale (skills-based vs. interactional group therapy) (Getter, Litt, Kadden, & Cooney, 1992)
	Psychodynamic Work and Object Rating Systems (psychodynamic group therapy) (Piper, McCallum, & Azim, 1992; Piper & McCallum, 2000)
	Comprehensive Psychotherapeutic Interventions Rating Scale (Trijsburg et al., 2002)
Therapeutic Factors	Critical Incident Questionnaire (Lieberman, Yalom, & Miles, 1973, p. 17) & The "Most Important Event" Questionnaire (Bloch, Reibstein, Crouch, Holroyd, & Themen, 1979, p. 258)
	Curative Climate Instrument (Fuhriman, Drescher, Hanson, Henrie, & Rybicki, 1986)
	Curative Factors Scale (Lieberman, Yalom, & Miles, 1973)
	Curative Factors Scale-Revised (Stone, Lewis, & Beck, 1994)
	Group Counseling Helpful Impacts Scale (Kivlighan, Multon, & Brossart, 1996)
	Therapeutic Factors Inventory (Lese & MacNair-Semands, 2000)
	Therapeutic Group Interaction Factors Scale (Hastings-Vertino, Getty, & Wooldridge, 1996)

Measures may fit more than one domain.

Table 3.3.   Searchable Sources of Measures for Group Work

Citations/URL	*Notes*
Buros Online (Tests in Print & Mental Measurements Yearbook)[1] http://buros .unl.edu/buros/jsp/search.jsp (also available through subscription through OVID/ SilverPlatter)	Buros online is a comprehensive bibliography access to all known commercially available tests that are currently in print in the English language. Guides readers to test reviews published in the Mental Measurements Yearbook series.
Educational Testing Service (ETS) Test Collection[1]http://www.ets.org/testcoll/ index.html	Includes an extensive library of 20,000 tests and other measurement devices from the early 1900s to the present (Web site). Includes group-related measures in database.
Health and Psychosocial Instruments (available by subscription through OVID)	Indexes tests, measures, survey instruments, rating scales, and questionnaires on human health and behavior. Includes group-based instruments.

All the sources may be available by subscription through local university; all include group-based instruments in their inventory.

[1]Free searches.

work journals provide free table-of-contents delivery. Table 3.4 provides a summary of relevant journals that offer free table-of-contents alerts, which are sent to the subscriber's e-mail address. These sites also permit users to sign up according to population or problem area, such as "Addictions counseling, treatment and recovery" (Haworth, as of May, 2006). As relevant material comes in, group workers may add it to a word-processor file or electronic bibliographic program (such as Endnote [http://www.endnote.com] or RefWorks [http:// www.refworks.com]) or print it out and put it into a binder for future reference. This passive methodology helps group workers build specific knowledge about their particular areas of interest and is particularly helpful for building important background knowledge. The active-search methodology, described next, will more likely yield evidence related to pressing foreground questions.

Specific Techniques for Searching for Evidence

This section of the chapter provides specific methods for undertaking a search for group-related evidence, integrating the principles outlined above. The first section discusses databases that one could search for evidence, and it is followed by a section on methods for searching the databases.

Sources of Evidence

Table 3.5 provides a list of specific sources of intervention research evidence. The first section of rows consists of sources that group workers may search for

Table 3.4. Peer-Reviewed Group Journals

Title (Publisher)	Provenance, Circulation, & Description (Ulrich's Periodicals Directory, 2005)	URLs of Journal and Free Table of Contents Delivery
Group Analysis: Journal of Group Analytic Psychotherapy (SAGE)	First published 1967, published quarterly. Circulation 1,250. Theory, practice, and experience of analytic group psychotherapy, using an integrative approach based on the view that humans are all primarily group beings.	http://www.sagepub.co.uk/journal.aspx?pid=105567 Free table of contents alerts: http://online.sagepub.com/cgi/alerts
Group Dynamics: Theory, Research, and Practice (APA)	First published 1997, published quarterly. Circulation 1,000. Covers empirical analyses of topics that extend knowledge of groups. Revitalizes the link between the scientific study of group dynamics and the application of that scientific understanding in applied settings.	http://www.apa.org/journals/gdn/papercall.html Free table of contents alerts: http://notify.apa.org/
Group Processes & Intergroup Relations (SAGE)	Sociology, begun 1998, published quarterly. Circulation 900. Focuses on basic and applied aspects of group and intergroup phenomena, ranging from small, interactive groups to large-scale social categories.	http://www.sagepub.co.uk/journal.aspx?pid=105568 Free table of contents alerts: http://online.sagepub.com/cgi/alerts
Groupwork (Whiting & Birch, London, UK)	First published 1988, published three times a year. Circulation 750. Covers group work of all types.	No Web site
International Journal of Group Psychotherapy (Guilford)	First published 1951, published quarterly. Circulation 5,400. Devoted to reporting and interpreting the research and practice of group psychotherapy. Official publication of the American Group Psychotherapy Association.	http://www.guilford.com/cgi-bin/cartscript.cgi?page=pr/jngr.htm&dir=periodicals/per_psych&cart_id=398891.32129 Free table of contents alerts: https://www.atypon-link.com/action/registration

(continued)

Table 3.4. (continued)

Title (Publisher)	Provenance, Circulation, & Description (Ulrich's Periodicals Directory, 2005)	URLs of Journal and Free Table of Contents Delivery
Journal of Child and Adolescent Group Therapy (Springer)	Published 1991 to 2001, when it ceased with volume 11. Covers issues in child, adolescent, and parent group therapy. Includes clinical reports and articles on new developments, theoretical issues, applications of group therapy and group methods, and the group process.	http://www.springerlink.com/content/105366/?p=2e139d88754a4ce6b3c5056ed1444491&pi=0
Journal of Groups in Addiction & Recovery (Haworth)	First published 2006; published quarterly.	http://www.haworthpress.com/store/product.asp?sid=VDARGJ2VSAAX9HKPPHHXC0CRC6U5AAD6&sku=J384 Free table of contents alerts: https://www.haworthpress.com/store/AlertServiceSplash.asp?home=root
Journal for Specialists in Group Work (Routledge, Taylor & Francis Group)	First published 1978, published quarterly. Circulation 6,000. Includes empirical research, history of group work, work with groups, theoretical discussions, and current group literature reviews. Journal of the Association for Specialists in Group Work, a Division of the American Counseling Association.	http://www.tandf.co.uk/journals/titles/01933922.asp Free table of contents alerts: http://www.informaworld.com/smpp/controlpanel~mode=alerts
Small Group Research: An International Journal of Theory, Investigation and Application (SAGE)	First published 1970, published bimonthly. Circulation 800. Addresses three vital areas of study: the psychology of small groups, communication within small groups, and the organizational behavior of small groups. Brings together research that probes all aspects of small group	http://www.sagepub.co.uk/journal.aspx?pid=105775 Free table of contents alerts: http://online.sagepub.com/cgi/alerts

	functioning, including processes, dynamics, outcomes, and relationship to environment. Formerly *Small Group Behavior* (first published in 1969); incorporates *International Journal of Small Group Research and Comparative Group Studies.*	https://www.haworthpress.com/store/product.asp?sku=J009 Free table of contents alerts: https://www.haworthpress.com/store/AlertServiceSplash.asp?home=root
Social Work with Groups (Haworth)	First published 1978, published quarterly. Circulation 1,012. Covers group work in psychiatric, rehabilitative, and multipurpose social work and social services agencies.	

Table 3.5. Sources of Research Evidence on Group Interventions/Techniques

Type	Sources	URL	Notes
1. Books (includes handbooks, guidebooks, encyclopedias, manuals, guidelines)	Bowker's *Books in Print*	http://www.booksinprint.com/bip/default.asp	Search titles, and restrict search to books. Check with research librarian for specific search strategies particular to that library catalog.
	Library of Congress[1] Local public and university library	http://catalog.loc.gov/ Check with local library and university for electronic access. Electronic card catalog of local library.	
2. Databases of systematic reviews or preappraised evidence	Agency for Healthcare Research & Quality[1]	http://www.ahrq.gov/clinic/epcix.htm	Includes free reviews.
	BMJ Updates	http://bmjupdates.mcmaster.ca/index.asp	Medical research. Current best evidence from research to support evidence-based clinical decisions. Includes searchable database and e-mail alerting service.
	Campbell Collaboration Library[1]	General Web site: http://www.campbellcollaboration.org/ To view current and proposed list of systematic reviews, access C2 RIPE at http://www.campbellcollaboration.org/frontend.aspx	Effects of interventions in the social, behavioral, and educational arenas. The main database is C2-RIPE, containing approved titles, protocols, reviews, and abstracts of Campbell reviews. It also contains refereed comments and critiques if they were submitted. Campbell also includes C2-SPECTR, a database of randomized or possibly randomized trials that can be searched. Group workers can subscribe to the Campbell e-mail list to be informed of new publications.

46

Resource	URL	Description
Centre for Evidence-Based Medicine (two sites)	http://www.cebm.net/	Provide support and resources to anyone who wants to practice or teach EBM (Web site).
	http://www.cebm.utoronto.ca/	Resources to practice and teach EBM for undergraduate, postgraduate, and continuing education for health-care professionals from a variety of clinical disciplines (Web site).
Centre for Evidence-Based Mental Health	http://www.cebmh.com/	News and information about mental health.
Clinical Evidence	http://www.clinicalevidence.com/ceweb/conditions/index.jsp	Health care.
Cochrane Collaboration Library[1]	http://www.cochrane.org/index.htm	Medical literature.
Evidence-Based Mental Health	http://ebmh.bmjjournals.com/	A quarterly digest of clinical research for clinicians in mental health. Includes link to journal *Evidence Based Mental Health*.
Evidence-Based Nursing	http://ebn.bmjjournals.com/	A journal with appraised abstracted research.
Evidence-Based Practice, Evaluation Center@HRSI	http://www.tecathsri.org/knowledge.asp	Includes a search screen for evidence-based practice resources.
Patient-Oriented Evidence that Matters (POEMs)	http://www.infopoems.com/	Medical literature includes two services: InfoRetriever provides clinicians with the best available evidence as they practice. Daily InfoPOEMs alert them to the latest developments in clinical medicine research.

(continued)

Table 3.5. *(continued)*

Type	Sources	URL	Notes
	Promising Practices Network	http://www.promisingpractices.net/	The Promising Practices Network Web site highlights programs and practices that credible research indicates are effective in improving outcomes for children, youth, and families.
	What works in education	http://whatworks.ed.gov/	What Works Clearinghouse collects, screens, and identifies studies of the effectiveness of educational interventions.
3. Government publications (also search individual government agencies, e.g., Center for Disease Control, National Institute of Drug Abuse, National Institute of Justice)	Catalog of U.S. Government Publications[1]	http://catalog.gpo.gov/F	The tool for finding federal publications; provides direct links to those that are available online.
	Government Printing Office[1]	http://bookstore.gpo.gov/	User may subscribe to new titles by topic (e-mail service).
4. Journals	ERIC	http://www.eric.ed.gov/	Education.
a. Free searches and/or limited free full-text journal articles	Google Scholar	http://scholar.google.com/	Specific search for scholarly literature, including peer-reviewed papers, theses, books, preprints, abstracts, and technical reports from broad areas of research. Searches a variety of academic publishers, professional societies, preprint repositories, and universities, as well as scholarly articles available across the Web.

Ingenta Connect	http://www.ingentaconnect.com/	A comprehensive collection of academic and professional publications.
Public Library of Science (PLoS)	http://medicine.plosjournals.org/perlserv/?request=index-html	Open-access journal published monthly by the Public Library of Science (http://www.plos.org). All works published in PLoS journals are distributed under the terms of the Public Library of Science Open-Access License, which permits unrestricted use, distribution, and reproduction in any medium, provided the original work is properly cited. Sign up for issue alerts, and you will receive by e-mail the table of contents each month: https://register.plos.org/plos-registration/register.action
PubMed	http://www.ncbi.nlm.nih.gov/entrez/query.fcgi?DB=pubmed	PubMed, a service of the National Library of Medicine, includes over 15 million citations for biomedical articles dating back to the 1950s. PubMed includes links to many sites providing full-text articles and other related resources (Web site).
Social Care Online (UK)	http://www.scie-socialcareonline.org.uk/	UK's most complete range of information and research on all aspects of social care—for free (Web site). Can subscribe for updates.
Turning Research into Practice (TRIP)	www.tripdatabase.com	Medical research, but includes psychosocial studies. As noted on its Web site, "the TRIP Database has the world's largest explicit collection of evidence-based articles." At time of writing, nonsubscribers allowed 5 free searches per week.

(continued)

Table 3.5. *(continued)*

Type	Sources	URL	Notes
b. Available by subscription or university affiliation (check with your university for availability or additional resources)	ACP Journal Club	http://www.acpjc.org/index.html (also check with library)	Purpose: "To select from the biomedical literature articles that report original studies and systematic reviews that warrant immediate attention by physicians attempting to keep pace with important advances in internal medicine. . . . The content is carefully selected from over 100 clinical journals through reliable application of explicit criteria for scientific merit, followed by assessment of relevance to medical practice by clinical specialists" (Web site). Includes group-based articles. Free searches, but access to text is limited to subscribers.
	CINAHL	Check with library	Indexes 800+ scholarly journals and other publications on nursing, allied health, biomedical, and consumer health topics.
	Criminal Justice Abstracts	Check with library	Indexes international scholarly journals and other publications in criminology and related disciplines.
	Education Full Text	Check with library	Indexes 550+ journals and other publications in education. Full text coverage begins with 1996.
	Expanded Academic ASAP	Check with library.	Indexes 1,000+ multidisciplinary scholarly and trade journals, popular magazines, and newspapers.
	InfoTrac OneFile	Check with library.	Indexes 6,000+ multidisciplinary scholarly and trade journals, popular magazines, and newspapers.

Lexis/Nexis Academic Universe	Check with library.	Full-text access to a wide range of news, business, legal, medical, government, statistical, and reference information (Web site).
Project Muse	Check with library.	Electronic full text of 100+ scholarly journals published by several university presses.
Psychological Abstracts (PsycINFO, Psyc-ARTICLES, PsycEXTRA)	Check with library.	PsycINFO (abstracts and citations to the scholarly literature in the behavioral sciences and mental health); PsycARTICLES (searchable database of full-text articles from 42 journals published by APA and allied organizations from 1988 to the present, with earlier years in production); PsycEXTRA (database of hard-to-find psychological information that does not appear in traditional scholarly publications but is from providers vetted by APA as credible sources of relevant content).
Social Sciences Full Text	Check with library.	Indexes 350+ international scholarly journals and popular magazines in the social sciences. Full text coverage begins in 1995.
Social Sciences Citation Index	Check with library.	Indexes 1,700+ multidisciplinary scholarly journals and other publications in the social sciences, with cited references.
Social Service Abstracts	Check with library.	Indexes 390+ scholarly journals and other publications in social work and related areas.
Social Work Abstracts	Check with library.	Indexes 450+ scholarly journals and other publications in social work and human services.
Sociological Abstracts	Check with library.	Indexes 2,600+ publications in sociology and related disciplines.

(continued)

Table 3.5. (continued)

Type	Sources	URL	Notes
5. Professional Group Work Associations and Divisions; Expert Panel Recommendations	American Group Psychotherapy Association	http://www.agpa.org/	
	American Psychological Association, Division 49–Group Psychology and Group Psychotherapy	http://www.apa.org/about/division/div49.html	
	American Society of Group Psychotherapy and Psychodrama	http://www.asgpp.org/	
	Association for Specialists in Group Work (best practices)	http://www.asgw.org/best.htm	
	Association for the Advancement of Social Work with Groups	http://www.aaswg.org/	
	National Guidelines Clearinghouse	http://guidelines.gov/	Public resource for evidence-based clinical practice guidelines.
6. Theses/Dissertations	UMI ProQuest Dissertations and Theses	http://www.umi.com/umi/dissertations/graddefault.shtml	Visitors can freely access the last 2 years of citations and abstracts in the Dissertation Abstracts database. To search the entire database, one must connect from a subscription institution.

This table includes the categories cited in Cournoyer, 2004, p. 46.

[1] Free searches. For sites without free full access, check with your local library, which may provide free access.

books, such as handbooks or manuals. However, because these sources, including treatment manuals, can be published without research support, they must be carefully evaluated for their level of rigor. Books may include original research but typically include reviews by the author(s), with varying degrees of critical review and recency. However, they can be helpful as starting points for finding research.

The second section of rows includes sources of systematic reviews or pre-appraised syntheses of evidence, representing the highest level of research evidence (Figure 3.1). Some of the sources offer free searches and reviews. These sites are regularly updated and may contain group-based research findings. One of the sites that include quality-filtered reviews of psychosocial research is the Campbell Collaboration. The Cochrane Collaboration site includes mostly medically related research. The sites included in this section of the table are only some of the relevant and available resources; there are many evidence-based research sites on the Internet. Many more are listed at a site titled "Netting the Evidence" (http://www.shef.ac.uk/scharr/ir/netting/).

The third set of rows includes government resources, most of which may be searched at no cost. In addition, one could search individual federal agencies or institutes, depending on the area in which group-based research is desired. For example, the U.S. Department of Justice includes the National Criminal Justice Reference Service database (http://www.ncjrs.gov/abstractdb/search .asp), which may be searched for group-related evidence.

To find journal articles, one may look in specific journals dedicated to group work (Table 3.4), but a more efficient strategy is to conduct an online search of databases that include group work journals. These will also include journals that are not dedicated to groups but which publish group work articles. The fourth section of rows in Table 3.5 includes sources that allow free searches and limited full-text access, as well as those that require subscriptions. Some full-text journals are free, such as those published at the Public Library of Science (PLoS). PLoS includes free downloads to PDA, and one may sign up for monthly e-mail delivery of tables of contents of issues posted on the site. Additionally, PubMed-indexed articles sometimes provide full text at no charge. In a notable development for public access to research knowledge, the National Institutes of Health (NIH) has requested that its grantees submit copies of publications to PubMed after they are submitted to scientific journals (Steinbrook, 2005). Thus, PubMed includes full-text access to journals that may include group-based research studies. The limitation of these sites is that they include journals and materials mostly related to medicine rather than psychosocial disciplines. However, they are invaluable resources that may be quickly searched, and they offer the potential for free access to full-text materials related to group work. The other journal sources are available by subscription or, for students, through affiliation with university libraries.

The fifth row identifies professional group work organizations that might also include sources (e.g., practice standards, practice guidelines, or best practices). The Web sites listed may be browsed or searched for relevant materials.

Sources for theses and dissertations are harder to access and often require interlibrary loans. Thus, they generally do not meet the criteria for timely access. However, many databases may be searched for free, and the thesis or dissertation desired may be available at a local university.

Where to begin a search? Ideally, one should begin with the highest level of research evidence indicated in Figure 3.1. Search first for empirically based syntheses or systematic reviews, then for empirically based original studies. If no studies are found, move down the table to find the next level of evidence.

How many sources to search? For interventions, begin with a search of at least one site that includes systematic reviews (e.g., Campbell Collaboration). If there are no reports in the systematic-review sites, include searches of three large databases that represent different disciplines (e.g., PsycINFO, Social Work Abstracts, and ERIC). For efficiency, include at least one database that also searches books and chapters, such as PsycINFO via ProQuest. If you have access only to free databases, search at least three (e.g., PLoS, Google Scholar, and Social Care Online). Include a search of the university or local library. Finally, review one or two relevant (i.e., related to the population involved) and recent (i.e., last 10 years) group work books. For techniques, the search may be narrower. At this time, there are few or no systematic reviews of techniques related to intervening in group processes. Search at least three large databases (either paid or free), include an electronic search of the university or local library, and review at least two relevant and recent group work books.

As an aid to readers, Table 3.6 includes a selection of systematic reviews, including meta-analyses, of group-based research across a range of areas. Some of the studies include reviews of group-based studies but also review individual and/or family interventions. The table shows the range of systematic reviews involving group work that are available. This list is not exhaustive, and new reviews are published regularly. Thus group workers should take measures to ensure that their search acquires the most *current* research evidence.

The systematic reviews in Table 3.6 relate to interventions intended to achieve problem-related distal outcomes (e.g., improved functioning at post-test and follow-up) and not specifically to techniques that group workers could use to improve group conditions within the life of the group (group-related proximal outcomes). Most systematic reviews evaluate the efficacy of a particular intervention and not factors within groups, such as leadership, processes, and structures, that relate to ultimate outcomes. Scant systematic reviews examine the evidentiary support associated with group factors that may improve group conditions and outcomes. However, several recent reviews of the level of empirical support for research in these areas have been published (Burlingame, Fuhriman, & Johnson, 2004b; Burlingame, Mackenzie, et al., 2004; Dies, 2003). Table 3.7 presents the research support associated with selected group processes. As indicated in the table, interpersonal feedback (giving and taking) and the alliance between the group members and the worker have the strongest empirical evidence related to positive client change.

Table 3.6. Sample of Recent Systematic Reviews of Group-Based Intervention Studies

Area	Reference
General Reviews of the Efficacy of Group Work	Burlingame, G. M., Fuhriman, A., & Mosier, J. (2003). The differential effectiveness of group psychotherapy: A meta-analytic perspective. *Group Dynamics: Theory, Research, and Practice, 7*(1), 3–12.
	Burlingame, G. M., MacKenzie, K. R., & Strauss, B. (2004). Small group treatment: Evidence for effectiveness and mechanisms of change. In M. J. Lambert (Ed.), *Bergin and Garfield's handbook of psychotherapy and behavior change* (5th ed., pp. 647–696). Hoboken, NJ: Wiley.
	Kösters, M., Burlingame, G. M., Nachtigall, C., & Strauss, B. (2006). A meta-analytic review of the effectiveness of inpatient group psychotherapy. *Group Dynamics: Theory, Research, and Practice, 10*(2), 146–163.
	McRoberts, C., Burlingame, G. M., & Hoag, M. J. (1998). Comparative efficacy of individual and group psychotherapy: A meta-analytic perspective. *Group Dynamics: Theory, Research, and Practice, 2*(2), 101–117.
	Tillitski, C. J. (1990). A meta-analysis of estimated effect sizes for group versus individual versus control treatments. *International Journal of Group Psychotherapy, 40*(2), 215–224.
	Toseland, R. W., & Siporin, M. (1986). When to recommend group treatment: A review of the clinical and the research literature. *International Journal of Group Psychotherapy, 36*(2), 171–201.
Problem/Challenge	
Alcohol and other drug treatment	Marques, A. C., & Formigoni, M. L. (2001). Comparison of individual and group cognitive-behavioral therapy for alcohol and/or drug-dependent patients. *Addiction, 96*(6), 835–846.
	Stinchfield, R., Owen, P. L., & Winters, K. C. (1994). Group therapy for substance abuse: A review of the empirical literature. In A. Fuhriman & G. M. Burlingame (Eds.), *Handbook of group psychotherapy: An empirical and clinical synthesis* (pp. 458–488). New York: Wiley.
	Waldron, H. B., & Kaminer, Y. (2004). On the learning curve: The emerging evidence supporting cognitive-behavioral therapies for adolescent substance abuse. *Addiction, 99 Suppl 2*, 93–105.
	Weiss, R. D., Jaffee, W. B., de Menil, V. P., & Cogley, C. B. (2004). Group therapy for substance use disorders: What do we know? *Harvard Review of Psychiatry, 12*(6), 339–350.

(continued)

Table 3.6. (continued)

Area	Reference
Bipolar	Huxley, N. A., Parikh, S. V., & Baldessarini, R. J. (2000). Effectiveness of psychosocial treatments in bipolar disorder: State of the evidence. *Harvard Review of Psychiatry, 8*(3), 126–140.
Bulimia[1]	Hartmann, A., Herzog, T., & Drinkmann, A. (1992). Psychotherapy of bulimia nervosa: What is effective? A meta-analysis. *Journal of Psychosomatic Research, 36*(2), 159–167.
	Lundgren, J. D., Danoff-Burg, S., & Anderson, D. A. (2004). Cognitive-behavioral therapy for bulimia nervosa: An empirical analysis of clinical significance. *International Journal of Eating Disorders, 35*(3), 262–274.
	Thompson-Brenner, H., Glass, S., & Western, D. (2003). A multidimensional meta-analysis of psychotherapy for bulimia nervosa. *Clinical Psychology: Science & Practice, 10*(3), 269–287.
Cancer	Campbell, H. S., Phaneuf, M. R., & Deane, K. (2004). Cancer peer support programs: Do they work? *Patient Education and Counseling, 55*(1), 3–15.
	Edwards, A. G., Hailey, S., & Maxwell, M. (2004). Psychological interventions for women with metastatic breast cancer. *Cochrane Database Systematic Review*, Issue 1. Art. No.: CD004253.pub2.
	Smedslund, G., & Ringdal, G. I. (2004). Meta-analysis of the effects of psychosocial interventions on survival time in cancer patients. *Journal of Psychosomatic Research, 57*(2), 123–131.
Cancer and HIV	Leszcz, M., Sherman, A., Mosier, J., Burlingame, G. M., Cleary, T., Ulman, K. H., et al. (2004). Group interventions for patients with cancer and HIV disease: Part IV. Clinical and policy recommendations. *International Journal of Group Psychotherapy, 54*(4), 539–556; discussion 557–562, 563–538, 569–534.
	Sherman, A. C., Leszcz, M., Mosier, J., Burlingame, G. M., Cleary, T., Ulman, K. H., et al. (2004). Group interventions for patients with cancer and HIV disease: Part II. Effects on immune, endocrine, and disease outcomes at different phases of illness. *International Journal of Group Psychotherapy, 54*(2), 203–233.
	Sherman, A. C., Mosier, J., Leszcz, M., Burlingame, G. M., Ulman, K. H., Cleary, T., et al. (2004a). Group interventions for patients with cancer and HIV disease: Part I: Effects on psychosocial and functional outcomes at different phases of illness. *International Journal of Group Psychotherapy, 54*(1), 29–82.

Topic	References
	Sherman, A. C., Mosier, J., Leszcz, M., Burlingame, G. M., Ulman, K. H., Cleary, T., et al. (2004b). Group interventions for patients with cancer and HIV disease: Part III. Moderating variables and mechanisms of action. *International Journal of Group Psychotherapy, 54*(3), 347–387.
Child and adolescent sexual abuse	Reeker, J., Ensing, D., & Elliott, R. (1997). A meta-analytic investigation of group treatment outcomes for sexually abused children. *Child Abuse and Neglect, 21*(7), 669–680.
Depression	Austin, M. P. (2003). Targeted group antenatal prevention of postnatal depression: A review. *Acta Psychiatrica Scandinavica, 107*(4), 244–250.
	Bledsoe, S. E., & Grote, N. K. (2006). Treating depression during pregnancy and the postpartum: A preliminary meta-analysis. *Research on Social Work Practice, 16*(2), 109–120.[1]
	Clarke, G. N., DeBar, L. L., & Lewinsohn, P. M. (2003). Cognitive-behavioral group treatment for adolescent depression. In A. E. Kazdin & J. R. Weisz (Eds.), *Evidence-based psychotherapies for children and adolescents* (pp. 120–134). New York: Guilford Press.
	McDermut, W., Miller, I. W., & Brown, R. A. (2001). The efficacy of group psychotherapy for depression: A meta-analysis and review of the empirical research. *Clinical Psychology: Science & Practice, 8*, 98–116.
HIV in men who have sex with men[1]	Johnson, W. D., Hedges, L. V., & Diaz, R. M. (2003). Interventions to modify sexual risk behaviors for preventing HIV infection in men who have sex with men. *Cochrane Database Systematic Review,* Issue 1. Art. No.: CD001230.
Medical self-help groups	Barlow, S. H., Burlingame, G. M., Nebeker, R. S., & Anderson, E. (2000). Meta-analysis of medical self-help groups. *International Journal of Group Psychotherapy, 50*(1), 53–69.
Mental disorders, adults[1]	DeRubeis, R. J., & Crits-Christoph, P. (1998). Empirically supported individual and group psychological treatments for adult mental disorders. *Journal of Consulting and Clinical Psychology, 66*(1), 37–52.
Obesity[1]	Ayyad, C., & Andersen, T. (2000). Long-term efficacy of dietary treatment of obesity: A systematic review of studies published between 1931 and 1999. *Obesity Reviews, 1*(2), 113–119.
Pain, dyspnea, and nausea and vomiting in patients near the end of life[1]	Pan, C. X., Morrison, R. S., Ness, J., Fugh-Berman, A., & Leipzig, R. M. (2000). Complementary and alternative medicine in the management of pain, dyspnea, and nausea and vomiting near the end of life. A systematic review. *Journal of Pain and Symptom Management, 20*(5), 374–387.

(continued)

Table 3.6. (*continued*)

Area	Reference
Parenting concerns	Barlow, J., & Coren, E. (2003). Group-based parent-training programmes for improving emotional and behavioural adjustment in 0–3 year old children. *Campbell Collaboration*, from http://www.campbellcollaboration.org/doc-pdf/grouppar.pdf. Barlow, J., Parsons, J., & Stewart-Brown, S. (2005). Preventing emotional and behavioural problems: The effectiveness of parenting programmes with children less than 3 years of age. *Child: Care, Health & Development, 31*(1), 33–42. Coren, E., & Barlow, J. (2002). Individual and group-based parenting for improving psychosocial outcomes for teenage parents and their children. *Campbell Collaboration*, from http://www.campbellcollaboration.org/doc-pdf/teenpar.pdf.[1] Coren, E., Barlow, J., & Stewart-Brown, S. (2003). The effectiveness of individual and group-based parenting programmes in improving outcomes for teenage mothers and their children: A systematic review. *Journal of Adolescence, 26*(1), 79–103.[1]
Pediatric chronic conditions	Plante, W. A., Lobato, D., & Engel, R. (2001). Review of group interventions for pediatric chronic conditions. *Journal of Pediatric Psychology, 26*(7), 435–453.
Post-Traumatic Stress Disorder[1]	Bisson, J., & Andrew, M. (2005). Psychological treatment of post-traumatic stress disorder (PTSD). *Cochrane Database Systematic Review*, Issue 3. Art. No.: CD003388.pub2.
Schizophrenia	Huxley, N. A., Rendall, M., & Sederer, L. (2000). Psychosocial treatments in schizophrenia: A review of the past 20 years. *Journal of Nervous and Mental Disease, 188*(4), 187–201.[1] Lawrence, R., Bradshaw, T., & Mairs, H. (2006). Group cognitive behavioural therapy for schizophrenia: A systematic review of the literature. *Journal of Psychiatric and Mental Health Nursing, 13*(6), 673–681. Lockwood, C., Page, T., & Conroy-Hiller, T. (2004). Effectiveness of individual therapy and group therapy in the treatment of schizophrenia. *JBI Reports, 2*(10), 309–338.[1] Mojtabai, R., Nicholson, R. A., & Carpenter, B. N. (1998). Role of psychosocial treatments in management of schizophrenia: A meta-analytic review of controlled outcome studies. *Schizophrenia Bulletin, 24*(4), 569–587.[1] Pekkala, E., & Merinder, L. (2002). Psychoeducation for schizophrenia. *Cochrane Database Systematic Review*, Issue 2. Art. No.: CD002831.[1]

Smoking	Manske, S., Miller, S., Moyer, C., Phaneuf, M. R., & Cameron, R. (2004). Best practice in group-based smoking cessation: Results of a literature review applying effectiveness, plausibility, and practicality criteria. *American Journal of Health Promotion, 18*(6), 409–423.
	Moher, M., Hey, K., & Lancaster, T. (2005). Workplace interventions for smoking cessation. *Cochrane Database Systematic Review,* Issue 2. Art. No.: CD003440.[1]
	Stead, L., & Lancaster, T. (2000). Group behaviour therapy programmes for smoking cessation. *Cochrane Database Systematic Review,* Issue 2. Art. No.: CD001007. Update in 2002, Issue 3, Art. No.: CD001007.

Populations

Caregivers in cancer and palliative care	Harding, R., & Higginson, I. J. (2003). What is the best way to help caregivers in cancer and palliative care? A systematic literature review of interventions and their effectiveness. *Palliative Medicine, 17*(1), 63–74.
Caregivers of adults with dementia	Acton, G. J., & Kang, J. (2001). Interventions to reduce the burden of caregiving for an adult with dementia: A meta-analysis. *Research in Nursing & Health, 24*(5), 349–360.
Caregivers of frail elderly[1]	Yin, T., Zhou, Q., & Bashford, C. (2002). Burden on family members: Caring for frail elderly: A meta-analysis of interventions. *Nursing Research, 51*(3), 199–208.
Child and adolescent group treatment	Ang, R. P., & Hughes, J. N. (2002). Differential benefits of skills training with antisocial youth based on group composition: A meta-analytic investigation. *School Psychology Review, 31*(2), 164–185.
	Casey, R. J., & Berman, J. S. (1985). The outcome of psychotherapy with children. *Psychological Bulletin, 98*(2), 388–400.
	Hoag, M. J., & Burlingame, G. M. (1997). Evaluating the effectiveness of child and adolescent group treatment: A meta-analytic review. *Journal of Clinical Child Psychology, 26*(3), 234–246.
	Prout, H. T., & DeMartino, R. A. (1986). A meta-analysis of school-based studies of psychotherapy. *Journal of School Psychology, 24,* 285–292.
	Prout, S. M., & Prout, H. T. (1998). A meta-analysis of school-based studies of therapy and psychotherapy: An update. *Journal of School Psychology, 36,* 121–136.
	Reddy, L. A., Atamanoff, T., Springer, C., Hauch, Y., Braunstein, D., & Kranzler, R. (2004). Psychosocial group prevention and intervention programs for children and adolescents. *Child and Adolescent Psychiatric Clinics of North America, 13*(2), 363–380.

(continued)

Table 3.6. (*continued*)

Area	Reference
	Stathakos, P., & Roehrle, B. (2003). The effectiveness of intervention programmes for children of divorce: A meta-analysis. *International Journal of Mental Health Promotion, 5*(1), 31–37.
	Weisz, J. R., Weiss, B., Alicke, M. D., & Klotz, M. L. (1987). Effectiveness of psychotherapy with children and adolescents: A meta-analysis for clinicians. *Journal of Consulting and Clinical Psychology, 55*(4), 542–549.
	Weisz, J. R., Weiss, B., Han, S. S., Granger, D. A., & Morton, T. (1995). Effects of psychotherapy with children and adolescents revisited: A meta-analysis of treatment outcome studies. *Psychological Bulletin, 117*(3), 450–468.
Children about family member's cancer[1]	Scott, J. T., Prictor, M. J., Harmsen, M., Broom, A., Entwistle, V., Sowden, A., et al. (2003). Interventions for improving communication with children and adolescents about a family member's cancer. *Cochrane Database Systematic Review,* Issue 4. Art. No.: CD004511.
Infertile couples[1]	Boivin, J. (2003). A review of psychosocial interventions in infertility. *Social Science & Medicine, 57*(12), 2325–2341.
Offenders	Duncan, E. A. S., Nicol, M. M., Ager, A., & Dalgleish, L. (2006). A systematic review of structured group interventions with mentally disordered offenders. *Criminal Behaviour and Mental Health, 16*(4), 217–241.
	Morgan, R. D., & Flora, D. B. (2002). Group psychotherapy with incarcerated offenders: A research synthesis. *Group Dynamics, 6*(3), 203–218.
	Wilson, D. B., Bouffard, L. A., & Mackenzie, D. L. (2005). A quantitative review of structured, group-oriented, cognitive-behavioral programs for offenders. *Criminal Justice & Behavior, 32*(2), 172–204.
Older adults[1]	Pinquart, M., & Sörensen, S. (2001). How effective are psychotherapeutic and other psychosocial interventions with older adults? A meta-analysis. *Journal of Mental Health & Aging, 7*(2), 207–243.
Parents of children with intellectual disabilities	Hastings, R. P., & Beck, A. (2004). Practitioner review: Stress intervention for parents of children with intellectual disabilities. *Journal of Child Psychology and Psychiatry, 45*(8), 1338–1349.
Sex offenders[1]	Kenworthy, T., Adams, C. E., Bilby, C., Brooks-Gordon, B., & Fenton, M. (2003). Psychological interventions for those who have sexually offended or are at risk of offending. *Cochrane Database Systematic Reviews,* Issue 4. Art. No.: CD004858.

| Survivors of child sexual abuse | Callahan, K. L., Price, J. L., & Hilsenroth, M. J. (2004). A review of interpersonal-psychodynamic group psychotherapy outcomes for adult survivors of childhood sexual abuse. *International Journal of Group Psychotherapy, 54*(4), 491–519. |
| | Kessler, M. R., White, M. B., & Nelson, B. S. (2003). Group treatments for women sexually abused as children: A review of the literature and recommendations for future outcome research. *Child Abuse and Neglect, 27*(9), 1045–1061. |

Theoretical Approaches

Group cognitive-behavioral therapy	Petrocelli, J. V. (2002). Effectiveness of group cognitive-behavioral therapy for general symptomatology: A meta-analysis. *Journal of Specialists in Group Work, 27*(1), 92–115.
Mindfulness-based stress reduction	Grossman, P., Niemann, L., Schmidt, S., & Walach, H. (2004). Mindfulness-based stress reduction and health benefits: A meta-analysis. *Journal of Psychosomatic Research, 57*(1), 35–43.
Multiple-family group treatment	McDonell, M. G., & Dyck, D. G. (2004). Multiple-family group treatment as an effective intervention for children with psychological disorders. *Clinical Psychology Review, 24*(6), 685–706.
Psychodramatic techniques	Kipper, D. A., & Ritchie, T. D. (2003). The effectiveness of psychodramatic techniques: A meta-analysis. *Group Dynamics, 7*(1), 13–25.

Studies may fall into more than one area. Systematic reviews synthesize empirical research using methods that maximize objectivity. These may include using quantitative statistical methods, such as those that include meta-analyses, or evaluating research using an external published standard, such as rating systems that rank the empirical rigor of research studies.

[1] This table includes published studies that are mainly about group work, except for these studies that include other modalities or treatments. These studies may include a comparison of group approaches with individual or family modalities.

Table 3.7.   Empirical Support Associated with Selected Group Processes

	Level of Empirical Support		
Area	Excellent—Very Good	Good—Promising	Mixed—Untested
Group structure		Pregroup preparation (good)	Composition (mixed)
		Early group structure (promising)	
Verbal interaction	Interpersonal feedback	Leader verbal style (promising)	Member self-disclosure (mixed)
Therapeutic relationship	Alliance	Group climate (promising)	Cohesion (mixed)
Therapeutic factors[1]		Differential client value across setting	Dynamic interplay

Excellent—Very Good: Treatment gains supported by two or more randomized clinical trials (RCT) or meta-analytic studies; Good—Promising: Limited RCT support or uncontrolled pre–post improvement; Mixed: contradictory evidence; Untested: Empirical examinations of existing protocols not located (Burlingame, Fuhriman, & Johnson, 2004, p. 52). *Source*: Burlingame, G. M., Fuhriman, A., & Johnson, J. E. (2004). Process and outcome in group counseling and psychotherapy. In J. L. DeLucia-Waack, D. A. Gerrity, C. R. Kalodner, & M. Riva (Eds.), *Handbook of group counseling and psychotherapy* (p. 55). Thousand Oaks, CA: SAGE. Adapted with permission.

[1]Therapeutic factors include instillation of hope, universality, imparting of information, altruism, recapitulation of primary family, development of socializing techniques, imitative behavior, interpersonal learning, cohesion, catharsis, and existential factors (Yalom, 1995).

Thus, these are areas in which group workers should seek to increase their competence.

Search the Sources using MAP and COMPASS

Given that there are many potential sources of group-based evidence, how does one undertake an effective and efficient search? First, make sure the question meets the principles of the MAP question noted in the previous chapter (i.e., the question is member-relevant, answerable, and practical). However, a MAP is not fully useful without a COMPASS so one can navigate an effective and efficient search.

The COMPASS search strategy consists of four elements: **CO**ncepts, **M**ethodology, **P**ublication, **A**nd **S**earch **S**tring. The purpose of this strategy is to help identify the key elements of the search process and produce needed results efficiently. These steps do not necessarily occur in a linear fashion. The process is iterative, involving judgment and trial and error. The steps are described next, followed by examples that expand upon and apply the elements.

The first step is to identify the concepts and keywords for the search. To do this, examine the MAP question and extract words related to the most important parts of the question. The following example serves as an illustration: "In parenting-skills groups for teenage mothers, are female-led groups more effective than male-led groups?" The concepts include the following: "parenting skills," "treatment groups," "teenage mothers," "female leaders," and "effective." However, in searching databases, it is important to include additional words, or keywords. To do this, one can add words using a common thesaurus (there are also thesauri associated with specific databases that may be used to find additional words, such as psychology's thesaurus of index terms [American Psychological Association, 2005b]). In addition, Table 3.8 includes group-related concepts and keywords that may be used (truncation is discussed below). Here are specific examples of concepts and keywords related to the MAP question above:

- "parenting skills": parenting abilities, parenting competence
- "treatment groups": group work, group counseling, group treatment, group therapy, group intervention, group psychotherapy, group approach (from Table 3.8, under "terms related to group work")
- "teenage mothers": adolescent mothers
- "female leaders": female group leaders, female leadership, group leadership, gender and leadership
- "effective": efficacy, effective, beneficial, helpful (from Table 3.8, under terms related to "intervention/prevention")

The goal of this first step is to generate a good number of keywords for an effective and efficient search.

The second and third steps tend to co-occur and involve, respectively, identifying the methodology sought and the publications (or sources) to search. With respect to methodology, the group worker needs to determine if the question relates to an intervention/technique (i.e., a question about a worker action), a survey (i.e., a question about frequency and distribution of a specified phenomenon that occurs among group members or in a group), or an assessment (i.e., a question about a group-based instrument).

If the worker is looking for an effective intervention (or strategy or technique) to implement in his or her groups (as in the example above), then the worker would seek the highest level of evidence related to interventions, such as systematic reviews or well-designed quantitative studies (Figure 3.1). In this case, the keywords might be "systematic review" and "randomized clinical trial." Publication sources of intervention research are included in Tables 3.4 and 3.5.

If the worker's question relates to survey methodology, such as "What size group do members like best?," the keywords for a search might be "survey" or "questionnaire." For the publication source, the group worker should seek the highest level of research evidence (top of Figure 3.1).

Table 3.8. Search Terms for Locating Group-Based Research

General Terms/Concepts	Related Words (Keywords) for Searching, Including Truncation
Terms Related to Group Work	
Group dynamics, group processes	group dynamic* (includes dynamic-s) group process* (includes process-es) group structure* (includes structure-s) Note: If a more specific search is desired, instead of using the general search terms above, use a more specific search term, such as "group cohesion," "group development," "group composition," or "group interaction."
Involvement/attendance	involve* (includes involve-ed, -ing) participat* (includes participat-e, -ion) engage* (includes engage-d, -ment) attend* (includes attend-s, -ed, -ing, -ance) interact* (includes interact-s, -ion, -ive)
Leadership	group leader* (includes leader-s, -ship) co-leader* (includes co-leader-ship
Membership	group membership group composition
"Task" groups	task group* (includes task group-s) work group* (includes work group-s) committee* (includes committee-s) team* (includes team-s) task force* (includes task force-s) board of directors coalition* (includes coalition-s) cabinet* (includes cabinet-s)
"Treatment" groups	group work group counseling group treatment* (includes group treatment-s) group therap* (includes group therap-y, -ies, -ist) group intervention* (includes group intervention-s) group prevention* (includes group prevention-s) group psychotherap* (includes group psychotherap-y, -ies) group approach
Terms Related to Research Design or Methodology (selective)	
Assessment/ measurement/instruments	assess* (includes assess-es, -ment, -ments) diagnos* (includes diagnos-is, -es, -tic) instrument* (includes instrument-s) measur* (includes measur-e, -es, -ement -ements)

(continued)

Table 3.8.   *(continued)*

General Terms/Concepts	Related Words (Keywords) for Searching, Including Truncation
Intervention/prevention	intervention* (includes intervention-s) prevention* (includes prevention-s) strateg* (includes strategy, -ies) technique* (includes technique-s) Effectiveness, Efficacy, Outcomes *Primary terms*[1] efficacy effective* (includes effective-ness) *Secondary terms*[1] benefi* (includes benefi-tted, -ts, -cial) helpf* (includes helpf-ul, -ulness) outcome* (includes outcome-s) result* (includes result-s) improve* (includes improve-s, -ment, ments)
Literature review	Primary terms[1] meta analys* (and meta-analys*)(includes analys-is, -es) systematic review* (includes review-s) systematic literature review* (includes review-s) Secondary terms[1] literature review review
Randomized trial	clinical trial* (includes trial-s) experimental design randomized clinical trial randomized controlled trial control group* (includes group-s)
Survey	survey* (includes survey-s) questionnaire* (includes questionnaire-s) opinion* (includes opinion-s) poll* (includes poll-s, -ing)

[1]Primary terms should be used first. If no results, include the secondary terms in a search.

If the worker needs information about an instrument related to group work, then keywords might include "measurement," "instruments," and "assessment." Specific instruments and sources to find instruments have been identified in Tables 3.1 through 3.3.

The fourth step is to construct the search string, or syntax, for the search desired. As referred to above, Table 3.8 includes keywords and truncated terms for searches. The words with asterisks are truncated to allow search engines to include variations in spelling or conjugation. To maximize the effectiveness of the searches, the keywords should be combined in a search string. For example, a search related to "treatment groups" should include all related keywords (Table 3.8). The search strategy would include the keywords, separated by the Boolean operator "OR," as follows: " 'group work' OR 'group counseling' OR 'group treatment' OR 'group intervention' OR 'group psychotherapy,' " and so on. Search engines may permit a more efficient strategy by including portions of the search strategy in parentheses. Thus, the previous example might be streamlined to " 'group' AND ('counsel*' OR 'intervention' OR 'psychotherap*,' etc.)." Consult the instructions of the specific database for its methodology for combining terms. Combining these keywords for treatment groups with a specific term for the situation would yield the best available research evidence from that data source. For example, if one has a question about the effectiveness of group work for adolescents who are depressed, the MAP question might be, "What group treatment is most effective in reducing depression among adolescents?" The concepts here are "group treatment," "effective," "depression," and "adolescents." Using Table 3.8 as a partial guide, one would construct the following search strategy, which includes the four major concepts:

- For effectiveness, one would include the terms "efficacy" or "effective*."
- For group treatment, one would include the search terms listed under "treatment groups" in Table 3.8. Thus the search strategy would be "group counseling" OR "group intervention*" OR "group prevention*" OR "group psychotherap*" OR "group therap*" OR "group treatment*" OR "group work" OR "group approach."
- "Depression."
- "Adolescen*" (which includes variations such as adolescents, adolescence).

The examples above relate only to interventions or techniques. If one needed to find a measure related to group work, one could construct a search strategy that includes the search terms in the row marked "Assessment/Measurement/ Instruments" in Table 3.8. These terms would be combined with one or more other search terms listed in the table to narrow the search. For example, if a group worker were searching for a measure of group development, the search strategy could include the following:

- "assess*" OR "instrument*" OR "measur*"
- "group development"

One additional consideration in searching for evidence is deciding what field or fields to search. When searching sources managed by the American Psychological Association (APA), one could consult its "field guide" (American Psychological Association, 2005a), *Thesaurus of Psychological Index Terms* (American Psychological Association, 2005b), and/or the APA Web site (http://www.apa.org). These resources would indicate that one could search by descriptor, key phrase, title, form or content type (e.g., literature review, meta-analysis), subject age group, or population group, to name a few. Most

---

Box 3.1.   Widening and Narrowing Searches

"Too *many* results!"—Strategies for narrowing searches

    Search only title or keyword
    Search only group-related literature (see Table 3.8 for keywords)
    Include more recent years
    Narrow to a particular demographic group
    Narrow to a particular publication type (e.g., peer-reviewed)
    Search for evidence at the highest possible level (Figure 3.1)
    Include Boolean terms NOT or AND

"Too *few* results!"—Strategies for expanding searches

    Search full text
    Add more databases
    Include fewer terms or concepts
    Broaden terms or concepts
    Widen date range
    Include all publication types
    Include Boolean OR instead of AND

---

databases also allow one to search the abstract, and some allow one to search the full text of publications. Each database may have different potential fields to search, and it is best to consult that database, or a reference librarian who manages that database, to get the best advice about which fields to search. As a general guide, search the title, keywords, and abstract for the presence of the keywords.

Depending on the yield in results, these four steps in COMPASS might be repeated and the contents revised depending on the results (for widening and narrowing searches, see Box 3.1). The next section will describe a specific application of MAP and COMPASS using one of the case examples cited earlier.

Examples of MAP and COMPASS

Two examples will be used to illustrate searching for evidence. The first example relates to finding evidence about the best change approach to use in a group. The second is an example of finding evidence related to a common concern in group work: helping members contribute verbally.

Keisha Smith: Refreshing an Existing Group Intervention

Readers may recall that Keisha Smith is a 32-year-old African American graduate student in counseling psychology. Keisha participated as a co-worker in several parenting groups that did not include specific content to help parents manage their children's behavior. After consulting with her supervisor, she decided that she would search for a research-based approach that might replace the existing, informally developed parenting group. From the last chapter, Keisha's MAP question was, "In the case of group work for parents and their children with behavior problems, what brief group intervention (2 to 4 sessions) could improve children's behavior at home?"

In terms of the COMPASS criteria for searching, the concepts or keywords include the following: "group work," "children," "behavior problems," and "parenting." If Keisha needed to expand the search to include more citations, she would add keywords. For this, a thesaurus is helpful, coupled with judgment and trial and error. In addition to a thesaurus, keywords related to group work can be found in Table 3.8. Based on these two sources, here are some examples:

- "Group intervention": group work, group treatment, group therapy, group psychotherapy, group counseling
- "children": children
- "behavior problems": problem behavior, challenging behavior, difficult behavior
- "parenting": parenting program, parenting skills

The methodology is an intervention. Keisha's question has to do with change theory. Keisha would search for a systematic review that aggregates and synthesizes the research on group work to improve parenting practices. Her search would include the terms related to interventions and literature reviews, as noted in Table 3.8.

The optimal publication sources meet the highest level of research evidence in Figure 3.1. These include databases of systematic reviews and peer-reviewed journals. In terms of actual sources (Table 3.5), Keisha would include a search of the Campbell Collaboration library, and if no results were obtained she would search Psychological Abstracts.

The last step in the search process is to construct the actual search string. Actual search strings would vary depending on which database is used, but the examples that follow are the procedures used for searching the Campbell Collaboration (C2) database and Psychological Abstracts.

At the time Keisha accessed the site, the C2 Register of Interventions and Policy Evaluation (C2-RIPE) did not have a search engine to search across and within reviews. However, she learned that she could search the Web page that listed the reviews, but with less than 100 actual or promised systematic reviews posted on C2-RIPE Keisha decided to use a broader search strategy for this source. Thus she used a more general search strategy consisting of the single word "parent." This strategy yielded six results. In examining the abstracts, two of the reviews seemed to have relevant content:

- Barlow, J., & Coren, E. (2003). Group-based parent-training programmes for improving emotional and behavioural adjustment in 0-3 year old children. *Campbell Collaboration*, from http://www.campbellcollaboration.org/doc-pdf/grouppar.pdf

- Coren, E., & Barlow, J. (2002). Individual and group based parenting for improving psychosocial outcomes for teenage parents and their children. *Campbell Collaboration*, from http://www.campbellcollaboration.org/doc-pdf/teenpar.pdf

The reports were available at no cost on the C2 Web site.

Although she had two potentially good sources of evidence, Keisha initiated one additional search for individual studies. She searched Psychological Abstracts, using PsycINFO via ProQuest. She searched both the citation and abstract using the advanced-search screen. She entered the following in the search screen: "(group intervention OR group work OR group treatment OR group therapy OR group psychotherapy OR group counseling OR group approach) AND children AND behavior AND parenting." This initial search yielded 286 articles—too many to browse. Keisha narrowed the search to the following: "(group intervention OR group work OR group treatment OR group therapy OR group psychotherapy OR group counseling) AND children AND behavior problem AND parenting program." She also set search limits to include only peer-reviewed journals and empirical studies. This search yielded 14 studies. In reviewing the titles and abstracts of the articles, Keisha thought the following two seemed appropriate and rigorous; both were available in her university's library:

- Bradley et al. (2003). Brief psychoeducational parenting program: An evaluation and 1-year follow-up. *Journal of the American Academy of Child and Adolescent Psychiatry*, *42*(10), 1171–1178.
- Hemphill, S. A., & Littlefield, L. (2001). Evaluation of a short-term group therapy program for children with behavior problems and their parents. *Behavior Research and Therapy*, *39*(7), 823–841.

In summary, Keisha had four promising sources of evidence, which she could then evaluate for rigor, impact, and applicability (as described in the next chapter). A summary of the results of her search is in Table 3.9.

Roselia Gomez: Seeking an Evidence-Supported
Strategy for Increasing Verbal Contributions

As readers may recall, Roselia is a 22-year-old Mexican American graduate student in social work. Her practicum is in a middle school where, as part of her experience, she is leading a small group for eighth-grade adolescents at risk of dropping out. The adolescents are second-generation Mexican Americans who are bilingual and, in Roselia's assessment, bicultural. There are five girls and three boys in the group, which has been meeting for five weeks. Roselia is concerned that a couple of the participants have said little or nothing since the group began. She believes that the group has developed beyond the initial stage of group development, a stage in which she expected the adolescent group members to be nervous about sharing. In addition, she has observed the members' interactions with others outside the group, and they suggest that the

Table 3.9.   Keisha Smith's Worksheet for Searching for Evidence Using MAP
                and COMPASS

MAP Question: "In the case of group work for parents and their children with behavior problems, what brief group intervention (2 to 4 sessions) could improve their child's behavior at home?"

COMPASS Element: Concepts	Keywords for Concepts
1. Group intervention	group work, group treatment, group therapy, group psychotherapy, group counseling, group intervention, group approach.
2. Children	children
3. Behavior problems	problem behavior, challenging behavior, difficult behavior
4. Parenting	parenting program, parenting skills

COMPASS Element	Finding
Methodology	Intervention
Publication(s)	Systematic reviews: Campbell Collaboration Peer-reviewed journals: Psychological Abstracts
Search String(s) by Publication source	Campbell Collaboration: "parent," C2-SPECTR
	Psychological Abstracts: "(group intervention OR group work OR group treatment OR group therapy OR group psychotherapy OR group counseling OR group approach) AND children AND behavior problem AND parenting program."

Citations with Abstract

Systematic review: Barlow, J., & Coren, E. (2003). Group-based parent-training programmes for improving emotional and behavioural adjustment in 0–3 year old children. *Campbell Collaboration*, from http://www.campbellcollaboration.org/doc-pdf/grouppar.pdf. Synopsis: Parenting practices play a significant role in the development of emotional and behavioural problems in children, and parenting programmes which are aimed at the parents of infants and toddlers thereby have the potential to prevent the occurrence of such problems. The findings of this review provide some support for the use of group-based parenting programmes to improve the emotional and behavioural adjustment of children under the age of 3 years. The limited evidence available concerning the extent to which these results are maintained over time, however, is equivocal, and it may be that during this period of rapid change in the infant's development, further input at a later date is required. More research is needed before questions of this nature can be answered.

Systematic review: Coren, E., & Barlow, J. (2005). Individual and group based parenting for improving psychosocial outcomes for teenage parents and their children. *Campbell Collaboration*, from http://www.campbellcollaboration.org/doc-pdf/teenpar.pdf. Synopsis: There is evidence from a range of studies which suggests adverse child outcomes for the children of teenage parents. Parenting programmes are increasingly being used to promote the well-being of parents and children, and this review aims to establish whether they can improve outcomes for teenage parents and their children. The findings of the review are based on a small number of studies, and are therefore limited. The results suggest, however, that parenting programmes may be effective in improving a range of psychosocial and developmental outcomes for teenage mothers and their children. Further research is needed, particularly that which includes long-term follow-up of the children of teen parents and the role of young fathers as well as young mothers.

(continued)

Table 3.9.   *(continued)*

Abstract: Bradley, S. J., Jadaa, D. A., Brody, J., Landy, S., Tallett, S. E., Watson, W., et al. (2003). Brief psychoeducational parenting program: An evaluation and 1-year follow-up. *Journal of the American Academy of Child and Adolescent Psychiatry, 42*(10), 1171–1178. Abstract: OBJECTIVE: Despite recognition of the need for parenting interventions to prevent childhood behavioral problems, few community programs have been evaluated. This report describes the randomized controlled evaluation of a four-session psychoeducational group for parents of preschoolers with behavior problems, delivered in community agencies. METHOD: In 1998, 222 primary caregivers, recruited through community ads, filled out questionnaires on parenting practices and child behavior. Parents were randomly assigned to immediate intervention or a wait-list control. The intervention comprised 3 weekly group sessions and a 1-month booster, the focus being to support effective discipline (using the video *1-2-3 Magic*) and to reduce parent-child conflict. RESULTS: Using an intent-to-treat analysis, repeated-measures analyses of variance indicated that the parents who received the intervention reported significantly greater improvement in parenting practices and a significantly greater reduction in child problem behavior than the control group. The gains in positive parenting behaviors were maintained at 1-year follow-up in a subset of the experimental group. CONCLUSIONS: This brief intervention program may be a useful first intervention for parents of young children with behavior problems, as it seems both acceptable and reasonably effective.

Abstract: Hemphill, S. A., & Littlefield, L. (2001). Evaluation of a short-term group therapy program for children with behavior problems and their parents. *Behavior Research and Therapy, 39*(7), 823–841. Abstract: The current study investigated the effectiveness of a short-term, cognitive behavioral program for 106 primary school-aged children referred with externalizing behavior problems and their parents, compared with 39 children and their parents on a waiting-list to be treated. Exploring Together comprised a children's group (anger management, problem solving, and social skills training), a parents' group (parenting skills training and dealing with parents' own issues), and a combined children's and parents' group (to target parent-child interactions). The program reduced children's behavior problems and improved their social skills at home. Changes in children's behaviors and social skills at home were generally maintained at 6- and 12-month follow-up. Implications of the findings for improving interventions for childhood externalizing behavior problems are discussed.

adolescents are not shy and that particular cultural issues do not explain their silence within the group. Also, when she has met with them individually she has not discerned any individual concerns, including gender or culture, that would contribute to their reluctance to speak. She could hear other group members benefiting from the group experience and helping others, but these members were not similarly involved in the group. Her question is, "How do I increase the verbal contributions of the silent group members?" This question meets the criteria of being member-relevant, answerable, and practical, and may be reworded (using the structure noted in Table 2.2) to more specifically read, "In the case of an adolescent who is not speaking in group, what worker strategy will increase verbal contributions in sessions?"

With respect to the COMPASS criteria, the concepts or keywords include the following: "adolescent," "not speaking," "strategy," and "group." As noted above, a thesaurus is helpful in expanding the number of keywords, if necessary. Here are specific examples related to the MAP question above:

- "adolescent": teen, young person, youth, youngster, minor, juvenile
- "not speaking": silent, quiet, uncommunicative
- "strategy": plan, approach, tactic, technique
- "group": group work, group treatment, group intervention, group therapy

The methodology is an intervention or strategy, and therefore Roselia would ideally seek a systematic review that synthesizes the outcome literature on interventions with demonstrable effectiveness in increasing verbal contributions. Thus, the first search would include the terms related to interventions and literature reviews in Table 3.8.

The preferred publication sources are those at the highest level of research evidence in Figure 3.1, such as databases of systematic reviews and peer-reviewed journals. Thus, in terms of actual sources (Table 3.5), Roselia would first search the Campbell Collaboration library. If no results were obtained from this, Roselia would search at least two journal database sites, such as the PLoS free database, followed by Psychological Abstracts and Social Work Abstracts. As a student in her educational counseling program, she would be able to access these latter two sources at no charge. Had she no access to these resources, then she would include at least two or three additional sources along the lines of those listed in Table 3.5.

Roselia's last step is to construct the actual search string for each of the databases. As noted above, actual search strings might vary depending on the database used, but the following discussion describes what she would use in searching the Campbell Collaboration (C2), PLoS, Psychological Abstracts, and Social Work Abstracts.

As noted above, C2-RIPE does not have a search engine for searching across and within reviews. However, one can search the Web page that lists the reviews. Because she expected relatively few systematic reviews related to her particular area of group work, Roselia searched the Web site using the general term "group." Three studies came up, but none was relevant.

Moving to PLoS, she used the advanced-search mode to search anywhere in the article. At the time of this writing, PLoS does not allow one to use "or." The options include "with all of the words," "with any of the words," and "with the exact phrase." Thus Roselia may need to run several quick searches. Here is the first one, including one of each of the keywords noted above and using "with all of the words" appearing "anywhere in article": "adolescent, silent, strategy, group." This initial search strategy yielded no results from PLoS, so words were substituted from the list above. Second and third searches with word substitutions also yielded no results.

For Psychological Abstracts, PsycINFO via ProQuest was used, and a search of the citation and abstract was carried out using the advanced-search screen. Unlike PLoS, ProQuest allows one to include the first search string constructed, which, for Roselia, was the following: (adolescen* OR teen*)

AND (silent OR quiet) AND (group work OR group treatment OR group therapy OR group counseling OR group psychotherapy OR group approach). This search yielded 12 articles. From a quick review of the abstracts, Roselia narrowed the list to three that looked promising:

- Hauserman, N., Zweback, S., & Plotkin, A. (1972). Use of concrete reinforcement to facilitate verbal initiations in adolescent group therapy. *Journal of Consulting & Clinical Psychology, 38*(1), 90–96.
- McCullagh, J. G. (1982). Assertion training for boys in junior high school. *Social Work in Education, 5*(1), 41–51.
- Sims, G. K., & Sims, J. M. (1973). Does face-to-face contact reduce counselee responsiveness with emotionally insecure youth? *Psychotherapy: Theory, Research & Practice, 10*(4), 348–351.

In an electronic search, Roselia found that the journals were available in her library.

In Social Work Abstracts, Roselia used the same search string as in PsycINFO, with "words anywhere." Her initial search yielded no records; nor did a subsequent search that added "youth" to the search string. Thus, the materials yielded in the PsycINFO search above provided the best results.

Roselia also reviewed a group work text she had on her shelf (Jacobs, Masson, & Harvill, 2002). Due to their scope, textbooks may not address particular practice issues in detail, but they sometimes provide evidence related to a particular concern and can also provide citations pointing to original research studies. The book Roselia chose happened to have material specifically related to how to deal with silent group members. Roselia decided that she would first review the articles above to see if a specific strategy had empirical support for increasing verbal contributions. A summary of the results from her search is in Table 3.10. Table 3.11 provides a blank worksheet for readers.

In this second scenario focusing on a practical issue in the life of a group, Roselia was able to find a few potential resources that might help her to increase verbal participation. The results suggested that there were no recent research studies, but there were good potential sources. Now Roselia must acquire the sources and carry out a critical review, which will be discussed in the next chapter.

The two cases also illustrate ideas for engaging in efficient searches within busy schedules. Box 3.2 summarizes strategies for managing the time needed to undertake a search for the best available evidence.

Conclusion

The first part of the chapter described the general principles of an effective and efficient search, describing where and how to look. Regarding where to look, the hierarchy of research merit was discussed and a distinction was made between group workers' desires for an intervention/technique and for a

Table 3.10. Roselia Gomez's Worksheet for Searching for Evidence Using MAP
and COMPASS

MAP Question: "In the case of an adolescent who is not speaking in group, what worker strategy will increase verbal contributions in session?"

COMPASS Element: Concepts	Keywords for Concepts
1. adolescent	teen, young person, youth, youngster, minor, juvenile
2. not speaking	silent, quiet, uncommunicative
3. strategy	plan, approach, tactic, technique
4. group	group work, group treatment, group intervention, group therapy, group approach

COMPASS Element	Finding
Methodology	Intervention or strategy (related to group processes)
Publication (s)	Systematic reviews: Campbell Collaboration
	Journals: PLoS, Psychological Abstracts, Social Work Abstracts
	Books: Group work
Search String(s) by Publication Source	Campbell Collaboration: "group," C2-SPECTR
	PLoS: "adolescent, silent, strategy, group," anywhere in article.
	Psychological Abstracts: "(adolescen* OR teen*) AND (silent OR quiet) AND (group work OR group treatment OR group therapy OR group counseling OR group psychotherapy OR group approach)," in citation and abstract.
	Social Work Abstracts: Same as Psychological Abstracts, with words anywhere.
	Books: personal library, which included one group work book

Results with Abstract

Abstract: Hauserman, N., Zweback, S., & Plotkin, A. (1972). Use of concrete reinforcement to facilitate verbal initiations in adolescent group therapy. *Journal of Consulting & Clinical Psychology, 38*(1), 90–96. Abstract: Administered token reinforcement to 6 disturbed hospitalized adolescents contingent upon their emission of verbal initiations in group therapy. Results support the hypothesis that adolescents who are typically nonverbal and considered poor candidates for verbal-type psychotherapy can be shaped into emitting a substantially higher rate of verbal initiations. Reversal procedures demonstrated the expected extinction effects. The procedures were successful enough that typical "silent" Ss were reappraised in terms of their verbal potential. Once the rate of initiations increased, peer group pressure used social reinforcement to bring about a decrease in silly, off-topic verbalizations and a subsequent increase of initiations which were appropriate and relevant to the interests of the group.

(*continued*)

Table 3.10.   *(continued)*

Abstract: McCullagh, J. G. (1982). Assertion training for boys in junior high school. *Social Work in Education, 5*(1), 41–51. Abstract: 18 11–14 yr old socially isolated males were administered a modified Rathus Assertiveness Schedule (RAS) and assigned to 1 of 3 groups: Group 1 received audio- and videotaped feedback, Group 2 received audiotaped feedback, and Group 3 received audiotaped feedback plus specific assertion problems for resolution. Each group underwent a highly structured training program that included (1) developing social skills; (2) expressing positive and negative feelings; (3) expressing one's needs, desires, and opinions; and (4) increasing personal assertiveness. Results indicate that assertion training in groups can be used effectively with male adolescents who are quiet, shy, and nonassertive and who are isolated or rejected by their peers. There was no difference in assertive behavior as a result of the type of feedback received. Program effectiveness was demonstrated by postintervention RAS scores, observations by the author, and feedback from Ss and teachers.

Abstract: Sims, G. K., & Sims, J. M. (1973). Does face-to-face contact reduce counselee responsiveness with emotionally insecure youth? *Psychotherapy: Theory, Research & Practice, 10*(4), 348–351. Abstract: Considers that, as a consequence of experience with inappropriate punishment, low levels of positive reinforcement, and reciprocal social interaction among the child's family members, emotionally insecure children may be inhibited by the cues they receive from the physical presence of the adult counselor. They may be less inhibited, however, if the adult counselor is not physically present. It is hypothesized that Ss receiving this sort of indirect counseling will talk more about group goals and school-related and personal problems, will initiate more discussion, be less silent, and less destructive in the group setting. 48 underachieving 8th-grade male students volunteered to be counseled. 12 biweekly, 50-min sessions were held with a direct and indirect group. In the indirect group the counselor was not present, did not inform group members about his whereabouts, and communicated by telephone. The hypotheses were supported. Possible explanations and a discussion of implications for treating adolescents are included.

Book: Jacobs, E. E., Masson, R. L., & Harvill, R. L. (2002). *Group counseling: Strategies and skills* (4th ed.). Pacific Grove, CA: Brooks/Cole-Thomson Learning. (no abstract)

---

measure of change. In describing how to look for evidence, specific techniques for searching were presented, including identifying sources of evidence and searching the sources using the COMPASS search strategy.

Two scenarios were presented, one in which a researcher seeks evidence related to a question about an intervention and another in which evidence related to a question about a strategy for enhancing group processes, such as verbal participation, is sought. There is considerably more empirical research related to change theories. The number of systematic reviews, which in themselves aggregate many individual studies, is impressive and growing. On the other hand, there are fewer rigorous research studies dealing with the second question. Although there is much research on group dynamics and nonparticipation, there is little research on techniques. There are many individual studies about strategies and skills of group practice, but the body of research is not sufficient to justify systematic reviews about specific strategies

Table 3.11.   Blank worksheet for searching for evidence using MAP and COMPASS

MAP Question:

COMPASS Element: Concepts	*Keywords for Concepts*
1.	
2.	
3.	
4.	
5.	
6.	
7.	

COMPASS Element	*Finding*
Methodology:	
Publication(s):	
Search String(s) by Publication Source:	

Citations with Abstract:

Box 3.2.   "I don't seem to have the time to do
an online search!"

1. Examine your schedule critically. Often there is time if the activity is considered important—or ethical (review Chapter 1 for ethical reasons for EBGW).
2. Conduct searches in stages, not in one sitting.
3. Prioritize—engage in active searches for the most pressing practice questions (see Box 2.1).
4. Let the evidence come to you—subscribe to passive searches, as described earlier in the chapter.
5. Perform a quick screen (scan) of the material by reviewing its abstract for relevance to the question.
6. Work with your agency to provide more time and resources. Ideas for advancing EBGW within the agency are described in the last chapter of this book.

for group work. However, the research is growing, and with advances in EBGW it may not be long before we can find useful and rigorous systematic reviews of the research evidence supporting particular practices related to the day-to-day challenges group workers face. The last part of the chapter provided some practical suggestions for undertaking searches. The next chapter provides the tools for critically evaluating the rigor, impact, and clinical applicability of the acquired evidence so as to yield the best available evidence.

4

Undertake a Critical Review of the Evidence: Evaluate Its Rigor, Impact, and Applicability

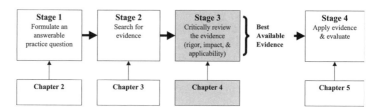

For evidence-based group work (EBGW) to be relevant for real-world practice, it is essential that group workers effectively and efficiently find and retrieve evidence. The previous chapter provided guides to completing an effective and efficient search for evidence. The purpose of this chapter is to offer guidance and tools for group workers attempting to critically evaluate the group-based evidence collected in their search. The chapter is divided into three sections. The first provides a discussion of the critical review system and an overview of the eight systems (guides) for critically evaluating evidence. The second section includes case examples illustrating how the guides may be used by group workers. The third section consists of the eight guides and details about each; these guides are consulted after evidence is acquired.

Introduction to the Systems for Evaluating Evidence

The guidelines provided here relate to critically reviewing interventions and techniques in group work and to evaluating instruments related to group work (e.g., group processes, leadership, structures).[1] Although there are comprehensive guidelines in the literature designed for researchers or expert committees, the guides included here are shorter and designed for clinicians. Abbreviated guides for evaluating evidence, designed for clinicians, have precedent in the literature (Miser, 2000b; Oxman & Guyatt, 1988; Shaughnessy et al., 1994; Slawson et al., 1994).[2] The guidelines incorporate elements of these abbreviated guides, in addition to elements from other sources, which are cited with the respective guideline.

The guidelines are divided into three areas in which group workers must make an assessment (partly based on Straus et al., 2005). First, workers should evaluate the research merit of the evidence, or its trustworthiness or validity (rigor). Second, group workers should evaluate the impact of the research—that is, how powerful the findings are, and in what direction. Third, they should evaluate the evidence with respect to its practice relevance and appropriateness (applicability). These three elements are important in determining whether evidence is appropriate for a clinical circumstance (Figure 4.1). Ideally, the evidence will be rigorous, have clear outcomes on which to act, and relate to a group worker's particular situation, all of which contribute to the *best available evidence*. However, there are many cases in which the quality within the three areas will vary, and group workers must use their own judgment to determine whether and how they should use the evidence. The following sections elaborate on these three areas.

Evaluating Research Merit: Rigor

Group workers assess a study's research merit by evaluating the rigor of the evidence, or its efficacy for achieving a desired outcome. As noted in Chapter 1, the preference is for research evidence that has been tested for accuracy and that increases the confidence that the intervention was specifically responsible for beneficial effects (American Psychological Association, 2002), as opposed

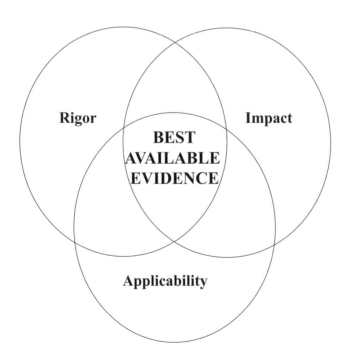

Figure 4.1. Best available evidence.

to authority-based evidence such as "the opinions of others, pronouncements of 'authorities,' unchecked intuition, anecdotal experience, and popularity (the authority of the crowd)" (Gambrill, 1999, p. 7). According to the hierarchy of research merit presented in the previous chapter (Figure 3.1), research-based studies provide the best source of research evidence, as they minimize bias. This may include strong quantitative and qualitative designs that are appropriate for the particular research question. Although the emphasis in this book is on questions that are best answered by quantitative methods, some questions are best answered by qualitative methods.

Qualitative research methods offer a valuable source of information in ways that quantitative methods can not. For example, qualitative designs are appropriate when research questions have to do with getting information about experiences of participants, questions about meaning, and examination of processes (Oktay, 2002). Researchers often use them to answer questions in areas in which there is little or no previous research. For example, qualitative methods are appropriate for studies of group member experiences with a particular intervention or leadership style. One study used focus groups to gain participant perspective about the cultural appropriateness of a potential group approach considered for widespread adoption across a state in the United States (Waites, Macgowan, Pennell, Carlton-LaNey, & Weil, 2004). Qualitative studies often yield data that can be used to generate hypotheses for testing in subsequent quantitative research. Studies may also examine both outcomes and processes using a combination of quantitative and qualitative analyses (often called mixed methods). These studies may provide a rich source of data about both the efficacy of an intervention and its acceptability to group members. Rigorous qualitative research studies reduce the amount of bias related generally to the selection of participants, methods of data collection, and analysis (further described below). Thus, qualitative methods are important for answering questions that are exploratory and descriptive.

For answering questions about causality, quantitative methods are best. Quantitative studies use "research methods that emphasize precise, objective, and generalizable findings" (Rubin & Babbie, 2005, p. 754), and include variables that can be handled numerically (Vogt, 1999). Among quantitative research studies, the controlled experiment is best for determining causal inferences; it is the best for determining whether an intervention was specifically responsible for effects.

> The main reason for the preeminence of the controlled experiment, however, is that researchers can have more confidence that the relations they study are the relations they think they are. . . . The unique and overwhelmingly important virtue of experimental inquiry, then, is control. In short, a perfectly conducted experimental study is more trustworthy than a perfectly conducted nonexperimental study. (Kerlinger, 1986, p. 293)

What distinguishes experimental from nonexperimental research "is the presence or absence of (a) manipulation of independent variables, and

(b) randomization" (Pedhazur & Schmelkin, 1991, p. 304). The most important concern in research design is ensuring that the independent variable (i.e., treatment, intervention, or prevention) most likely contributed to the change in the dependent variable (i.e., the outcome of interest). The advantage of control is that it minimizes bias.

Good experimental designs reduce four systematic errors or biases concerning selection, performance, attrition, and detection (Higgins & Green, 2005). *Selection bias* occurs when researchers manipulate assignment into groups; this bias is minimized when researchers use a table of random numbers or other method that conceals assignment from researchers. *Performance bias* results when there are "systematic differences in the care provided to the participants in the comparison groups other than the intervention under investigation" (Higgins & Green, 2005, p. 81). Researchers minimize this bias when group members and researchers are blind to assignment to condition. *Attrition bias* refers to systematic differences when there is a loss of participants in the study. Attrition may result in creating nonequivalencies between groups, a problem that researchers must reduce. Researchers often resolve this problem by using intent-to-treat analysis, which tracks all participant outcomes regardless of whether participants received the full treatment. *Detection biases* refer to systematic differences in observations or outcome assessment. Studies that blind those who are collecting data from the experimental condition reduce this bias, particularly with outcome measures that are subjective and require considerable interpretation (e.g., impressions of how the group is doing).

Rigorous quantitative methods are best for demonstrating efficacy. Treatment efficacy is defined as "the systematic and scientific evaluation of whether a treatment works" (American Psychological Association, 2002, p. 1053) and is typically undertaken in a well-controlled experimental setting. Efficacy studies tend to maximize internal validity and thus reduce the likelihood of biases noted above. Relatedly, treatment *effectiveness* has to do with "how well an efficacious treatment can be transported from the research clinic to community and private practice settings" (Chambless & Ollendick, 2001, p. 3). Most researchers have emphasized efficacy research, which maximizes internal validity, whereas effectiveness research tends to emphasize external validity, or how the research may apply in naturalistic settings in clinics and in the community. Ideally, research should be both efficacious and effective in different clinical contexts, which improves the applicability of an intervention or technique.

Many potential guidelines could be used to determine whether biases or errors have been minimized, and whether an intervention or technique is most likely responsible for an outcome. The criteria included in the guidelines were selected based on three considerations.

First, the criteria should allow the worker to detect the best indicators of bias. As noted in the *Cochrane Handbook* (Higgins & Green, 2005), there is no gold standard for determining the true validity of an experiment. The *Handbook* noted that there were 34 scales or checklists for assessing the validity of randomized clinical trials based on generally accepted criteria and concluded that "none of the currently available scales for measuring the validity or 'quality' of trials can be recommended without reservation" (Higgins & Green, 2005, p. 83). However, although guidelines require judgment, they are helpful in reducing biases.

Although there is no one best way for reducing biases, domains are consistent across most systems, many of which are based on expert opinion or consensus. However, one system includes domains supported by empirical research—that is, the domains have been associated with biased results in biomedical research (Agency for Healthcare Research and Quality, 2002a).[3] The Agency for Healthcare Research and Quality (AHRQ) undertook an extensive review of over a hundred methods for evaluating the quality of research. The authors reviewed 1,602 publications identifying 121 systems as the basis of their report about methods for rating systematic reviews, randomized clinical trials, observational studies (e.g., nonrandomized), and diagnostic test studies (Agency for Healthcare Research and Quality, 2002b). Their review yielded 19 systems for rating individual study quality and 7 strength-of-evidence grading systems that met their criteria for tapping essential domains across the four areas of research reviewed. According to the AHRQ, these domains or criteria regarding study quality had empirical support for biased outcomes—that is, these domains were the best indicators of bias in research. The guidelines provided in this book for rating the quality of literature reviews (systematic and nonsystematic), randomized clinical trials, nonrandomized studies, and multiple studies/reports include those criteria for detecting bias. Other sources are reported as each guideline is presented.

The second practical consideration was that the criteria needed to be as brief as possible, because they have to be suitable for practice. The guidelines presented here balance rigor with brevity in an attempt to include the smallest number of items necessary to make an accurate judgment in the areas of rigor, impact, and applicability. The guidelines are appropriate for a general assessment of the rigor of a research study. Research is needed to examine the validity of the brief guidelines, specifically for psychosocial groups.

Third, because evidence can be derived from multiple sources, group workers need separate guidelines to evaluate each type of evidence. There is no one-size-fits-all research evaluation tool, and different guides are needed for evaluating the range of research that group workers might encounter in a search. However, although group workers should evaluate evidence within its own classification (e.g., RCTs, qualitative, authority-based), a particular category of research might be qualitatively better than others for answering a particular research question. For example, an authority with impeccable credentials (thus ranking high in terms of authoritative evidence) might state that if you employ a particular type of technique, cohesion will increase in your groups (without an accompanying reference to specific research findings). That evidence, although strong on its own merits, should be ranked low, as it is a statement of causality. A quantitative research study is stronger evidence, as it utilizes the best design for determining causality (see Figure 3.1). Authoritative sources generally rank lower than evidence derived from quantitative research with respect to answering the question, "What is the likelihood of an action leading to a desired outcome?"

Thus, the criteria regarding rigor provide group workers with an assessment of the level of bias or error of evidence that has an empirical basis (e.g., quantitative and qualitative research) and evidence that is authority-based. Those with the least amount of error represent stronger research. All research has biases; workers should select studies with the smallest amount. In addition, strong studies use the best *type* of research to answer a particular research question. For determining causality, that research is the controlled experiment. For getting detailed feedback about group member experiences, qualitative methods are best.

Evaluating Impact

A second area that group workers need to consider in evaluating evidence is the strength and direction of the findings—that is, the impact of the intervention or technique. Rigorous studies must have clear (consistent and powerful) findings to be useful. Group workers can evaluate this by examining whether the outcomes are significant both statistically and clinically. Most studies report statistical significance, but not all studies report clinical significance (also called practical significance). Such an evaluation determines whether there is meaningful change among group members. Rigorous studies should report both statistical and clinical significance. Group workers must evaluate the magnitude of the effects of the intervention or technique. Are the findings sufficiently clear and powerful to change practice? Group workers should generally not use interventions/techniques with unequivocally negative or damaging outcomes.[4] To evaluate impact, most of the guidelines require group workers to evaluate a study's report on statistical and clinical significance on primary outcomes and to consider the direction of the findings. These criteria are discussed when the guidelines are presented.

The areas of rigor and impact are the most technical of the guidelines. Although group workers with graduate degrees are qualified to rate these areas adequately, group workers or the organizations in which they work may have access to a consultant or research specialist with stronger qualifications and allotted time to complete a review of rigor and impact. As local research specialists, these individuals have superior qualifications to complete a review and would also understand the group work population. In these circumstances, the specialist would rate rigor and impact, or at least the areas of impact and rigor that are not understood by the group worker. However, in most circumstances consultants are not available, and group workers will need to make decisions about the quality of rigor and impact on their own (see Box 4.1 for further discussion).

**Box 4.1.   Are Clinical Group Workers Qualified
to Evaluate Research Rigor and Impact?**

Implicit in the discussion about rating evidence in the text is the assumption that clinicians—as opposed to academics or researchers—should make critical decisions about the quality of evidence in rigor and impact. Group workers need to engage in an evaluation of rigor and impact for practical and ethical reasons. As noted in the text, an ideal situation would be for group workers to have access to a local research consultant who would evaluate the rigor and impact of the acquired evidence. A comparable situation would be for preappraised evidence (such as from the Campbell Collaboration) to be readily available; this evidence would provide a review and recommendation about the research quality (i.e., rigor and impact) of evidence related to the clinical questions group workers face. This is why meta-analyses; systematic reviews published in reputable, peer-reviewed journals; and expert panel opinions based on such reviews are the strongest sources of research evidence—the evidence's research merit and impact has already been critically weighed by experts, and the findings have been published in reputable outlets. However, at this time preappraised evidence sources do not provide answers to most of the clinical questions group workers face. Indeed, very few group work studies have been critically appraised for rigor and impact. Thus, from a practical perspective alone, group workers *must* engage in a critical review. From an ethical perspective, group workers are ultimately responsible for knowing the quality of the evidence they use and should not fully trust off-the-shelf interventions or products that say "evidence-based." Even preappraised evidence from reputable sources must be screened by the group worker, although such evidence is likely to be sound.

The other question is, "What qualifications are needed to evaluate rigor and impact?" The author is not aware of any standards developed from research to answer this question and thus offers an opinion based on tradition and experience (i.e., authority-based evidence). Admittedly, an academic, researcher, or doctoral-level clinician would likely more fully understand the technical aspects and nuances of research (the assessment of rigor is time consuming and difficult without formal training in epidemiology [Slawson et al., 1994] or intervention methodology). Thus, group workers must be educated and trained in evaluating the level of rigor of research evidence, at least enough to be able to distinguish good- from poor-quality research. To do this, a college-level foundation course in human-services research methods should provide minimal background for conducting an effective review *if* the course includes content and accountability (e.g., graded work) in research bias and *critical* evaluation of empirical research using guidelines that are similar to those presented in this chapter. Group workers without this background or who need help using the guides may establish a partnership with a colleague who has the necessary ability or form a journal club, a collection of individuals who meet on a regular basis to critically review research studies (Straus et al., 2005). In addition, some organizations employ research specialists who could be involved in reviewing the sections on rigor and impact in the guides. However, the group worker would be ultimately responsible for deciding whether to use the intervention/technique.

Evaluating Applicability

In addition to assessing its research rigor and impact, group workers evaluate evidence for its clinical applicability, also called "clinical utility" or "directness" (American Psychological Association, 2002, p. 1053; Atkins, Eccles, et al.,

2004; Rosenthal, 2004, p. 21). Applicability essentially describes how relevant, suitable, and supportable an intervention or technique is for a particular clinical situation. Applicability is related to external validity, defined as "the extent to which the findings of a study are relevant to subjects and settings beyond those in the study" (Vogt, 1999, p. 105). Studies that are more likely to have conditions representing real-world practice settings have better external validity than those that can not be created outside the context of the research study. To evaluate applicability, the group worker uses clinical expertise, defined as "the basis of judgments as to how research findings are used with individual clients" (Gilgun, 2005, p. 53) (Figure 1.1). This takes into account several factors, including client preferences and values.

To evaluate the evidence's applicability, group workers compare information from the evidence about the intervention/technique with their own situation in three areas: agency setting, leader, and group variables.

The agency setting reported in the evidence is compared with that of the group worker to determine whether there are substantial differences that would affect applicability. The agency setting may dictate what kind of intervention may be utilized or how much flexibility the worker has in offering different kinds of services or strategies. Some agencies may encourage innovation and provide support and supervision. On the other hand, financial costs of carrying out the strategy or intervention may be prohibitive, or there may be no physical space or staff to support a particular group intervention. Evaluating the setting requires discretion; "however, large differences in location should raise caution in your mind" (Miser, 2000b, p. 44).

With respect to the group worker, does the evidence fit in with his or her professional values and ethical guidelines? Does the worker (and clinical supervisor, if applicable) have the competence—the knowledge, skills, and experience—to use the evidence in practice? Is the competence of the worker comparable to the competence and support of the worker who originally utilized the evidence (American Psychological Association, 2002)? Are there other relevant differences between the worker and the original user of the evidence that might affect implementation, such as gender, race and/or ethnicity, language, and socioeconomic background? Broadly, what other generalizability or dissemination issues related to translating the evidence from its original setting to the current situation are important to consider? Applicability with respect to the group worker is particularly important if the intervention/technique is incompatible with a worker's values or if the worker lacks the competence or supervision to apply the evidence, indicating that the evidence should not be used or should be used only after the worker has further training.

Applicability also involves considering the values and needs of individuals and the group in weighing the evidence. Is this evidence appropriate and relevant for the individuals within this group? Is the evidence or information likely to help clients in *this* group? How would client characteristics influence the utility of the evidence for this situation (American Psychological

Association, 2002)? Workers should consider group members' age, gender, culture, ethnicity, race, language, problem or diagnosis, developmental level, acculturation, and socioeconomic status (SES) in determining the appropriateness of the evidence. At the group level, workers should consider how similarities or differences in composition (e.g., age, gender, group size, race/ethnicity) and setting (e.g., school, clinic) between the evidence source and the target group might affect the appropriateness of the evidence (*how* similar or different is expanded upon in the next section). In addition, workers should consider the group's culture and values in determining the suitableness of evidence. Workers should be prepared to share the rationale behind the selection of evidence (Pollio, 2002). Further, *involving* the group or members in the selection of possible evidence could help in determining how relevant and appropriate that evidence is. This gives clients and groups the opportunity to participate actively in the helping process. As with potential incompatibilities with certain leader variables, if the intervention/technique is not consistent with group member values or if group members are not going to support the intervention/technique, it should generally not be used (further discussed in the first guideline, below).

One of the questions that arises when evaluating applicability is, "How similar does the evidence have to be to apply to my situation?" This question is addressed in the next section.

How *Applicable?*

The text has included questions group workers should ask and answer to determine whether an intervention or technique might be applicable to their situation. However, the questions include language that requires judgment, such as knowing if there are "relevant differences" or if clients "are similar to those in the study." The question is, how different and how similar? This concern is particularly relevant for group workers in localities in which clients are culturally different from those involved in the research study, a concern acknowledged in medicine: "[c]linicians managing patients who differ economically, racially, or culturally from those recruited in typical clinical trials face particular challenges in addressing applicability" (Dans, Dans, Guyatt, & Richardson, 1998, p. 545). For example, is a cognitive-behavioral group intervention for white, Anglo adolescents, delivered in a U.S. urban setting and led by a white group leader with a European American value perspective, applicable for a group of aboriginal youth in a northern Canadian province (McKenzie & Morrissette, 1993)?

The medical field has perhaps been at the forefront in attempting to deal with this question using research findings and has provided guidelines that include relatively objective methods for determining "similarity," where the data are available (Dans et al., 1998; Oxman, Cook, & Guyatt, 1994; Sheldon, Guyatt, & Haines, 1998). These guidelines include considering pathophysiologic differences in illnesses that may negatively affect treatment response, knowing about contraindications that would reduce the benefit of treatment, determining the client's absolute risk of an adverse event without treatment, or determining whether the relative risk reduction attributed to the treatment is likely to be different because of the patient's physiological or clinical characteristics (Dans et al., 1998; Sheldon et al., 1998). The same guidelines also include questions that are less research determined (but that may be equally important), such as considering social or cultural factors that might affect the suitability of treatment or its acceptability, as well as client preferences (Sheldon et al., 1998, p. 141). In short, there is a balance of factors, including using research findings and judgment in considering how sociodemographic factors may be relevant in determining applicability.

The author is not aware of any research-based guides in the psychosocial literature that indicate when research might be considered "applicable." Although the literature discusses sociocultural variables and their effects on group processes and outcomes and presents case studies or models for working with diverse groups (DeLucia-Waack & Donigian, 2003; DeLucia-Waack, Gerrity, Kalodner, & Riva, 2004; Greif & Ephross, 2004; Toseland & Rivas, 2005, pp. 128–150), there is no rigorous outcome research manipulating cultural variables to determine their *specific* effect on group processes or outcomes. Group-related protocols state that "unfortunately, little research reveals how group therapy should be adapted to meet such [cultural] difference, and many of the findings that do exist are contradictory. Further, any generalizations about cultural groups may not apply to individuals because of variance in levels of acculturation and other experiential factors" (Center for Substance Abuse Prevention, 2005, p. 47). Thus, group workers need to use judgment informed by knowledge, values, and skills related to competency for working across diverse groups. The Association for Specialists in Group Work developed the *Principles for Diversity-Competent Group Workers* (Association for Specialists in Group Work, 1998), and group workers should be familiar with them. The application of these principles was illustrated in an example of a group for ethnic-minority adolescents delivered in a predominantly white residential treatment center (Merchant & Butler, 2002). The need for cultural sensitivity in group work is well established: "[c]ultural sensitivity in responding to the ethnic realities of our clients is the *sine qua non* for effective group work in multicultural contexts" (Chau, 1990, p. 10).

In answering the question "Should this apply?," it is perhaps best to begin with the question, "Why should this *not* apply?" In the medical field, one perspective is to "ask whether there are compelling reasons why the results should not be applied to the patient. A compelling reason usually won't be found, and most often you can generalize the results to your patient with confidence" (Guyatt, Sackett, & Cook, 1994, p. 61). There is good evidence in the psychosocial prevention literature that the concern with whether evidence will apply may be overstated; that is, treatment effects have been reported across gender, race/ethnic group, and class for many prevention programs. In their review of the research evidence, Elliot and colleagues concluded, "The *a priori* assumption that these effects are always present and that every program must have a separate treatment or curriculum for each sex and racial/ethnic group is unwarranted" (Elliott & Mihalic, 2004, p. 51). Thus, it is recommended that a group worker consider carefully the possible reasons for *not* applying the evidence.

In determining whether evidence should not apply, particularly when considering sociodemographic variables (e.g., age, gender, culture, race/ethnicity), the following steps are suggested:

1. Undertake a self-assessment to determine the degree to which you are a diversity-competent group worker (Association for Specialists in Group Work, 1998). If an honest self-assessment indicates minimal competence, consider what attitudes and beliefs, knowledge, and skills are needed, and proceed with the position that you have cultural blind spots and likely need external guidance in determining applicability (see Step 4).
2. Examine the evidence (e.g., research article) for possible subgroup responses to the intervention or technique. Check the sample section to see if particular subgroups that may represent your particular group are included, and then check the findings section for results.
3. Consider the group with which you wish to apply the findings. Is there any reason to think that the results would be different had your group members been involved in the research study (Centre for Evidence Based Social Services, 2004)?
4. Consult a cultural guide (i.e., someone from the culture in which you wish to apply the evidence) or guides (i.e., focus group, advisory group) that can serve as an initial and ongoing source of consultation.

If there are no compelling reasons that the study may not be appropriate, apply the findings in consultation with the group and monitor processes and outcomes; these steps are further discussed in the next chapter. The next section introduces the guidelines for critically reviewing group-based evidence, followed by case examples to illustrate how some of the guides are used.

Guidelines for Evaluating Group-Based Evidence:
Overview, Rating, and Scoring

When this book was written, there were no guidelines that included items relevant for groups and which gave simultaneous attention to the three areas important in determining the best available evidence: rigor, impact, and clinical applicability. This chapter includes eight systems for rating evidence from quantitative and qualitative studies, authorities, multiple studies/reports, literature reviews (systematic and nonsystematic), and group-based measures (Table 4.1). As indicated in Table 4.1, quantitative research studies may include grouped designs and single-case designs involving groups. Grouped designs may consist of randomized clinical trials and nonrandomized studies, also called analytic, primary studies (Miser, 2000a).

Table 4.1.   Guidelines for Evaluating Group-Based Evidence Cited in Chapter 4

Type of Evidence	Table #
A. Quantitative research studies	
1. Grouped designs	
a. Randomized clinical trials	4.2
b. Nonrandomized studies	4.3
2. Single-case designs	4.4
B. Qualitative research studies (includes case studies)	4.5
C. Authorities	4.6
D. Literature reviews (systematic and nonsystematic)	4.7
E. Multiple studies/reports	4.8
F. Instruments and measures	4.9

A group worker selects the appropriate guide to use to evaluate the particular evidence acquired. In some cases, more than one guide may be needed to evaluate the quality of evidence, such as studies that include both quantitative and qualitative methods. If the choice is clear as to which guide is appropriate, readers may refer to the respective guide later in the chapter, where each guide is presented and further described. If readers are unclear about which guide to use, they should consult Figure 4.2, which includes a decision tree for selecting the appropriate guide for evaluating evidence.

Structure and Scaling

The guides for evaluating each type of relevant research are presented as tables later in the chapter. Each guide has three general sections that rate the (1) rigor or validity of the study, (2) impact of the evidence, and (3) applicability for the group situation. All three are needed to determine the best available evidence.[5] The guidelines are designed to assign value to studies that do not simply *report* biases or errors but rather *minimize* them. For example, studies should not merely report data about the validity and reliability of measures used but rather should *include* measures that are reliable and valid. In addition, the emphasis in this book is on evidence that can directly inform worker actions. Thus, the guidelines emphasize interventions or techniques that workers can utilize for positive change.

Each guide has three columns. The first column includes the general descriptors, labeled "criteria." The second column has the specific numbered items and descriptions of the items. In the third column, the rating is documented using a response scale. There are two response scales, one for rating

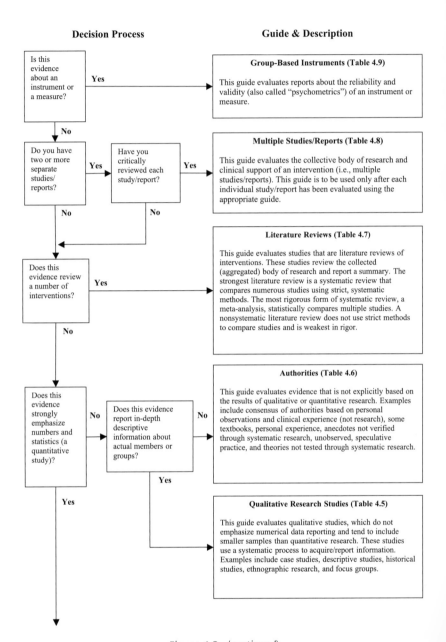

Decision Process **Guide & Description**

Is this evidence about an instrument or a measure? — **Yes** →

Group-Based Instruments (Table 4.9)

This guide evaluates reports about the reliability and validity (also called "psychometrics") of an instrument or measure.

No

Do you have two or more separate studies/reports? — **Yes** → Have you critically reviewed each study/report? — **Yes** →

Multiple Studies/Reports (Table 4.8)

This guide evaluates the collective body of research and clinical support of an intervention (i.e., multiple studies/reports). This guide is to be used only after each individual study/report has been evaluated using the appropriate guide.

No **No**

Does this evidence review a number of interventions? — **Yes** →

Literature Reviews (Table 4.7)

This guide evaluates studies that are literature reviews of interventions. These studies review the collected (aggregated) body of research and report a summary. The strongest literature review is a systematic review that compares numerous studies using strict, systematic methods. The most rigorous form of systematic review, a meta-analysis, statistically compares multiple studies. A nonsystematic literature review does not use strict methods to compare studies and is weakest in rigor.

No

Does this evidence strongly emphasize numbers and statistics (a quantitative study)? — **No** → Does this evidence report in-depth descriptive information about actual members or groups? — **No** →

Authorities (Table 4.6)

This guide evaluates evidence that is not explicitly based on the results of qualitative or quantitative research. Examples include consensus of authorities based on personal observations and clinical experience (not research), some textbooks, personal experience, anecdotes not verified through systematic research, unobserved, speculative practice, and theories not tested through systematic research.

Yes

Yes

Qualitative Research Studies (Table 4.5)

This guide evaluates qualitative studies, which do not emphasize numerical data reporting and tend to include smaller samples than quantitative research. These studies use a systematic process to acquire/report information. Examples include case studies, descriptive studies, historical studies, ethnographic research, and focus groups.

Figure 4.2. (*continued*)

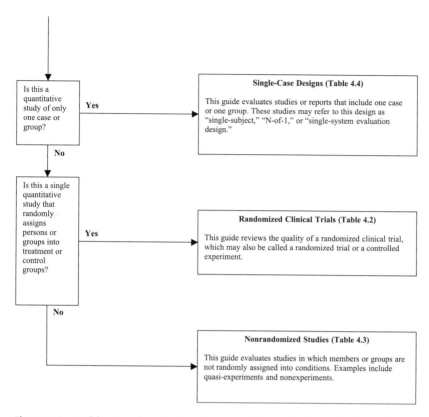

Figure 4.2. Decision tree for selecting the appropriate guide for evaluating evidence.

rigor and impact and a second for rating some items related to applicability. In rating rigor and impact, group workers rate the degree to which the study provides evidence that the item is present (ranging from 3, "strong evidence," to 0, "no evidence"). Some items include the words "if applicable," recognizing that not all items may apply. However, in most cases group workers provide a numerical rating for all items. If there is no evidence, one should simply rate it so. In one of the response scales for rating applicability, group workers rate the degree of truth of each statement (ranging from 3, "true," to 0, "untrue"). All items must be rated; there is no item that is "not applicable."

Several examples illustrate items in the guides and the use of the response scales. For example, in the Guide to Evaluate a Group-Based Nonrandomized Study (Table 4.3), Item 1 under Rigor asks if the nonrandomized design was adequately justified by the researchers. If the study provided "strong" evidence, the group worker would assign a value of "3" in the third column under "rating." In a second example, Item 12 under Rigor of the Guide to Evaluate a Group-Based Randomized Clinical Trial (Table 4.2) asks if multiple sources (e.g., group member, group leader) or methods (observation, self-report) were used to collect information in the study. However, not all randomized studies include multiple measures of sources, either because of limited resources or because the sources were not available. In this case, the group worker provides a rating of "N/A," or not applicable. In a third example, also from Table 4.2, Item 9 under Applicability asks if "the intervention/technique fits in with my agency's values and views about treatment." If the group worker does not believe the intervention would be acceptable to the agency because it is not part of the "established" treatments offered by the agency, then the rating will be "0," or "untrue." Additional examples of the items and how they are scored can be found in the examples provided below and in the explanation of the items themselves.

Scoring

Group workers should not simply tally the mean numbers or responses to get an overall score (Higgins & Green, 2005). Rather, each major section—rigor, impact, and applicability—should be evaluated separately, as well as each numbered section (e.g., "research design," "measurement," and "statistical analyses") in each of these three major parts. For example, in evaluating a study's research design using the Guide to Evaluate a Group-Based Randomized Clinical Trial (Table 4.2), group workers should not simply add up the ratings from the subsections of randomization, equivalence, number of participants, and so on to derive a sum score. Rather, group workers should obtain a *general* assessment of how well a study performs within that section by considering how many items or subsections were rated in the high range (i.e., moderate and high evidence) versus in the low range (i.e., weak or no evidence). This approach also gives the group worker some flexibility to weigh certain items more heavily (or lightly) than others when making a determination about the rigor, impact, or applicability of a study. Merely averaging or summing scores would level the weights of all items, which may not always be appropriate or desirable.[6] Thus group workers need to exercise judgment in obtaining an overall indication of a study's rigor, impact, and applicability. The case examples below illustrate how group workers arrive at a general assessment.

At the end of each section on rigor, impact, and applicability, group workers consider the evidence from their review and provide an overall rating within these three areas. There is a final question at the end of each guideline that asks for a decision about whether to use the evidence in practice, based on weighing the relative merits of rigor, impact, and applicability. More details about how this is done are discussed below at the end of the applicability section under the heading "Evaluation of a Randomized Clinical Trial."

The guides are located in the last section of the chapter, and each is accompanied by an introduction and an explanation of items to facilitate interpretation and use. Some examples of how the guides may be used in practice are now presented. Readers are encouraged to examine the respective guides as they are introduced in the case examples below.

Case Examples in Group Work

In this section, examples are provided to illustrate how the guides may be used in the three case examples used in the book. Specifically, five of the guides are used to evaluate six different pieces of evidence (one systematic review, two randomized clinical trials, one nonrandomized study, one single-subject design, and one authority-based item). For more information about these specific guides, consult the appropriate table at the end of the chapter.

Keisha Smith: Refreshing an Existing Group Intervention

Keisha's MAP (member-relevant, answerable, and practical) question was, "In the case of group work for parents and their children with behavior problems, what brief group intervention (2 to 4 sessions) could improve their child's behavior at home?" Keisha's search yielded a few promising articles, which will be used as examples of how to use some of the guidelines.

Keisha's first search was for a systematic review that might recommend a particular group approach. Her search yielded two systematic reviews from the Campbell Collaboration. The first one involved teenage parents of infants; after doing a quick screen of the abstract and sample section of the article (in the methods section), Keisha decided that it did not seem appropriate for her situation (Coren & Barlow, 2002). The other article evaluated group-based parent training programs that included adult parents but also included infants (Barlow & Coren, 2003). Although her group consisted of older children, she decided she would not rule out including this study, which is included here to illustrate how the guide may be used. The other two articles she found were individual studies of two different parenting groups (Bradley et al., 2003; Hemphill & Littlefield, 2001). These three studies will be reviewed using the respective guidelines.

Evaluation of a Systematic Review

Keisha used the guide for evaluating a literature review to examine Barlow and Coren's report (Barlow & Coren, 2003) with respect to its rigor, impact, and applicability (Table 4.7). In evaluating the *rigor* of the systematic review, Keisha found most of the information she needed in the first half of the study.[7] She found strong evidence for a clear and thorough search strategy. However, the study received a mixed assessment in terms of quality. It provided strong evidence for identifying the method of study quality but weak evidence for using two independent evaluators (both authors did the review), and there was no indication that evaluators were blind to the studies' authors, institutions, and results. Thus there was weak to moderate evidence of a sound evaluation of study quality. With respect to the study's synthesis and analysis, it is clear that the authors accounted for differences in study quality and about the studies' heterogeneity. However, the authors did not consider the possible effects of dependence of observations in the original studies. Thus there was moderate evidence for a good synthesis and analysis of the literature. Finally, there was strong evidence that the authors considered potential conflicts of influence. To obtain an overall rating of the study's rigor, Keisha considered the range of scores and judged that the level of evidence for the rigor of the study was moderate to strong. Thus she concluded that this systematic review had good rigor and that she could be relatively confident in its findings.

The second area that Keisha reviewed was *impact*—in what direction and how powerful were the study's main findings.[8] The systematic review found five studies with sufficient data to combine the results in two meta-analyses within the same study: one outcome that included parent and independent reports of children's behavior, and a second that involved limited follow-up data. Keisha examined the outcomes across the studies involved in the two small meta-analyses and concluded that there was moderate evidence of consistent findings (they all seemed to be in the same direction). In evaluating the power of the findings, Keisha found that the authors provided effect sizes for outcomes and follow-up, with confidence intervals (CI) and interpretations of these effect sizes. The effect sizes for parent and independent person reports of children's behavior were mixed; the first was nonsignificant but positive, and the second was significant with a moderate effect size (ES -0.54, CI -0.84 to -0.23), respectively. The second meta-analysis that involved limited follow-up data showed a nonsignificant difference favoring the intervention group. From an examination of these results, there is only weak evidence for consistent, powerful, and positive outcomes. Keisha concurred with the reviewers' conclusions that "the findings from this review provide some support for the use of group-based parenting programmes to improve the emotional and behavioural adjustment of children under the age of 3 years" (Barlow & Coren, 2003, p. 22).

The third area that Keisha reviewed was *applicability*: how relevant, suitable, and supportable this intervention is for her situation. The information about the intervention/strategy was mostly in the appendix of the article (p. 23), although the title gave some immediate information about the sample. Keisha examined the information and concluded that it provided weak evidence. In particular, little or no information was provided about the group approaches. This would make it difficult to determine whether the study's conclusions were applicable for her situation. She concluded that in the absence of this information and because the intervention involved parenting younger children—and as she had another study that seemed more relevant—she would not use this particular review.

Although the study turned out not to be useful to Keisha, it suggested that group-based parent training programs might be helpful, and it made her optimistic that studies involving older children would also be beneficial. In addition, the review gave an example of how a group worker would use the guideline to evaluate the most rigorous form of a literature review, a systematic review. The next study she found was a nonrandomized study.

Evaluation of a Nonrandomized Study

Keisha next examined what appeared to be a more relevant study (Hemphill & Littlefield, 2001); the intervention was short term and involved older children who were closer to the age of the children in her group. To determine which guideline to use, Keisha needed first to do a quick screen of the study. She examined the abstract and quickly learned that it was a quantitative outcome research study. However, the abstract did not make clear whether the study was an experiment, specifically an RCT. To determine this, she checked the "Methods" section to see whether participants were randomly assigned to conditions. The section did not explicitly state the design, and, to confuse matters, the section used the term "control group," which is usually reserved for RCTs (studies should more clearly state the designs used). Keisha could not confirm the design until she performed a search for an electronic version of the article using the term *random* and found, in the "Results" section, a statement that the researchers did not use random assignment. Thus, Keisha would use the guide for evaluating non-RCTs. In general, as this was a non-RCT, Keisha could not be as confident that the intervention contributed to the outcomes (due to the inherently weak research design) as she could have been with a study that used a strong randomized design (although there are excellent nonrandomized designs that arguably control more biases than some poorly executed "randomized" designs!).

Keisha first examined the study's rigor using the guide (Table 4.3). To find information about the research design, she examined the "Methods" section, particularly the section on participants. In her review, Keisha found the research design to be of mixed quality. On the one hand, the authors justified their nonrandomized design, provided strong evidence that they attended to issues of attrition and follow-up, and, although they did not do a power analysis specifically to indicate the adequacy of their sample size,[9] included a good number of participants in each group (106 in the treatment groups, 39 in the control group). On the other hand, the design was weak in the remaining five areas. Thus Keisha concluded that there was weak to moderate evidence for a rigorous research design. She then examined the study's measures. Although the study provided only general information about the quality of the instruments used (stating that "they are reliable and valid"), Keisha knew enough about them (Achenbach's Child Behavior Checklist and Teacher Report Form) to conclude that there was strong evidence for their reliability and validity. In addition, because it included parent and teacher versions of the Achenbach measures, the study scored high in using multiple sources to collect information. However, the study did not indicate whether participants were aware of treatment conditions or study hypotheses. Thus, Keisha's overall rating of the measures was moderate to strong. She found the information related to statistical analyses in the section on results (in well-organized studies, the statistical methods are often in an earlier, separate section titled "Data Analysis," or simply "Analysis"). Although the study accounted for pretest differences, there were no indicated analytical methods to account for missing data or for dependence of observations. Thus, her review indicated that there was weak evidence for sound statistical analysis. Under sponsorship and support, Keisha noted a potential conflict of interest in that the second author of the study developed the program evaluated by the study. The authors did not allay any concerns about this potential source of bias. In sum, Keisha concluded that the study had weak to moderate evidence for a rigorous study.

To find information about the study's *impact*, Keisha looked in the "Results" (sometimes titled "Findings") section. She quickly noticed that this article included both statistical and clinical significance, so an evaluation of whether a practical, beneficial change was observed could be made. There were a number of analyses of statistical significance in the study, so Keisha had to examine each to determine whether most of the outcome measures had significant outcomes (Item 1), which they mostly did. As the authors of the study noted,

> children's externalizing and internalizing behavior problems at home, but not at school, showed statistically significant reductions at the end of the program, relative to an untreated control group. ET [Exploring Together, the group intervention] also improved children's social skills at home compared with the control group. Six- and 12-month follow-up suggested that the reduction in children's behavior problems and the gains in social skills at home at the end of ET were at least maintained, if not further improved. (Hemphill & Littlefield, 2001, p. 838)

To determine clinically significant change, the study reported categorical shifts in client performance on the Achenbach measures. There was some evidence that some children's behavior problems and prosocial behaviors at home moved to within the normative range, indicating that there was moderate evidence for clinically significant change. There was clear evidence that the group intervention was helpful. Keisha concluded that there was moderate to strong evidence that the intervention had impact.

Keisha found most of the information about the first section of *applicability* in the methods section of the study (in subsections titled "Participants," "Treatment Program"), which is conventional in a quantitative research study. Overall, the authors of the report provided good detail about the group members and group leadership but little information about the group intervention and group processes (e.g., how cohesive or interactive the groups were). A training manual was referenced, but it was not published or readily available online. Without knowing the essential ingredients of the intervention, Keisha would not use the approach in her setting.

Hemphill and Littlefield's study illustrates that although a study might have some rigor and impact, it may not be applicable because essential information about the group intervention or service was not available. The example underscores the need to conduct a thorough search to yield an adequate body of evidence, because some of the evidence may not be usable.

Evaluation of a Randomized Clinical Trial

The other study that Keisha found was an RCT of a brief parenting program (Bradley et al., 2003). The group intervention was a four-session psychoeducation group for parents of preschoolers (3- to 4-year-olds) with behavior problems. The study tested the efficacy of three weekly group sessions and a 1-month booster in supporting effective discipline and reducing parent–child conflict. The study reported improved parenting practices and problem behavior (see abstract cited in Table 3.9 for more information). The abstract clearly indicated that the study was an RCT.

In evaluating the study's rigor, Keisha was able to find the information she needed relatively quickly. The information was clearly organized, with most of the information needed to evaluate rigor located in the "Methods" section (although the information about intent-to-treat analysis was mentioned only in the abstract). She gave the study a mixed rating for rigor. Some items had weak or no evidence (e.g., concealed randomization, blind to condition, leader confound, multiple sources in measurement), others had moderate to strong evidence (e.g., number of participants, instruments, and analytical methods), and a last set had ratings between weak and moderate. Thus, she rated the study's rigor as weak to moderate.

Keisha found the information about impact quickly in the "Results" section, where the study reported both statistical and clinical significance. The study defined clinical significance as larger reductions in the number of families in the clinical range on the parenting scale as compared with the wait-list control group. In Keisha's assessment, the study provided strong evidence for powerful and positive outcomes.

Keisha found information about applicability in the "Methods" ("Subjects" and "Procedure" subsections) and "Results" ("Demographic" subsection) sections. With respect to providing information about the intervention, the study had generally good ratings. It had a moderate to strong rating for providing information about group members and describing parts of the group approach. Particularly important, the parenting support video described in the article ("1-2-3 Magic") was available in her local public library, and a brief manual was available from the author by e-mail (which the author readily forwarded as an e-mail attachment). On the other hand, the study provided little evidence for information about leadership and group composition, which would make strict replication of the study conditions difficult. However, Keisha thought that she could integrate into her groups the essential ingredients identified in the study—that is, the video and leader facilitation of exploration of strategies and members' support of one another, as well as the brief manual, which provided good information about the essential content of the sessions. Overall, Keisha rated the study as having moderate evidence for a description of the intervention. Had she not been able to acquire the manual, her rating would have been weak to moderate with respect to evidence regarding the group approach.

With respect to her situation, she rated the intervention as generally applicable. The question that remained was whether the video would be attentive to racial and cultural concerns, which she and her supervisor would evaluate before use. Assuming the video was not racially or culturally insensitive, Keisha would use it to stimulate group discussion about how racial or cultural differences might affect parenting practices.

Overall, she thought the intervention would be applicable to her situation. In weighing the study's rigor, impact, and applicability (and in consultation with her supervisor), Keisha decided to use the brief intervention in the group. Although important process and structure details about the group intervention were missing, this article is a good example of an intervention that could be flexibly integrated into various types of groups. Success of the groups would be measured in the application and evaluation stage of evidence-based group work.

The three examples reported in Keisha's search show the importance of including a number of potential sources. Although titles emerging in a search might look promising, a further examination might indicate that critical information about the intervention or technique is not available, leading to a dead end. A quick screen helps in narrowing the amount of useful evidence. In this case, only one study was sufficiently rigorous, impactful, and applicable, which made it the best available evidence.

Keisha's case is an example of evaluating evidence concerning problem-related distal outcomes (interventions). The next case illustrates how to evaluate evidence on group-related proximal outcomes, techniques, or strategies for increasing within-group factors.

Roselia Gomez: Seeking an Evidence-Supported Strategy for Increasing Verbalization

Roselia's MAP question was, "In the case of an adolescent who is not speaking in group, what worker strategy will increase verbal contributions in session?" Roselia's question was different from Keisha's in that it related to using a technique in an existing group; that is, it had to do with group-related proximal outcomes. As noted in an earlier chapter, Roselia's search yielded one group text and three journal articles that needed to be further screened. From a quick scan of the article abstracts, she decided that one was not practical, as it required audio and video feedback tools (McCullagh, 1982), and another involved leaderless groups, which were not used in her agency (Sims & Sims, 1973). This left the third article, and although it was over 30 years old, it seemed relevant, as it used reinforcement to enhance verbal participation (Hauserman, Zweback, & Plotkin, 1972). Thus she had two sources that she would review: the article obtained from the library, and the group text in her office. These two sources offered two different approaches and methods of evaluation—one based explicitly on behavioral theory involving the individual within the group using single-subject design (SSD) and the other directly manipulating the communication structure and based on anecdotal experience. Following are examples of how Roselia evaluated these articles using two different guides, one to evaluate an SSD and the other to evaluate authority-based evidence.

Evaluation of a Single-Subject Study

The research study (Hauserman et al., 1972) involved a single group of six hospitalized adolescents and utilized token reinforcement contingent upon the adolescents' emission of verbal initiations in group therapy. The researchers used an SSD to test the hypothesis—whether youth who are typically nonverbal in group can be encouraged (through reinforcement) to increase their verbal initiations (see Table 3.10 for the abstract of the article). Roselia evaluated the article in the areas of rigor, impact, and applicability to her group.

In assessing the study's rigor, Roselia found that the research design, measurement system used (two observer raters), analyses, and quality of source provided moderate to strong evidence for a rigorous study (a few items such as follow-up, fidelity to protocol, and sponsorship/support were not applicable). Roselia next evaluated the impact of the study. The study did not calculate statistically significant outcomes but provided a graphic display. Visual analysis clearly indicated that the strategy, contingent token reinforcement, was effective in increasing spontaneous verbal contributions by group members. Concerned that the study considered any type of verbal contribution acceptable, Roselia found that the authors of the study left it to the discretion of the group leaders to reinforce "relevant" verbal contributions (p. 95). In sum, although there were no statistical analyses, the study gave sufficiently strong evidence for meaningful and powerful outcomes.

The last section Roselia reviewed was the study's applicability. The authors provided moderate to strong evidence about the group members, approach, leadership, and components. In evaluating her situation, Roselia's rating was mostly "somewhat true" for setting, leader, and group variables, except in the area of competence and resources. In terms of resources, she thought the lack of observers was a relatively minor concern (she could do the observations on her own) but that the strategy was too complex, requiring resources (e.g., setting up a token system) and energy that did not seem to fit the situation. A more significant concern was her lack of experience and supervision in utilizing the strategy. Without these, she considered it unethical to use the strategy. Thus, she did not consider the strategy appropriate for her situation and decided she would consider a simpler approach if one could be found.

This first review is a good example of a study that, despite being rigorous and having clinical impact, should not be applied. In this case, it does not represent the best available evidence. At this point Roselia would evaluate the other evidence she found.

Evaluation of Authority-Based Evidence

As noted earlier, Roselia also reviewed a group work text she had on her shelf (Jacobs, Masson, & Harvill, 2002), which included material specifically related to dealing with silent group members. Roselia evaluated the quality of the material using the guide for evaluating authority-based evidence. Specifically, she found a section in the book (Jacobs et al., 2002, pp. 184–195) on the use of rounds, defined as "an activity where every member is asked to respond to some stimulus posed by the leader" (Jacobs et al., 2002, p. 184). Jacobs and colleagues (pp. 171–175) noted eight different reasons for which a group member may be silent. Roselia thought that the most applicable reason (for her purposes) for the lack of verbal participation was fear/anxiety about speaking within the group. She decided to use the three different rounds that Jacobs and colleagues discussed, which grow in response time from shortest to longest: (1) a *designated* word or phrase round where members respond with either yes or no; (2) a word or phrase round in which members may respond freely but briefly; and (3) a comment round where group members may respond at length. Roselia would begin with the first type of round, ending the session with the two members who had been most quiet in the group. After this, she would vary the rounds as the sessions progressed until they were unnecessary—when the quiet group members would at least occasionally respond without prompting.

With respect to rigor, Roselia knew that, because it was authority-based evidence, it was not the optimal source for determining with much certainty that an action would likely lead to a desired effect. Using the guide, she rated the authority as having moderate rigor (on the relevant items, Roselia rated the collected qualifications of the three authors).

She rated the impact of the technique as having strong evidence. Before giving this rating, Roselia also sought confirmatory advice from her supervisor and from a co-worker who had experience in group work. When queried independently, both reported that the approach would likely have a good effect in drawing out the silent members.

There was strong evidence that the technique was applicable for her situation. This was confirmed after she discussed the approach with her supervisor and co-worker. In the end, she decided that she would use this evidence in this situation.

Roselia's example illustrates that although evidence may have very high rigor (e.g., a research study), it may not be applicable in every situation. Authority-based evidence was the best available evidence in this example. Sometimes poor applicability will override strong rigor and high impact, as in this case.

James Herrera: Increasing Attendance
in Groups for Adolescents with Alcohol
and Other Drug Problems

James's MAP question was, "What strategy can increase attendance to a majority of members in a group for adolescents with AOD problems?" Although the search was not described in the text, the most promising evidence yielded in James's search of the literature was an RCT of a behavioral, contingency management (CM) procedure for reducing cocaine use and enhancing group therapy attendance among adults in community-based clinics (Petry, Martin, & Simcic, 2005). In that study, group members earned the opportunity to win prizes for submitting cocaine-negative urine samples and attending group sessions. James was interested in this study because a quick screen indicated that it involved AOD groups (adults, while his groups involved older adolescents), and the results seemed to indicate increased session attendance. By examining the abstract in the quick screen, James learned that the study was an RCT; thus he would use the guide for evaluating a randomized clinical trial. James's question related exclusively to increasing attendance, so he focused on the part of the study relating to attendance.

In evaluating the study's rigor, James noted that overall the study used good research methods (moderate to strong evidence for sound research methods). Although the study provided no evidence for a couple of items ("concealed randomization" and "blind to treatment condition"), it was strong in most of the other areas. A few areas of the guide were not applicable. For example, follow-up was not relevant because James was more concerned about how attendance changed within the study than how it might have related to cocaine abstinence. The items about assessors being blind to treatment condition (Item 11) and the use of multiple sources and multiple methods (Item 12) were both not applicable because of the objective, relatively unbiased measure being used—that is, whether the individual attended sessions.

With respect to impact, James was primarily interested in examining outcomes related only to attendance in groups. The study gave strong evidence for statistical significance (the CM condition had a significantly higher weekly therapy attendance rate than the control condition) but also provided a source of meaningful change, although the authors did not call it "clinical significance." They noted that the number of group sessions attended was "correlated with cocaine abstinence, and each group session attended during treatment was associated with a 17% increase in the probability of reduced cocaine use 12 weeks after the study" (Petry et al., 2005, p. 358). Overall, James rated the study as providing strong evidence for powerful and positive outcomes for CM to improve attendance.

In the area of applicability, the study provided little information about the intervention/strategy. The researchers provided some information about group members and timing of sessions and offered good and critical information about the CM technique, but they gave little or no information about group composition, format, leadership, or components. In rating the situation, James noted that the setting and leadership criteria were mostly true. With respect to the group, James believed the approach would fit with the values of the members of his group and that they would support the approach. He asked for feedback from some of the group members from the first group in which he was a co-worker, and they thought the approach would have been a good motivator in helping them increase their attendance. When he evaluated the item related to group member similarity (Item 13), James noted that the original study involved adults (mean age about 40 years) with serious AOD problems, and he had concerns of whether the results of the study were likely to apply to his group. He decided that although there is a marked developmental difference between an adolescent and a middle-aged adult, the CM approach should work with either group as long as the prizes are developmentally relevant. Essentially, he could not see any relevant sociodemographic variables that would preclude the results of the study applying to his group members. James decided that in view of the study's rigor, impact, and applicability, he would use the evidence in his situation.

These three cases illustrate how group workers may use the guides to evaluate quantitative research, authorities, and literature reviews (meta-analysis). As illustrated, the group workers used the guides to get a general impression of the rigor, impact, and clinical applicability of the evidence. In evaluating rigor, the most technical part of the guides, group workers should not get bogged down by any one item, leading them to perhaps give up on a critical review out of frustration, as one item is not likely to change the overall rating on rigor. A general rating is more important than the results of any one item. After a few trials using the guides, group workers will become more efficient and effective with them. The examples also illustrated how the group workers made clinical decisions based on weighing the relative merits of the evidence in the three domains.

Eight Guides for Evaluating Group-Based Evidence

The remaining section of the chapter describes each guideline as presented in Table 4.1. If readers have a question about which guide to use, they should consult Figure 4.2. Although the materials build on the efforts of others (documented at the bottom of each guide) and many items apply to all modalities, as far as the author is aware, these are the first guidelines designed specifically for group workers that include in each guide an assessment of rigor, impact, and clinical applicability for determining the best available evidence. Although the items are based on standards developed and tested by others, the specific guidelines need validation in research studies involving groups. Group workers need to use clinical judgment in using these guides, which provide a general assessment of the rigor, impact, and applicability of evidence.

Guide to Evaluating a Group-Based Randomized
Clinical Trial

The strongest quantitative group research design is the randomized clinical trial (RCT). (For questions about which guide to use, consult Figure 4.2.) There are many examples of such studies (Avants, Margolin, Usubiaga, & Doebrick, 2004; Cordioli et al., 2003; DiNitto, Webb, & Rubin, 2002; Rosenblum, Magura, Kayman, & Fong, 2005). For determining causality, an RCT is likely to have the highest rigor when compared with a study that did not randomly assign participants to conditions. These studies maximize internal validity, defined as "the extent to which the results of a study (usually an experiment) can be attributed to the treatments rather than to flaws in the research design. In other words, internal validity is the degree to which one can draw valid conclusions about the causal effects of one variable on another" (Vogt, 1999, p. 143). Highly controlled experiments limit the confounding effects of extraneous variables in explaining how the independent variable (treatment or intervention) affects the dependent variable (the outcome, such as depression, drug use). However, there are variations in quality across RCTs. Table 4.2 provides guidelines for evaluating the strength of an RCT's rigor, impact, and applicability. Only items that need additional commentary are discussed in the text below. The elements included in Table 4.2 are drawn from a number of sources (Agency for Healthcare Research and Quality, 2002a; Atkins, Best, et al., 2004; Centre for Evidence Based Social Services, 2004; Gibbs, 2003; Higgins & Green, 2005; Kratochwill, 2002, 2003; Lewis-Snyder, Stoiber, & Kratochwill, 2002; Miser, 2000b; Pyrczak, 2005; Straus et al., 2005). To illustrate how a group worker would use the guide, the chapter provides two examples (Keisha Smith and James Herrera).

Explanation of Items in Table 4.2

Rigor   *Item 1.* Individual group members should be randomly assigned to conditions (i.e., treatment, untreated control, or comparison). There must be a control or comparison group so that the researcher can determine whether the treatment group did better than the group with no treatment or an alternate treatment. Control groups typically involve no treatment. Comparison groups may receive any of the following: a usual intervention without the addition of the experimental treatment, an alternative intervention, a wait-list group treatment that is delivered at a later time but that initially involves only the pretest and post-test measures, or a placebo in which the condition receives attention but no effective treatment.

Item 2. To reduce selection bias (systematic differences between groups), the process of randomization should be concealed from study personnel and group members (Higgins & Green, 2005; Straus et al., 2005). This is to prevent the possibility of people "tinkering with which groups people were allocated to" (Centre for Evidence Based Social Services, 2004). Group

Table 4.2. Guide to Evaluating a Group-Based Randomized Clinical Trial

Criteria	Items/Descriptions	Rating The study provided: 3—strong evidence 2—moderate evidence 1—weak evidence 0—no evidence N/A—not applicable
A. Rigor (Did the study use sound research methods?)		
1. Research Design		
Randomization	1. Individuals were randomly assigned to conditions *and* individuals were randomly assigned to groups within conditions (with no exceptions made to assignment).	_____
	2. Randomization was concealed from group members and study personnel to avoid selection bias.	_____
Equivalence	3. Groups were equivalent at the beginning of the study on key variables.	_____
Number of participants	4. There were a sufficient number of participants. This is best determined by a power analysis, but a study that includes *at least* 25 participants per condition offers some evidence that this criterion is met.	_____
Blind to condition	5. Group members, group workers, and assessors (i.e., those completing assessment measures) were blind to (unaware of) treatment condition, or at least to the hypotheses of the study.	_____
Leader confound	6. The researchers reduced the personal effect of particular group leaders. This may be accomplished by assigning group leaders to all treatments, counterbalancing group leaders across conditions, or a statistical analysis that controls for group leader effect across conditions.	_____

Attrition	7. All participants/groups who/that began the study were accounted for at the end of the study and at follow-up (strongest evidence = all were accounted for, but no less than 80% at post-test and 70% at follow-up).[a]	
Follow-up	8. Follow-up of members was sufficiently long—at least 6 months after the end of the study, with strongest evidence at 1 year or more (lower the rating one point if follow-up did not consist of at least 70% of original study participants).	
Fidelity to protocol	9. Fidelity to the intervention/technique was maximized by (a) training leader, (b) leader use of a manual or guide, (c) supervision, and (d) optimally, monitoring sessions by two or more independent raters (using audio or videotape, session checklists).	
2. Measurement	10. Instruments used to measure primary outcomes or processes were reliable and valid (see text for further definitions). If multiple observers were used to collect data, rater agreement was at least 70% or 0.70 (higher levels of agreement indicate stronger evidence).	
	11. Those who completed the measures were blind to (unaware of) the treatment condition or at least the study hypotheses (if applicable).	
	12. If applicable, multiple *sources* (at least two, such as group member, group leader, parent, independent observer) or multiple *methods* (at least two, such as observation, self-report, rating by others) were used to collect information.	
3. Statistical Analyses	13. Analytical methods were used to account for any missing data, study withdrawals, or loss to follow-up (if applicable). A method of accounting for missing data is imputation, and a method to account for withdrawals or loss to follow up is intent-to-treat analysis.	
	14. Analyses were done at the group level using statistical procedures that accounted for the dependence of observations (e.g., multilevel analyses such as *Hierarchical Linear Modeling* [HLM]).	

(continued)

105

Table 4.2. *(continued)*

Criteria	Items/Descriptions	*Rating* The study provided: 3—strong evidence 2—moderate evidence 1—weak evidence 0—no evidence N/A—not applicable
4. Sponsorship/Support	15. If applicable, potential conflicts of interest were identified and, if present, dealt with to allay concerns about sponsor influence over the research.	_____
5. Quality of Source	16. The study is in a publication or source employing blind peer review.	_____
Summary	Overall, what is the level of evidence for the rigor of the study?	_____

B. Impact (How powerful and in what direction were the main findings?)

1. Statistical Significance	1. The study had statistically significant outcomes for most of the primary outcome measures for each key construct (e.g., if the study used three measures of depression, at least two had significant outcomes), at $p < 0.05$. Rate highest a study that demonstrates statistically significant change on all measures.	_____
2. Clinical Significance	2. The results using the primary outcome measures were *clinically* significant. This can be demonstrated statistically with reports of reliable change index (RCI), effect size (ES), or, more rarely, absolute risk reduction (ARR) or numbers needed to treat (NNT) with accompanying 95% confidence interval (CI). It may also be demonstrated by categorical changes in client functioning (e.g., improved, unchanged, deteriorated), which the authors must fully explain (see text for further discussion).	_____

3. Direction of Findings

If the results of the analyses were statistically and/or clinically significant, there was clear evidence that the intervention/technique was helpful.

Summary   Overall, what is the level of evidence for powerful and positive outcomes?

C. Applicability (Is this intervention/technique relevant to my situation?)

1. Intervention/Technique

Group members   1. The characteristics of group members were identified (age, gender, race/ethnicity, language/acculturation, developmental level, problem/diagnoses, socioeconomic status).

Group approach(es)   2. The intervention/technique was detailed (e.g., a manual or session outline was provided or available).

3. The timing of sessions was detailed (number of sessions, how often, how long each session lasted).

4. Group composition was detailed (size, gender, age, race/ethnicity, criteria for membership).

5. Group format was identified (closed, open, slow open) and location specified.

Group leadership   6. Group leadership was adequately described (number of leaders, co-leadership, race/ethnicity, gender, training/education/experience).

Group components   7. The study included measures of group processes or dynamics (e.g., cohesion, engagement, therapeutic alliance, interaction) to help in replication.

Summary   Overall, what is the level of evidence about the intervention/technique?

(continued)

Table 4.2. *(continued)*

Criteria	Items/Descriptions	Rating The statement is: 3—true 2—somewhat true 1—somewhat untrue 0—untrue
2. Situation		
Setting	8. I have adequate resources (e.g., finances, physical space, staff) to provide the same intervention/technique in my setting.	_____
	9. The intervention/technique fits in with my agency's values and views about treatment.	_____
	10. The intervention/technique is compatible with my professional values and ethical guidelines. [b]	_____
Leader	11. I have the competence (knowledge, skills, and experience) or appropriate supervision to use the intervention/technique in practice. [b]	_____
	12. There are no other relevant differences between me and the group leader in the study that might affect implementation, such as gender, race and ethnicity, language/acculturation, and socioeconomic background.	_____
Group	13. My group members are sufficiently similar to those in the study in terms of sociodemographic variables that the results are likely to apply (consider age, gender, culture, race/ethnicity, language/acculturation, problem/diagnosis, developmental level, and socioeconomic status). (When there are differences in sociodemographic variables, rate this item positively if the differences are not likely to affect how the intervention/technique would likely perform with your group members.)	_____

14. The intervention/technique fits in with my group members' norms, culture, or values (if possible, involve group members in rating this item).[b]

15. My group members are likely to support this intervention/technique (if possible, involve group members in rating this item).[b]

Summary   Overall, this intervention/technique is applicable for my situation.

Decision: Considering the study's rigor, impact, and applicability, should I use this evidence in this situation? Circle one: yes / probably / probably not / no

Material in this table is drawn from a number of sources (Miser, 2000b; Agency for Healthcare Research and Quality, 2002a; Gibbs, 2003; Kratochwill, 2002, 2003; Lewis-Snyder, Stoiber, & Kratochwill, 2002; Atkins et al., 2004; Centre for Evidence Based Social Services, 2004; Higgins & Green, 2005; Pyrczak, 2005; Straus, Richardson, Glasziou, & Haynes, 2005).

[a] Source: Kratochwill (2003). Also, Straus et al. (2005, p. 121) noted that at least one medical journal requires 80% or more follow-up in a study for it to be considered for publication.

[b] In general, a rating of "untrue" or "somewhat untrue" in these items indicates that the intervention/technique should not be used.

members should then be randomly assigned to groups within conditions, a procedure that increases the likelihood that member characteristics are randomly distributed across groups within conditions. If this is not done, group member similarities may become clustered in particular groups within conditions. These compositional variables, not created by chance, might unexpectedly add an unchecked extraneous variable. It should be noted that researchers in clinical studies in community settings may not always be able to control variations in composition if they are to maintain some principle of composition. These situations should be acknowledged in such studies and an effort made (if possible) to distribute characteristics equally across groups.

Item 3. Randomization can sometimes result in unbalanced or nonequivalent groups on variables of interest. Researchers should demonstrate that the treatment and control groups were equivalent at the start of the study on important variables (Kratochwill, 2002, p. 30; Straus et al., 2005, p. 117). The researchers must answer the question, "Were there any key differences between the groups at baseline, which might, in part, account for any differences in outcome (known as confounders)?" (Centre for Evidence Based Social Services, 2004). If there are occasions when variables are important to match, random assignment can be coupled with matching groups on variables of interest, such as age or gender.

Item 4. Research studies must provide evidence that there was a sufficiently large number of participants (after attrition) to yield enough statistical power for detecting differences (Kratochwill, 2003). A common general guideline has been to require that each condition have a minimum number of participants, generally 25 to 30 (Chambless et al., 1996; Chambless & Hollon, 1998). A more effective and respected method is for researchers to conduct a power analysis to determine the required number of participants needed for a particular effect size (small, medium, large) given a particular probability value (e.g., $p < 0.05$). If there were insufficient participants, the study may not have been able to detect a difference simply because too few people took part (Centre for Evidence Based Social Services, 2004). Thus, in using the guide, workers should remember that studies that support the adequacy of the sample size by using a power analysis (with moderate power) employ the best method. However, studies that have at least 25 participants per condition (i.e., the traditional cutoff) are adequate and are better than studies that include fewer participants.

Item 5. To reduce leader, member, and study personnel influence on outcomes, it is best to blind them to treatment condition after assignment. This procedure helps prevent group members, leaders, or personnel from making progress judgments based on expectations of performance. Double-blind studies are common in medical trials in which researchers can make the substances consumed look similar (Miser, 2000b). Double-blind studies are not common in psychosocial research but may appear in situations in which researchers create a comparison condition that includes a benign alternative treatment. It is also important to have assessors who are blinded to condition

(Centre for Evidence Based Social Services, 2004), and there is an item in the guide that evaluates for this specific concern (in the section on measurement, described below). However, if members, leaders, and study personnel cannot be blinded to conditions, blinding them to the hypotheses of the study may prevent the potential bias of fulfilling expectancies of outcomes (Stinchfield, Owen, & Winters, 1994, p. 478).

Item 6. In studies that include more than one group worker or group condition, researchers must minimize the "personal effect" of a particular group worker (Pyrczak, 2005, p. 104). In such studies,

> [g]roup therapy conditions were frequently confounded with the therapist variable. This confound occurred because each group therapy condition was conducted by a different therapist, that is, the therapist variable was nested, rather than crossed, with treatment conditions. Therefore, it is unknown how much of the effect is due to the group therapy condition and how much is attributable to the particular therapist conducting the group. (Stinchfield et al., 1994, p. 478)

To reduce this agent-by-condition confound, group workers can be assigned to deliver all treatments, or they can be counterbalanced across treatment groups or conditions. As an acceptable alternative, researchers can control for group worker effects using particular statistical analysis (Kratochwill, 2003, p. 30), which the researchers must document.

Item 7. Strong experimental designs control for attrition bias (Higgins & Green, 2005). Attrition bias occurs when researchers do not account for participants who begin the study but drop out before the end of the study or before follow-up. This generates the problem of potentially creating substantive differences between subjects (i.e., group members or entire groups) who began the study and those who dropped out (Kratochwill, 2003, p. 31). Most studies will have dropouts, but the strongest studies minimize the number of dropouts to the standards presented in Item 7. Sometimes researchers will account for dropouts using a procedure called intent-to-treat analysis, which is further described in the subsection on statistical analysis below. If they used such a procedure, item 7 would be rated positively.

Item 9. Fidelity to the intervention or technique is important to ensure that what the researchers purport to be responsible for change was accurately delivered. Fidelity to the intervention can be determined by a number of methods in a research study, identified in Table 4.2, including training, use of a guide, supervision, and audio or video monitoring. The strongest research includes all of these. In addition, strong research may also detail how the manual was adapted during intervention. A manual or guideline is essential for replicating the intervention or technique in practice (see Box 4.2 for more on manualized group curricula).

Item 10. A common form of reliability reported is internal consistency. Sources may report this as "coefficient alpha," "Cronbach's alpha," "alpha," or "α"; it is a correlation coefficient with a range of 0.00 to 1.00. A value of 0.70

Box 4.2.   Manualized Group Interventions

Manualized group interventions have many strengths, including the ability to help group workers deliver the "active ingredients" of the proposed intervention. However, they have two potential limitations. First, they may give the impression of a script and suggest that *any* deviation is forbidden. Overly rigid requirements for maintaining the elements of the manual might potentially override important issues that may arise in the group and are not included in the manual. Manuals may create a dependence on a script and neglect important opportunities to deal with processes in a group to make the group function more effectively. This concern is not necessarily about the use of manuals per se but the strict application of any type of structure, such as group activities. Sticking firmly to a script or agenda may prevent leaders from identifying and working with processes or themes within the group that may affect participation. Thus, manuals should allow some latitude, flexibility, or creativity in application, as long as the *essential* elements of the session (which must be identified in the manual) are covered.

Second, manuals might not include information about group processes, structures, or leadership that is important for success. A recent example of a manual that includes information about group process is *Making Choices: Social Problem-Solving Skills for Children* (Fraser, Nash, Galinsky, & Darwin, 2000). Manuals should include information about the best compositional dynamics for success, particular leader strategies that are helpful for dealing with challenging or opportunistic group situations, and what to expect from group members. Thus, manualized group interventions can maximize the likelihood that essential components of the intervention are delivered, and, rather than being mechanistic, they can be sensitive to group dynamics and group work practice principles (Galinsky, Terzian, & Fraser, 2006).

---

suggests that the measure has *adequate* internal consistency (Kratochwill, 2003, p. 26). However, this is a *minimal* threshold; reliability of 0.80 is *good* reliability (Bloom, Fischer, & Orme, 2003). Thus, 0.70 indicates minimal evidence (i.e., "weak" evidence) of reliability, and a higher coefficient indicates stronger evidence. Some researchers may also include reports of rater agreement (interrater reliability) about measures. If they do, the agreement should be at least 70%, or 0.70 (Bloom et al., 2003; Gibbs, 2003, p. 165), which is a minimal threshold (i.e., "weak" evidence), with 80% or 0.80 representing *good* agreement between raters (Bloom et al., 2003) and thus stronger evidence. In addition, if researchers in the study used raters or observers to collect data, the study should include information about rater agreement (also known as interrater, interobserver, or interjudge agreement), which should be at least 70% or 0.70.

With respect to validity, researchers must present data that indicate that each of the primary measures used in the study measured what it was intended to measure (Lewis-Snyder et al., 2002, p. 430). There are many forms of validity. The simplest, weakest form of validity is face validity, which asks, "Does this measure appear to measure what it is supposed to measure?" Stronger forms of validity are empirically based and include criterion validity ("Does this measure correlate with a criterion with which it is supposed to correlate?"; this may include concurrent and predictive validity) and construct validity ("Does this measure perform as expected against other related constructs?"; this might include convergent or divergent validity, or it may be determined using confirmatory or exploratory factor analysis).

Item 11. As noted in Item 5, raters who have completed measures should ideally not know which condition their subjects were from, or at least should not be aware of the hypotheses of the study ("blind" to condition or hypotheses, respectively) (Centre for Evidence Based Social Services, 2004). The concern here is minimizing detection biases—that is, systematic differences in observations or outcome assessments (Higgins & Green, 2005). Studies that blind those who collect data to the experimental condition reduce this bias, particularly with outcome measures that are subjective and require considerable interpretation (e.g., impressions of how the group is doing) (Higgins & Green, 2005). Sometimes this concern is not applicable when the measures are objective, simple, and relatively bias free, such as binomial ratings of whether an individual attends group or not.

Item 12. Although not all studies can include multiple measures and sources (i.e., they have limited resources or multiple sources are not available), there are many that can and should. Such rigorous measurement systems use multiple methods and multiple sources on each variable (Pyrczak, 2005, p. 86). Multiple (i.e., at least two) assessment methods may include observations, self-reports, or behavior ratings (Kratochwill, 2003, p. 27) and multiple sources such as group leader, group member, or independent observer (Kratochwill, 2003; Lewis-Snyder et al., 2002, p. 430). Sometimes multiple measures or sources are not needed, as in the case of data not subject to significant bias, such as attendance or whether an individual is incarcerated.

Item 13. There are two areas related to statistical analyses that need to be rated: how the study dealt with subject dropouts, and missing data. In their review of methods for evaluating study quality, the AHRQ (Agency for Healthcare Research and Quality, 2002b) identified dealing with dropouts and missing data (by using appropriate analytic techniques for addressing study withdrawals, loss to follow-up, and missing data) as essential to identifying and minimizing bias. Thus, RCTs must indicate how they dealt with this issue. Group members may drop out or may not complete all group sessions, and researchers need to record these events and, more rigorously, track these members regardless of whether they completed the entire trial. To accomplish this, rigorous RCTs include "intent-to-treat" analysis, in which all group members "are analyzed in the groups to which they were initially assigned, regardless of whether they received their assigned treatment" (Straus et al., 2005, p. 122). If researchers document no dropouts or missing data, these analytical methods are not applicable.

Item 14. A long-standing and critical concern in group-based research is controlling for the unit of analysis (Glisson, 1986), which may be defined as the person or things being studied (Vogt, 1999). In group-based research, the unit of analysis could be the individual group member or the group as a whole.

Knowing which to control for is important, because a concern in aggregating people in groups is that it creates a potential violation of an important statistical assumption of independence of observations. This creates a problem called collinearity (also called multicollinearity), which occurs when predictor variables correlate with each other. "This, in turn, leads to an underestimate of the standard errors of conventional statistical tests, resulting in spurious 'significant' results" (Johnson, Burlingame, Olsen, Davies, & Gleave, 2005, p. 311). Members within a group are not independent of each other; they are influenced by and influence others in the group. This statistical problem has been a long-standing concern in group-based research (Baldwin, Murray, & Shadish, 2005; Burlingame, Kircher, & Taylor, 1994) and should be corrected using specific statistical procedures. One method of controlling for this concern is to utilize hierarchical analyses that separate individual and group effects, such as the Hierarchical Linear Modeling (HLM) that has been used in rigorous group-based research (Johnson et al., 2005; Kivlighan & Tarrant, 2001; Shechtman, 2003). Thus, the strongest group-based research studies control for this effect by using hierarchical models that simultaneously analyze data at the individual and group levels (Johnson et al., 2005; Kratochwill, 2003).

Item 15. Another factor related to biased results in biomedical research is funding or sponsorship (Agency for Healthcare Research and Quality, 2002a). Rigorous studies identify the type and sources of support for the study and identify methods by which the researchers have minimized bias.

Item 16. A lesser factor in determining study quality is to consider the quality of the publication source. Merely examining author credentials or prestige of publisher is not adequate for determining scientific quality. As Oxman and Guyatt (1988) have noted, "experts reviewing the same topic often come to different conclusions" (p. 698). However, having two or more independent raters helps to reduce mistakes (random errors) and biases (systematic errors), and if there is good agreement among reviewers the reader can have more confidence in the findings from the review (Oxman et al., 1994).[10]

Impact   Item 1. The impact of a group intervention is determined by examining the strength and direction of the changes in measured outcomes. Statistically significant changes should be at least $p < 0.05$ (i.e., there is at most a 5% chance that differences were due to chance). In cases where multiple measures were used to assess primary constructs, there must be a demonstration of significance in most of the measures (Kratochwill, 2003, p. 31). Thus, if a study used three measures of anxiety, at least two must be statistically significant. Studies that demonstrate statistically significant change on all measures show the strongest evidence of statistically significant change.

Item 2. Studies should report clinical significance. One problem with statistical significance is that it is a function of sample size, and when sample size exceeds 200 respondents significant results may be obtained due solely to the increased statistical power from the sample size (Hair, Anderson, Tatham, &

Black, 1998). As Kratochwill has noted, "Although statistical significance is a necessary criterion for intervention outcome efficacy, it is not sufficient in that statistically significant effects do not guarantee effects of practical importance" (Kratochwill, 2003, p. 31). Thus, the efficacy of group work can not be determined simply by statistical significance; one must also examine how members benefited from the modality.

Clinical significance (also called practical significance) broadly means "the extent to which treatment makes a difference, one of practical or applied value in everyday life" (Kazdin, 1999, p. 338). However, there is disagreement about how it should be operationalized and measured (Kazdin, 1999, 2001, 2006). Many definitions associate clinical significance with changes that are sufficient to "resolve or significantly ameliorate the problem for which the client [or group member] sought treatment" (Kazdin, 1977, p. 427). However, research studies may differ on definitions of clinically meaningful change. Thus, group workers reviewing the evidence should be alert to the different ways in which significance could be defined and measured:

> In contrast to criteria based on statistical significance, judgments regarding clinical significance are based on external standards provided by interested parties in the community. Consumers, clinicians, and researchers all expect psychotherapy to accomplish particular goals, and it is the extent to which psychotherapy succeeds in accomplishing these goals that determines whether or not it is effective or beneficial. The clinical significance of a treatment refers to its ability to meet standards of efficacy set by consumers, clinicians, and researchers. (Jacobson & Truax, 1991, p. 12)

Clinically significant change can be demonstrated through various means. Meaningful improvement in psychotherapy research can be assessed by examining effect sizes (the higher the better, depending on the measure's scoring direction), confidence intervals (CIs, the range within which a true score lies 95% of the time), elimination of the presenting problem, comparison against norms or a clinical cutoff score, evaluation of quality of life, improvements beyond a minimum criterion (e.g., 1.5 standard deviations from the mean), and categorizing client change as recovered, improved, unchanged, or deteriorated, often determined by using the Reliable Change Index (RCI) (Atkins, Bedics, McGlinchey, & Beauchaine, 2005, p. 982; Jacobson & Truax, 1991, p. 12; Kazdin, 2006; Kendall & Flannery-Schroeder, 1998; Miser, 2000b).[11]

Other methods for determining clinical significance include assessing the risks and benefits of therapy. These methods are rarely used in group treatment RCTs but are often used in medical research or in systematic reviews. Two frequent methods include absolute risk reduction (ARR) and numbers needed to treat (NNT), with accompanying CIs. Essentially, these methods ask the question, "Are the treatment benefits worth the potential harms and costs?" (Miser, 2000b, p. 46). The following is an overview of these two approaches, in case the reader encounters these methods in group-based studies. More details about these approaches and methods for calculating them can be found elsewhere (Higgins & Green, 2005, pp. 222–223; Straus et al., 2005, pp. 124–130).

ARR may be defined as "the absolute arithmetic difference in rates of bad outcomes between experimental and control participants in a trial" (Straus et al., 2005, p. 284) and is accompanied by a 95% CI.[12] To obtain the ARR, one must first obtain the percentages of those who improved by the end of the trial (a) in the treatment group (TG) and (b) in the comparison or control group (CG). The ARR is then calculated as TG minus CG (Straus et al., 2005, p. 126). For example, if in an RCT with a one-year follow-up 60% of group members reported no depression in the experimental condition compared with 45% of those in the comparison group, the ARR would be 15% (60% – 45%). This is the amount of change attributable to treatment effects.

NNT is defined as "the number of [group members] who need to be treated to achieve one additional favourable outcome" (Straus et al., 2005, p. 284). Put another way, it is the number needed to treat to prevent one additional bad outcome (Straus et al., 2005, p. 126). It is calculated as the inverse of the ARR ($1/_{ARR}$) and considers "the likelihood of an outcome or side effect. Generally, the less common a potential outcome (e.g., death), the greater the number of patients that would require treatment to prevent one outcome" (Miser, 2000b, p. 53). NNTs are accompanied by a 95% CI and a time frame specific to that study's treatment period. In general, a smaller NNT is desirable; "however, we should also consider the seriousness of the outcome that we are trying to prevent" (Straus et al., 2005, p. 126). Using the example cited in the previous paragraph, the NNT for the experimental group treatment would be 7 ($1/_{15\%}$), which is the number of group members who need to be part of the experimental group treatment to have one additional good outcome. This number is relatively low, but a worker needs to consider whether it is *sufficiently* low because of the outcome variable of depression, and if suicidality may be a concern. Group workers should examine the article to determine how the authors interpreted the NNT and if their reasoning is justified. If the comparison or control group did *better* than the treatment group, then the results would yield the number needed to harm (NNH), defined as "the number of [group members] who, if they received the experimental treatment, would result in one additional [member] being harmed, compared with [members] who received the control treatment" (Straus et al., 2005, p. 285).

Most research studies do not include any measure of clinical significance (Fidler et al., 2005). As noted above, with the exception of some meta-analyses discussed later in the chapter, few group-based individual studies report ARR and NNT. Most use the other methods (e.g., RCI), and some use more than one method within the same study (e.g., Bright, Baker, & Neimeyer, 1999; Erickson, 2003; Hepler, 1991; McLean et al., 2001; Openshaw, Waller, & Sperlinger, 2004; Perri et al., 2001; Schnurr et al., 2003; Whipple et al., 2003). Group workers must learn to recognize and interpret clinical significance scores in research studies and should be cautious about accepting the findings of a study that does not include clinical significance. Studies that include *some* indicator of clinical significance should be rated as stronger than those that do not. The best way to find this information is to look in the analysis (or statistics) or results sections of a research study for the methods associated with any of the following terms: *clinical significance, practical significance,* or *substantive significance.* Although researchers should provide an interpretation of their reports of clinical significance, not all do. Thus, group workers should have a basic understanding of how to interpret it using the information above. When studies provide the raw data but do not report clinical significance, group workers may calculate the less technical forms themselves to derive the impact of the research study. To calculate the effect size, group workers may consult relatively nontechnical guides (Bloom et al., 2003, p. 358; Gibbs, 2003, p. 163).

Summary of Impact. When providing an overall rating of impact, the group worker must determine the level and direction of outcomes. Do the results indicate a substantial positive impact of the group intervention? This could be determined by looking for the presence of "moderate" to "strong" evidence across the three impact items. Was the group intervention clearly helpful to group members? In some cases, the impact might not be clear or consistent across the sample within a study, and group workers can rate the study accordingly. For example, powerful effects with a subsample that represents the population that a group leader is working with are particularly meaningful.

Applicability   *Items 1–7.* The study or source must provide sufficient detail about the intervention/technique to allow the reader to make a judgment about applicability. Unfortunately, group research often does not provide adequate information about the group intervention/technique, which creates two problems. First, "the large number of studies that fail to provide the basic details of the study and its components significantly attenuates the possibility of offering substantive conclusions" (Burlingame, MacKenzie, et al., 2004, p. 680). It also makes it difficult, if not impossible, to make comparisons with one's group situation. Thus, studies should include sufficient information about the group members, group approach, leadership, and group components to allow comparisons with the current situation. If little or no information is in the study, the overall applicability rating will be low.[13]

Items 8–15. These items assess whether a group worker's setting, leader qualities, and group are sufficiently supportive, compatible, commensurate, and similar to utilize the intervention/technique. The items require the group worker to make an assessment as to whether the evidence "fits" the situation. It is important to note that unlike other parts of the guidelines, items in applicability have "veto" power in the worker's decision of whether to use evidence at all, even if the evidence is rigorous and has impact. In general, any rating of "untrue" or "somewhat untrue" on any of the following items indicates that the intervention/technique should not be used:

- *Item 10*: "The intervention/technique is compatible with my professional values and ethical guidelines"
- *Item 11*: "I have the competence (knowledge, skills, and experience) or appropriate supervision to use the intervention/technique in practice"
- *Item 14*: "The intervention/technique fits with my group members' norms, cultures, or values" (if possible, involve group members in rating this item)
- *Item 15*: "My group members are likely to support this intervention/technique" (if possible, involve group members in rating this item)

Item 13. When evaluating the evidence using this item ("My group members are sufficiently similar to those in the study in sociodemographic variables that the results are likely to apply"), it is important to consider the phrase "the results are likely to apply." Are there compelling reasons to expect different results if the study involves *your* group members? Sometimes there might be apparent differences between the study sample and your own group, but the differences may not be relevant in affecting outcomes. For example, there are likely no compelling reasons that a study using contingency management techniques with adults would not apply to a group of adolescents (for additional discussion, see the earlier section in this chapter titled "*How Applicable?*").

Items 14–15. In most cases, the group worker would rate the items without direct group input. However, these items about the group members' norms, culture, or values and their support of the intervention/technique should involve the group members, if possible. If no group members are available (e.g., while a group is being planned), a representative group member could be involved.

Decision. Deciding whether to use the evidence involves weighing rigor, impact, and applicability and determining whether the intervention or strategy should be used in this situation. There is no research-based algorithm for making a final decision, so all three areas should be considered equally important (except in the case of the applicability items noted above). Group workers need to weigh the benefits and harms of the intervention or technique, and then make a decision. In its guide to evaluating clinical guidelines, the GRADE Working Group (Atkins, Best, et al., 2004) offered some definitions in categorizing the benefits and harms of an intervention:

Net benefits = the [intervention/technique] clearly does more good than harm
Trade-offs = there are important trade-offs between the benefits and harms
Uncertain trade-offs = it is not clear whether the [intervention/technique] does more good than harm
No net benefits = the [intervention/technique] clearly does not do more good than harm

After weighing the relative benefits and harms in this situation, the decision to utilize the intervention/technique may be classified into one of two categories: "yes or no," indicating a judgment that most well-informed people would make; and "probably do it or probably don't do it," a judgment that a majority of well-informed people would make but a substantial minority would not (adapted from Atkins, Best, et al., 2004). If the decision is to "probably" use the intervention/technique, proceed with caution and monitor the effects upon the group and group members.

Guide to Evaluating a Group-Based Nonrandomized Study

Quantitative studies that do not randomize may be called quasi-experiments, pre-experiments, nonexperiments, or, more broadly, "observational studies" (Agency for Healthcare Research and Quality, 2002b, p. 5). (For questions about which guide to use, consult Figure 4.2.) Since they do not randomize participants into groups and because they lack the strict controls of a randomized clinical trial (RCT), these studies are inherently weaker in design (in particular, selection bias) and can not yield the best evidence that an intervention or technique results in a desired outcome (Figure 3.1). Thus, these studies should be critically evaluated within their own category, with the understanding that they are inherently weaker in design than RCTs in determining causality.

Nonrandomized studies vary widely in quality. Some may manipulate independent variables and have some statistical controls, while others may not alter or control any research conditions. Examples include nonrandomized comparison group designs, single-group designs, and time-series designs. Because of the lack of randomization, one can not determine whether the treatment or intervention contributed to outcomes more than any other possible extraneous variable.

In their review of high-performing scales for rating observational (nonrandomized) studies, the AHRQ cited five elements that maximized rigor: subjects were comparable, intervention(s) were detailed for all conditions, outcome measures were specified, statistical methods were used to assess confounding, and potential biases due to funding or sponsorship were reduced. The guideline to evaluating a single nonrandomized study (Table 4.3) includes these elements as well as items that were previously discussed in the RCT guideline. Only the five unique items are discussed here. To illustrate how a group worker would use the guide to evaluate a nonrandomized study, an example is provided in the chapter (Keisha Smith).

Explanation of Items in Table 4.3

Rigor *Item 1.* Researchers must adequately justify the reason for using a nonrandomized quantitative design. To do this, the researchers should favorably answer the following questions, posed by the Centre for Evidence Based Social Services (2004):

> Was a quasi-experimental study the right sort of research design to use to answer the question? Did the study aim to find out about the effectiveness of an intervention or service, but it would have been very complicated or impossible to

Table 4.3. Guide to Evaluating a Group-Based Nonrandomized Study

Criteria	Items/Descriptions	Rating The study provided: 3—strong evidence 2—moderate evidence 1—weak evidence 0—no evidence N/A—not applicable
A. Rigor (Did the study use sound research methods?)		
1. Research Design		
	1. The nonrandomized design was adequately justified by the researchers.	_____
	2. If more than one condition, group members were assigned or recruited into each condition in a way that minimized bias and confounders (e.g., same criteria for inclusion or exclusion were applied to all conditions).	_____
Equivalence	3. The groups were equivalent at the beginning of the study on key variables.	_____
Number of participants	4. There were a sufficient number of participants. This is best determined by a power analysis, but a study that includes *at least* 25 participants per condition offers some evidence that this criterion is met.	_____
Blind to condition	5. Group members, group workers, and assessors (i.e., those completing assessment measures) were blind to (unaware of) treatment condition (or at least to the hypotheses of the study).	_____
Leader confound	6. The researchers reduced the personal effect of particular group leaders. This may be accomplished by counterbalancing group leaders across conditions, counterbalancing group leaders across conditions, or a statistical analysis that controls for group leader effect across conditions.	_____

120

Attrition	7. All participants/groups who/that began the study were accounted for at the end and at follow-up (strongest evidence = all were accounted for, but no less than 80% at post-test and 70% for follow-up).[a]
Follow-up	8. Follow-up of members was sufficiently long—at least 6 months after the end of the study, with strongest evidence at 1 year or more (lower the rating one point if follow-up did not consist of at least 70% of original study participants).
Fidelity to protocol	9. Fidelity to the intervention/technique was maximized by (a) training leaders, (b) leader use of a manual or guide, (c) supervision, and (d) optimally, monitoring sessions by two or more independent raters (using audio or videotape, session checklists).
2. Measurement	10. Instruments used to measure primary outcomes or processes were reliable and valid (see text for standards). If multiple observers were used to collect data, rater agreement was at least 70% or 0.70 (higher levels of agreement indicate stronger evidence).
	11. Those who completed the measures were blind to (unaware of) the treatment condition or at least the study hypotheses.
	12. If applicable, multiple *sources* (at least two, such as group member, group leader, parent, independent observer) or multiple *methods* (at least two, such as observation, self-report, rating by others) were used to collect information.
3. Statistical Analyses	13. Analytical methods were used to take into account potential confounders (e.g., covariate analyses when nonequivalence was evident).
	14. Analytical methods were used to account for missing data, study withdrawals, or loss to follow-up (if applicable). A method to account for missing data is imputation, and a method to account for withdrawals or loss to follow up is intent-to-treat analysis.
	15. Analyses were done at the group level using statistical procedures that accounted for the dependence of observations (e.g., multilevel analyses such as Hierarchical Linear Modeling [HLM]).

(continued)

Table 4.3. (continued)

Criteria	Items/Descriptions	Rating The study provided: 3—strong evidence 2—moderate evidence 1—weak evidence 0—no evidence N/A—not applicable
4. Sponsorship/Support	16. If applicable, potential conflicts of interest were identified and, if present, dealt with to allay concerns about sponsor influence over the research.	
5. Quality of Source	17. The study is in a publication or source with blind peer review.	
Summary	Overall, what is the level of evidence for the rigor of the study?	
B. Impact (How powerful and in what direction were the main findings?)		
1. Statistical Significance	1. The study had statistically significant outcomes for most of the primary outcome measures for each key construct (e.g., if the study used three measures of depression, at least two had significant outcomes), at $p < 0.05$. Rate highest a study that demonstrates statistically significant change on all measures.	
2. Clinical Significance	2. The results using the primary outcome measures were *clinically* significant. This can be demonstrated statistically with reports of reliable change index (RCI), effect size (ES), or more rarely, absolute risk reduction (ARR) or numbers needed to treat (NNT) with accompanying 95% confidence interval (CI). It may also be demonstrated by categorical changes in client functioning (e.g., improved, unchanged, deteriorated), which the authors must fully explain (see text for more discussion).	
3. Direction of Findings	3. If the results of the analyses were statistically and/or clinically significant, there was clear evidence that the intervention/technique was helpful.	
Summary	Overall, what is the level of evidence for powerful and positive outcomes?	

1. Intervention/Technique

Group members

1. The characteristics of group members were identified (age, gender, race/ethnicity, language/acculturation, developmental level, problem/diagnoses, socioeconomic status). _____

Group approach(es)

2. The intervention/technique was detailed (e.g., a manual or session outline was provided or available). _____

3. The timing of sessions was detailed (number of sessions, how often, how long each session lasted). _____

4. Group composition was detailed (size, gender, age, race/ethnicity, criteria for membership). _____

5. Group format was identified (closed, open, slow open) and location specified. _____

Group leadership

6. Group leadership was adequately described (number of leaders, co-leadership, race/ethnicity, gender, training/education/experience). _____

Group components

7. The study included measures of group processes or dynamics (e.g., cohesion, engagement, therapeutic alliance, interaction) to help in replication. _____

Summary

Overall, what is the level of evidence about the intervention/technique? _____

The statement is:
3—true
2—somewhat true
1—somewhat untrue
0—untrue

2. Situation

Setting

8. I have adequate resources (e.g., finances, physical space, staff) to provide the same intervention/technique in my setting. _____

9. The intervention/technique fits in with my agency's values and views about treatment. _____

10. The intervention/technique is compatible with my professional values and ethical guidelines.[b] _____

Leader

11. I have the competence (knowledge, skills, and experience) or appropriate supervision to use the intervention/technique in practice.[b] _____

(continued)

123

Table 4.3. (continued)

Criteria	Items/Descriptions	Rating The statement is: 3—true 2—somewhat true 1—somewhat untrue 0—untrue
	12. There are no other relevant differences between me and the group leader in the study that might affect implementation, such as gender, race/ethnicity, language/acculturation, and socioeconomic background.	
Group	13. My group members are sufficiently similar to those in the study in terms of sociodemographic variables that the results are likely to apply (consider age, gender, culture, race/ethnicity, language/acculturation, problem/diagnosis, developmental level, and socioeconomic status). (When there are differences in sociodemographic variables, rate this item positively if the differences are not likely to affect how the intervention/technique would likely perform with your group members.)	
	14. The intervention/technique fits in with my group members' norms, culture, or values (if possible, involve group members in rating this item).[b]	
	15. My group members are likely to support this intervention/technique (if possible, involve group members in rating this item).[b]	
Summary	Overall, this intervention/technique is applicable for my situation	

Decision: Considering the study's rigor, impact, and applicability, should I use this evidence in this situation? Circle one: yes / probably / probably not / no

Material in this table is drawn from a number of sources (Miser, 2000b; Agency for Healthcare Research and Quality, 2002a; Kratochwill, 2002, 2003; Lewis-Snyder, Stoiber, & Kratochwill, 2002; Gibbs, 2003; Atkins et al., 2004; Centre for Evidence Based Social Services, 2004; Higgins & Green, 2005; Pyrczak, 2005; Straus, Richardson, Glasziou, & Haynes, 2005).

[a] Source: Kratochwill (2003). Also, Straus et al. (2005, p. 121) noted that at least one medical journal requires 80% or more follow-up in a study for it to be considered for publication.

[b] In general, a rating of "untrue" or "somewhat untrue" in these items indicates that the intervention/technique should not be used.

have conducted a randomised controlled trial? Do the researchers justify why a randomised controlled trial would not have been possible or desirable?

Item 2. In cases where there is more than one condition, researchers must assign individuals or groups to conditions using the same criteria, to minimize selection bias.

Item 3. To maximize equivalence, researchers should statistically test for similarity between groups by comparing pretest scores on salient variables.

Items 6 and 9. Unlike RCTs where the intervention is administered in a controlled manner, nonrandomized studies may deliver the group intervention based on clinical needs, resulting in potential differences in delivery across settings, groups, or group workers (Agency for Healthcare Research and Quality, 2002a). Thus, it is important to document and monitor the delivery of the intervention.

Item 13. If the groups are not equivalent, researchers should use statistical methods that control for pretest differences. To do this, researchers may use covariate analyses that adjust for the confounding factors (Centre for Evidence Based Social Services, 2004). Ultimately, these methods are not as good as randomization, as researchers can not be certain about which variables are the most important to control.

Guide to Evaluating a Single-Case Design in Group Work

A design referred to as a *single-subject, single-case, N-of-1,* or *single-system evaluation design* may be defined as "a set of empirical procedures used to observe changes in an identified target (a specified problem or objective of the client) that is measured repeatedly over time" (Bloom et al., 2003, p. 37). (For questions about which guide to use, consult Figure 4.2.) Single-subject designs (SSDs) have been used in group work, though less often than group designs. A number of important features distinguish SSDs from group designs. First, the researcher and practitioner is often a single person operating with a desire to improve his or her practice (Johnson, Beckerman, & Auerbach, 2001). Second, the data often concern not only the individuals within the group but also the group as a whole, or how the whole group is functioning (Johnson et al., 2001). Third, SSDs may deliberately involve only a few participants within a group. Fourth, analyses may involve visual rather than statistical analysis tailored for a small number of subjects (i.e., non-normal distributions). Fifth, with SSDs workers have the flexibility to change the type or degree of intervention while the study is ongoing, allowing them to search for a more effective treatment (e.g., ABC to ABCD and AB^1B^2 to $AB^1B^2B^3$) (Newman & Wong, 2004). In contrast, between-group studies do not change in response to incoming data. Thus there may be some similarity in group designs and SSDs in which a single group score is generated, even if the purposes and practices of the two are different.

The third point above raises an important consideration in research using SSDs in groups. Such designs should not only focus on individual outcomes but include elements representing the larger gestalt of the group: "Designs based on observing and recording change in clients, one-by-one, do not give attention to all of the relevant group information" (Fike, 1980, p. 42). As Fike has noted, SSDs should also include other variables in assessment that reflect the *group* experience, such as member satisfaction with the group, nature of interactions, cohesion, and leadership. One consequence of not doing this is attributing change (or the lack of change) strictly to the group intervention when other factors such as leadership, physical environment, or quality of member interactions may have a more important role (this is also a problem with most group designs). It was noted in the second chapter of this book that there are multiple areas of group work (i.e., change theory, individual group member, group structures, group processes, and leadership) that are related to therapeutic outcomes in groups (Burlingame, MacKenzie, et al., 2004). Thus, although an SSD can assess individual problems within groups, its optimum application in group work includes evaluating group elements and/or the group as a whole.

There are different ways that SSDs may be classified depending on how they are conceptualized (Bloom et al., 2003; Hayes, 1981). One method is to classify them as basic single-system designs, multiple-baseline designs, or multiple-treatment designs.

In the first type of design, a single individual, group, behavior, or setting is involved. SSDs may involve comparison within groups (or series) where changes in individual or group conditions are measured at different periods of an intervention or strategy. In this design, there is typically a baseline phase (labeled A) and an intervention phase (labeled B). The basic single-case design has a single baseline and treatment phase (A-B; this may also be called an interrupted time-series design), but in this design treatment may also be withdrawn for a phase to better control for extraneous factors (A-B-A-B, withdrawal/reversal). The use of withdrawal increases the rigor of the design. Essentially, replication is the primary means of maximizing internal validity in SSDs. The A-B-A, B-A-B, and A-B-A-B designs are basic experimental designs (Bloom et al., 2003). This first type of SSD involves examining the same individual, behavior, and setting.

A second design involves examining multiple baselines simultaneously. Group workers would consider this design when it may not be advisable or possible to remove treatment, which the first type of design often requires. By including multiple baselines that occur simultaneously, these designs might track the same behavior across several group members, or they might track several behaviors across the same group member. This design allows group workers to monitor behaviors within the same group or across different groups. Depending on how they are constructed, multiple-baseline designs can provide a strong basis for causal inference and can serve as a suitable alternative to the experimental designs noted above (Bloom et al., 2003, pp. 429, 436).

The third set of SSDs involves multiple treatments in which the group leader uses different interventions or strategies and measures their effectiveness. These designs are complex and idiosyncratic, depending on how the researcher conceptualizes the way the interventions should be implemented and tested. These interventions may be successive, alternating, or interacting (see Bloom et al., 2003, pp. 458–495, for further discussion and examples).

A statistical concern with time-series data is that the observations may not be independent. In SSDs that include multiple observations across time, there is a concern about the likely correlation of adjacent observations in a series of observations, "known as *series dependency*, and . . . quantified by a type of correlation known as *autocorrelation*" (Bloom et al., 2003, p. 533, italics in original). There are ways for transforming these autocorrelated data (Bloom et al., 2003, pp. 538–542), which the researcher should specify. Thus, group researchers need to indicate whether the observations were independent, as well as the basis of that determination.

SSDs have been embraced across professional realms including social work, psychology, and counselor education (Barlow & Hersen, 1984; Bloom et al., 2003; Hayes, 1992; Horner et al., 2005; Lundervold & Belwood, 2000; Tripodi, 1994). They are also considered a valid source of data in determining empirically supported and empirically validated interventions (Chambless et al., 1998; Chambless & Hollon, 1998). Many group texts include SSDs as a valuable evaluation method (Garvin, 1997; Rose, 1977, pp. 62–72; Toseland & Rivas, 2005; Zastrow, 2001). However, despite the widespread application and support of the method, SSDs are generally underutilized by practitioners (Foster, Watson, & Young, 2002; Galassi & Gersh, 1993; Gerdes, Edmonds, Haslam, & McCartney, 1996). In group work, a number of SSD studies have been published (Cetingok & Hirayama, 1983; Edleson, Miller, Stone, & Chapman, 1985; Hauserman et al., 1972; Johnson et al., 2001; O'Brien, Korchynsky, Fabrizio, McGrath, & Swank, 1999; Patterson & Basham, 2002; Petry, Martin, & Finocche, 2001).

The guide in Table 4.4 rates the quality of the rigor, impact, and applicability of the SSD. Many items in the section on rigor and impact are based mostly on Kratochwill and colleagues (Kratochwill, 2003, pp. 66–113) and on other sources (Bloom et al., 2003; Pyrczak, 2005).[14] The discussion below is on areas of the guideline that need explanation or which have not been discussed earlier. To illustrate the use of the guide, an example involving Roselia Gomez is included in the chapter.

Explanation of Items in Table 4.4

Rigor   *Item 1.* The design should have sufficient controls for the worker to be able to infer causality. There are basic designs that do not adequately control for errors; these are called *case study* designs, *basic single-system* designs, or *variations* on such designs (Bloom et al., 2003). Case study designs do not include baselines and do include B or B-C designs (i.e., two different successive

Table 4.4.   Guide to Evaluating a Single-Case Design in Group Work

Criteria	Items/Descriptions	Rating The study provided: 3—strong evidence 2—moderate evidence 1—weak evidence 0—no evidence N/A—not applicable
A. Rigor (Was the intervention/technique responsible for change?)		
1. Research Design		
Type of design	1. The study used an experimental design that included a withdrawal-reversal period (e.g., ABA, ABAB, BAB) *or* a suitable alternate design was documented as having sufficient controls to infer causality.	_____
Baseline	2. There was evidence of stability in the baseline (i.e., no slopes or trends in scores over at least three measurement periods). The exception to this is when there is a clear countertherapeutic trend in the baseline, which can permit a strong demonstration of treatment effects.	_____
Follow-up	3. In cases where intervention effects are expected by the end of the group or beyond, the follow-up of members was sufficiently long (at least 6 months after the end of the study with strongest evidence at 1 year or more).	_____
Fidelity to protocol	4. If the group leader used a particular theoretical approach, fidelity to the intervention/technique was maximized by (a) training leader, (b) leader use of a manual or guide, (c) supervision, and (d) optimally, monitoring sessions by two or more independent raters (using audio or videotape, session checklists).	_____

128

2. Measurement

5. Instruments used to measure primary outcomes or processes were reliable and valid (see text related to randomized clinical trials for further definitions). If multiple observers were used to collect data, rater agreement was at least 70% or 0.70 (higher levels of agreement indicate stronger evidence). ____ ____

6. If applicable, multiple *sources* (at least two, such as group member, group leader, parent, independent observer) or multiple *methods* (at least two, such as observation, self-report, rating by others) were used to collect information. ____ ____

3. Analyses

7. The author justified the use of visual or statistical analysis of outcomes. ____ ____

8. If statistical analyses were used with SSDs using repeated observations over time, the researchers included an analysis of independence of observations (e.g., autocorrelation analyses). ____ ____

4. Sponsorship/Support

9. If applicable, potential conflicts of interest were identified and, if present, dealt with to allay concerns about sponsor influence over the research. ____ ____

5. Quality of Source

10. The study is in a publication or source with blind peer review. ____ ____

Summary:

Overall, what is the level of evidence for the rigor of the study? ____ ____

B. Impact (How powerful and in what direction were the main findings?)

1. Statistical Significance

1. If there were statistical analyses, the study had significant outcomes for most of the primary outcome measures for each key construct (e.g., if the study used three measures of depression, at least two had significant outcomes), at $p < 0.05$. Rate highest a study that demonstrates statistically significant change on all measures.

129

(continued)

Table 4.4. (continued)

Criteria	Items/Descriptions	Rating The study provided: 3—strong evidence 2—moderate evidence 1—weak evidence 0—no evidence N/A—not applicable
2. Clinical Significance	2. If statistical analyses were performed, the results using the primary outcome measures were *clinically* significant. This can be demonstrated with reports of effect size (ES), two standard-deviation band tests, improvement scores to within the range of a nonclinical population, or other identified indicator of practical significance.	
	3. If there was a visual analysis of outcomes, there was a clear effect in any of the following areas: (a) strong degree of change in level between adjacent phases, (b) minimal score overlap between baseline and intervention phases, (c) change in trend between adjacent phases. At least three data points are needed to estimate variability and scores should appear stable (note: an unstable baseline moving in a countertherapeutic direction is satisfactory background with which to demonstrate treatment effects).	
3. Direction of Findings	4. If the results of the analyses were statistically and/or clinically significant, there was clear evidence that the intervention/technique was helpful.	
Summary:	Overall, what is the level of evidence for powerful and positive outcomes?	
C. Applicability (Is this intervention/technique relevant to my situation?)		
1. Intervention/Technique		
Group members	1. The characteristics of group members were identified (age, gender, race/ethnicity, language/acculturation, developmental level, problem/diagnoses, socioeconomic status).	

Group approach(es)	2. The intervention or technique was detailed so it could be replicated (e.g., guideline or session outline provided).	_____
	3. The timing of sessions was detailed (number of sessions, how often, how long each session lasted).	_____
	4. Group composition was detailed (size, gender, age, race/ethnicity, criteria for membership).	_____
	5. Group format was identified (closed, open, slow open) and location specified.	_____
Group leadership	6. Group leadership was adequately described (number of leaders, co-leadership, race/ethnicity, gender, training/education/experience).	_____
Group components	7. The study included measures of group processes or dynamics (e.g., cohesion, engagement, therapeutic alliance, interaction) to help in replication.	_____
Summary:	Overall, what is the level of evidence about the intervention/technique?	

2. Situation

The statement is:
3—true
2—somewhat true
1—somewhat untrue
0—untrue

Setting	8. I have adequate resources (e.g., finances, physical space, staff) to provide the same intervention/technique in my setting.	_____
	9. The intervention/technique fits in with my agency's values and views about treatment.	_____
Leader	10. The intervention/technique is compatible with my professional values and ethical guidelines.[a]	
	11. I have the competence (knowledge, skills, and experience) or appropriate supervision to use the intervention/technique in practice.[a]	

(continued)

Table 4.4. *(continued)*

Criteria	Items/Descriptions	*Rating* The statement is: 3—true 2—somewhat true 1—somewhat untrue 0—untrue
	12. There are no other relevant differences between me and the group leader in the study that might affect implementation, such as gender, race and ethnicity, language/acculturation, and socioeconomic background.	_____
Group	13. My group members are sufficiently similar to those in the study in sociodemographic variables that the results are likely to apply (consider age, gender, culture, race/ethnicity, language/acculturation, problem/diagnosis, developmental level, and socioeconomic status). (When there are differences in sociodemographic variables, rate this item positively if the differences are not likely to affect how the intervention/technique would likely perform with your group members.)[a]	_____
	14. The intervention/technique fits in with my group members' norms, culture, or values (if possible, involve group members in rating this item).[a]	_____
	15. My group members are likely to support this intervention/technique (if possible, involve group members in rating this item).[a]	_____
Summary:	Overall, this intervention/technique is relevant and appropriate for my situation	_____

Decision: Considering the study's rigor, impact, and applicability, should I use this evidence in this situation? Circle one: yes / probably / probably not / no

Material in the sections on rigor and impact are based mostly on Kratochwill (Kratochwill, 2003, pp. 66–113) and on other sources (Bloom, Fischer, & Orme, 2003; Pyrczak, 2005).

[a] In general, a rating of "untrue" or "somewhat untrue" in these items indicates that the intervention/technique should not be used.

interventions). The other set is the basic SSD involving the baseline and intervention, designated as A-B. Both these sets of designs, though commonly used, are weak in terms of determining causality. Stronger designs that control for internal validity threats include multiple-baseline designs and withdrawal-reversal designs. Examples include A-B-A, A-B-A-B, and B-A-B, described as "powerful designs for drawing causal inferences" (Bloom et al., 2003, p. 360). In particular, Bloom and colleagues consider the latter two the strongest of the three experimental designs. In essence, treatment effects need to be replicated at least once (e.g., through reversal phases or multiple baselines) to demonstrate that the observed improvements were not due to chance.

Multiple-baseline and multiple-treatment SSDs introduce their own strengths and limitations. In the case of multiple-baseline treatments, researchers should demonstrate, through sufficient discussion and references, how their particular design controls for other potential explanations for outcomes. Sometimes researchers may randomly assign phases or interventions to phases, or they may randomly select target problems or behaviors to be monitored to determine effects of the intervention. A concern with group-based multiple-baseline and multiple-treatment designs is that observations (e.g., behaviors) may not be completely independent. For example, Rose (1977, pp. 70–72) described an example of a group worker who monitored the effects of a particular intervention on three interactive behaviors (suggestion-giving responses, information-giving responses, and positive affectual responses) in a group of four hospitalized, chronic schizophrenic clients. Ideally, behaviors should be independent in a multiple-baseline design "to prevent the treatment of one behavior causing changes in the alternative behaviors" (Rose, 1977, p. 70), which is not always possible in groups. However, although the behaviors were not independent, substantial positive changes clearly followed the introduction of the treatment (see Rose, 1977, p. 71, for a graphic display of results). To strengthen the design in this example, the order in which each behavior (or problem) was treated could have been randomly selected (Rose, 1977) if the behaviors or problems were of equal priority (Bloom et al., 2003, p. 435). In addition, researchers can randomly assign phases, or interventions to phases, to determine effects of the intervention (Bloom et al., 2003). Ultimately, researchers need to make it clear that the "practitioner's efforts are causally related to the observed change" (Bloom et al., 2003, p. 435) and that there is not some other explanation. Thus, a researcher using a multiple-baseline or multiple-treatment design must indicate how the design was sufficiently rigorous to control for rival explanations for outcomes.

Item 2. The baseline should be sufficiently stable to allow the worker to determine treatment effects; that is, there should not be any systematic increase or decrease in an outcome variable during the baseline phase. The exception to this occurs when the data are unstable and trending in a counter-therapeutic direction, which can be an opportunity to demonstrate particularly strong treatment effects. In this case, not only did the treatment help but it was also able to reverse a pattern of clinical decline.

Item 3. With respect to follow-up, studies of the effects of an intervention on a group member's problem, behavior, or well-being should monitor effects beyond the end of the group. For example, studies of the effects of a group intervention on member depression should include an extended follow-up to determine whether the results attributed to the intervention last beyond the treatment group experience. This would not be relevant for techniques used to change group conditions during the life of the group, such as techniques to increase a member's responsiveness to other group members' feedback.

Item 7. Most researchers analyze outcomes visually as opposed to statistically. The researchers should support, with discussion and references, the method used. In cases involving a series of observations over time, rigorous SSDs should include information about how researchers dealt with the non-independence of observations, such as by using autocorrelation analyses.

Impact   *Item 2.* In addition to reporting statistical significance, researchers should determine whether there was clinically significant change. Some of the common standards for evaluating statistical outcomes are cited in Item 2. Additional markers of clinical significance, which relate to social validity, may be used, such as a group member's subjective evaluation that he or she is doing better, or approval from significant others.

Item 3. There are no precise methods for visual analyses, but the information noted in Item 3 may be used as a guide. Sometimes researchers will use a combination of statistical and visual approaches, such as statistical process control charts, a graphical analytical strategy (Callahan & Barisa, 2005; Orme & Cox, 2001).

Guide to Evaluating a Group-Based Qualitative Study

Qualitative studies are exploratory when their purpose is to gain a detailed understanding of participants, issues, concerns or problems, and strengths and assets. (For questions about which guide to use, consult Figure 4.2.) Studies may report outcome findings through a process of culling lengthy narratives from participants. Mostly verbal data are collected. Examples of qualitative studies in group work include descriptive studies, historical studies, focus groups, and case studies (Brownlee & Chlebovec, 2004; Doel, 2004; Jones & Hodges, 2001; Linton & Hedstrom, 2006; Waites et al., 2004; Zaidi & Gutierrez-Kovner, 1995). Qualitative methods are particularly suited for use in evaluating self-help groups (Kurtz, 1997). Qualitative studies may be used to gain an understanding of what group members might want or the receptivity of group members or group workers to a certain approach, or to report both processes and outcomes of a particular group on a small number of group members.

Qualitative methods may be used for their own sake because they are the best means of answering a particular research or practice question, but they may also serve as a foundation for a larger or quantitative inquiry. As such, they may test the feasibility of a larger-scale study or be used to develop methods for use in a subsequent inquiry. The Campbell Collaboration has acknowledged the value of qualitative inquiry in intervention development:

> Qualitative studies in the relevant field can (a) contribute to the development of a more robust intervention by helping to define an intervention more precisely, (b) assist in the choice of outcome measures and assist in the development of valid research questions, and (c) help to understand heterogeneous results from studies of effect. (Campbell Collaboration, 2001)

Although the purposes and data are different from those in quantitative methods, qualitative inquiry should be systematic to improve accuracy of reporting. The items in Table 4.5 separate good-quality from poor-quality qualitative inquiry and are derived from a number of sources (Centre for Evidence Based Social Services, 2004; Kratochwill, 2003; Mays & Pope, 1995; Pyrczak, 2005; Straus et al., 2005, pp. 143–146). The guide is appropriate for qualitative inquiry that uses (a) a justifiable qualitative methodology (e.g., focus group, case study, narrative, ethnography, grounded theory), (b) procedures for observations and recording, and (c) data analyses. Studies that do not include these criteria are not appropriate for this guide and are best evaluated using the guide for evaluating authoritative evidence (Table 4.6).

Explanation of Items in Table 4.5

Rigor   The section on rigor (Items 1–21) helps to identify qualitative studies that use appropriate, acceptable, and systematic methods to reduce bias.

Items 1–2. The first requirement of a rigorous qualitative study is that it document the appropriateness of the methodology used.

Item 3. Because researchers do not typically base qualitative studies on previous empirical inquiry, the study should also describe the theoretical framework that guided the research.

Items 4–6 (Selection of participants). The study should also clearly document how researchers selected participants and the number of participants who did not provide data.

Item 7. In data collection and coding, researchers should also explicitly connect to the study's theoretical framework the method used to record observations (i.e., the coding system).

Item 14. The method of data analysis must be explicit and acceptable. Examples include grounded theory, framework analysis, and discourse analysis, which may specify additional types of analysis. For example, grounded theory includes three stages in the analysis process: open coding, axial coding, and selective coding (Strauss & Corbin, 1990). Constant-comparison method is another type of analysis used in grounded theory research. A number of group-based studies use grounded theory as a form of inquiry; these have utilized open coding, axial coding, and the constant-comparison method (Brownlee & Chlebovec, 2004; Linton & Hedstrom, 2006).

Table 4.5. Guide to Evaluating a Group-Based Qualitative Study

Criteria	Items/Descriptions	Rating The study provided: 3—strong evidence 2—moderate evidence 1—weak evidence 0—no evidence N/A—not applicable
A. Rigor (How confident can I be that the results of the investigation were accurate?)		
Appropriateness	1. The researchers adequately conveyed (i.e., through discussion and references) that qualitative methodology was appropriate for answering the research question.	_____
	2. The specific qualitative methodology (e.g., grounded theory, focus groups, participant observation, discourse analysis, framework analysis) was described and justified.	_____
	3. The theoretical framework used in the study was made clear.	_____
Selection of participants	4. The method of selecting participants (e.g., random, snowball) was explicit and justified.	_____
	5. The number of participants who did not provide data (by refusal or lost contact) was recorded.	_____
	6. The number of participants in the study was justified.	_____
Data collection/coding	7. The coding system was clearly linked to the study's theoretical framework.	_____
	8. The methods of data collection were explicit and justified (i.e., where data were collected, by whom, how they were collected, and how long it took).	_____
	9. Data were collected in the same way from all participants.	_____
	10. Data were collected by more than one rater/observer.	_____

	11. Procedures were identified for testing consistency of ratings/observations (e.g., using interrater reliability) and for reconciling differences between ratings/observations.	_____
	12. Instruments used had acceptable reliability and validity (i.e., as documented by study authors).	_____
	13. The researchers stated that the study materials (e.g., transcripts, apes) were available for examination by other researchers.	_____
Data analysis	14. The methods of data analysis (e.g., grounded theory, framework analysis, discourse analysis) were clearly described and justified.	_____
	15. The researchers sought feedback from the participants for accuracy before reporting the results.	_____
	16. The data were examined by at least one additional independent evaluator to determine congruence of conclusions and, if more than one rater was involved, the extent of independent rater agreement was evaluated.	_____
Findings	17. Findings were clearly linked to the observations made in the study.	_____
	18. Findings were supported with examples from participants or descriptions of observations.	_____
Investigator bias	19. The researchers critically examined their role for potential bias and influence on participants (e.g., during data collection) or on the study's findings.	_____
	20. Potential conflicts of interest were identified and, if present, dealt with to allay concerns about sponsor influence over the research.	_____
Quality of source	21. The study is in a publication or source with blind peer review.	_____
Summary	Overall, what is the level of evidence for the rigor of the study?	_____

(continued)

137

Table 4.5. (*continued*)

Criteria *Items/Descriptions*	*Rating* The study provided: 3—strong evidence 2—moderate evidence 1—weak evidence 0—no evidence N/A—not applicable
B. Impact (How powerful were the findings/recommendations?)	
1. The study's conclusions/recommendations were strong.	_____
2. There was clear evidence that the intervention/technique was helpful.	_____
C. Applicability (Is this intervention/technique relevant to my situation?) **1. Intervention/Technique**	
Group members 1. The characteristics of group members were identified (age, gender, race/ethnicity, language/ acculturation, developmental level, problem/diagnoses, socioeconomic status).	_____
Group approach(es) 2. The theoretical approach(es) was (were) detailed (manualized, session outline provided).	_____
3. The timing of sessions was detailed (number of sessions, how often, how long each session lasted).	_____
4. Group composition was detailed (size, gender, age, race/ethnicity, criteria for membership).	_____
5. Group format was identified (closed, open, slow open) and location specified.	_____
Group leadership 6. Group leadership was adequately described (number of leaders, co-leadership, race/ethnicity, gender, training/education/experience).	_____
Group components 7. The study included measures of group processes or dynamics (e.g., cohesion, engagement, therapeutic alliance, interaction) to help in replication.	_____
Overall, what is the level of evidence about the intervention/technique?	

138

The statement is:

3—true
2—somewhat true
1—somewhat untrue
0—untrue

Setting	8. I have adequate resources (e.g., financial, physical space, staff) to provide the same intervention/technique in my setting.[a]
	9. The intervention/technique fits in with my agency's values and views about treatment.[a]
Leader	10. The intervention/technique is compatible with my professional values and ethical guidelines.[a]
	11. I have the competence (knowledge, skills, and experience) or appropriate supervision to use the intervention/technique in practice.
	12. There are no other relevant differences between me and the group leader in the study that might affect implementation, such as gender, race and ethnicity, language/acculturation, and socioeconomic background.
Group	13. My group members are sufficiently similar to those in the study in sociodemographic variables that the results are likely to apply (consider age, gender, culture, race/ethnicity, language/acculturation, problem/diagnosis, developmental level, and socioeconomic status). (When there are differences in sociodemographic variables, rate this item positively if the differences are not likely to affect how the intervention/ technique would likely perform with your group members.)
	14. The intervention/technique fits in with my group members' norms, culture, or values (if possible, involve group members in rating this item).[a]
	15. My group members are likely to support this intervention/technique (if possible, involve group members in rating this item).[a]
Summary	Overall, this intervention/technique is applicable for my situation

Decision: Considering the study's rigor, impact, and applicability, should I use this evidence in this situation? Circle one: yes / probably / probably not / no

Material in this table is drawn from a number of sources (Mays & Pope, 1995; Kratochwill, 2003; Centre for Evidence Based Social Services, 2004; Pyrczak, 2005; Straus, Richardson, Glasziou, & Haynes, 2005, pp. 143–146).

[a] In general, a rating of "untrue" or "somewhat untrue" in these items indicates that the intervention/technique should not be used.

Item 15. Feedback from group members and independent evaluators helps to achieve accuracy of observations and conclusions, respectively.

Impact   *Items 1–2*. In qualitative research, the impact may be determined by "impressive" (Straus et al., 2005, p. 144) results. Are the researchers clear and unequivocal about the results? Are the results clear and powerful enough for workers to consider a change in practice?

Guide to Evaluating Authority-Based Evidence in Group Work

Authority-based evidence is not explicitly based on the results of qualitative or quantitative research. An example is a statement of an expert, which may or may not be based on the expert's experience, and which is not typically based on results of a systematic evaluation. (For questions about which guide to use, consult Figure 4.2.) The term *authority* is used loosely, as it can include a range of individuals including authors of books, manuals, or pamphlets; colleagues; consultants; and television personalities. It may also include groups of individuals who present a consensus statement about areas of practice in which there may not be research but there is a need for "experts" to pool their personal observations, clinical experience, and judgment (Figure 3.1). It might also include untested group theories. Personal experience may also be a source, as long as it is not based on the results of a formal inquiry (i.e., based on results of systematic practice evaluation). In other cases, a group worker may have no experience about a situation or no opportunity to consult with an authority about a practice question, and the worker must use his or her own critical-thinking abilities in generating an answer (i.e., speculative practice). These particular situations are anecdotally called "flying by the seat of one's pants" and represent times when a group worker might resort to using authoritative evidence. The key difference between authority-based evidence and research-based evidence is that the latter reflects the results of systematic inquiry that reduces bias, whereas the former is often based on unsupported or undocumented statements. The statement may or may not be accurate, but there is no *research* evidence provided to support it, apart from perhaps a statement by the authority that this will work based on the authority's general experience or opinion.

Although authority-based evidence is less rigorous and secure in answering the question "What is the likelihood of an action achieving a desired outcome?" it has its place in generating evidence in cases where there is no evidence from formal research inquiry. Such evidence may be constructive at the beginning or end of the stages of inquiry. For example, authorities may be helpful to workers in getting ideas for practice or generating questions for practice. At the end of a search for research evidence, authorities may be consulted in helping workers evaluate the relevance and appropriateness of research evidence. In addition, authorities can be the *only* source of evidence when there is no research evidence available and a rapid answer is needed.

Thus, although evidence-based group workers must make every effort to find and evaluate research evidence, at times the only source of help to answer a pressing practice problem may be an authority.

How can a group worker evaluate the quality of authority-based evidence? Unlike some of the other guides in this chapter, there are no research-based guidelines to evaluating authority-based evidence. However, two sources were used in developing the guidelines in Table 4.6 (Cournoyer, 2004, pp. 146–147; Shaughnessy et al., 1994). To illustrate how a group worker could use the guide to evaluate authority-based evidence, a case example is provided in the chapter (Roselia Gomez).

Explanation of Items in Table 4.6

Preliminary question, top of table. The first step in evaluating authority-based evidence is to ensure that a review for *research-based* evidence has been undertaken and that there are no other appropriate sources available. If there is no research evidence available, group workers can assess the quality of the evidence using the rest of the guideline.

Rigor   The section on rigor (Items 1–7) helps workers assess the confidence they may have in the authority and the accuracy of the information.

Impact   *Items 1–2.* These two items assess the strength of the authority's recommendation. If more than one authority was used, the consistency and strength of recommendations is determined.

Decision. Because opinions among professional experts can vary (Galanter & Patel, 2005; Spodick, 1975), group workers should strive to get different perspectives on the practice problem, if practical. Before making a final decision about a course of action, in the absence of any research evidence, group workers should try to seek one or two additional authorities (triangulation) to determine whether the desired intervention/technique is a viable approach and is likely to achieve the desired effect. If two written sources are not readily available, two colleagues, blind to each other's responses, could be asked the MAP question to see if each offers the same, or at least a similar, proposed intervention/technique. Alternatively, the colleagues could review the desired intervention/technique to confirm that it is likely to achieve the desired effect.

Guide to Evaluating a Group-Based Literature Review (Systematic and Nonsystematic)

A type of research called an integrative, secondary study (Miser, 2000a) is an aggregation and synthesis of primary studies and may appear as a descriptive summary or a sophisticated meta-analysis that includes quantitative evaluation of the findings of original research studies. (For questions about which guide to use, consult Figure 4.2.) In contrast with literature reviews that

Table 4.6. Guide to Evaluating Authority-Based Evidence in Group Work

Preliminary question: Was an adequate search for *research* evidence conducted, which yielded no suitable material? If the answer is no, a search should first be undertaken for research evidence.

Criteria	Items/Descriptions	Rating Strength of evidence: 3—strong evidence 2—moderate evidence 1—weak evidence 0—no evidence N/A—not applicable
A. Rigor (How confident can I be that the information from the source is accurate?)		
	1. The authority has excellent training, knowledge, and experience in group work.	_____
	2. The authority's group work knowledge (degrees, training), experience (years), and/or writings relate specifically to my group work situation (e.g., population, problem area).	_____
	3. The authority's affiliation (e.g., university, clinic, association) is relevant for establishing expertise.	_____
	4. If the source is media (printed, audio, or video), the publisher/producer is reputable (e.g., well known, objective, academic, peer reviewed).	_____
	5. The authority is objective and scholarly (i.e., does not force a viewpoint, seems accurate, is logical, and has depth).	_____
	6. The information/material is well documented (i.e., references are included, experience is cited).	_____
	7. The authority appears to have no potential conflict of interest (e.g., the authority does not derive a source of income in giving a particular response). If so, any conflict was dealt with to allay concerns about affecting an objective answer to the question.	_____
Summary:	Overall, what is the level of evidence for the accuracy of the source/information?	_____

...were the recommendations?

1. If from more than one authority, their recommendations were consistent.

2. The authority's (or authorities') recommendations were clear and strong.

C. Applicability (Is this intervention/technique relevant to my situation?)
1. Intervention/Technique

Group members

1. The characteristics of group members were identified (age, gender, race/ethnicity, language/acculturation, developmental level, problem/diagnoses, socioeconomic status).

Group approach(es)

2. The theoretical approach(es) was (were) detailed (manualized, session outline provided).

3. The timing of sessions was detailed (number of sessions, how often, how long each session lasted).

4. Group composition was detailed (size, gender, age, race/ethnicity, criteria for membership).

5. Group format was identified (closed, open, slow open) and location specified.

Group leadership

6. Group leadership was adequately described (number of leaders, co-leadership, race/ethnicity, gender, training/education/experience).

Group components

7. The authority included measures of group processes or dynamics (e.g., cohesion, engagement, therapeutic alliance, interaction) to help in replication.

Summary

Overall, what is the level of evidence about the intervention/technique?

2. Situation

Setting

8. I have adequate resources (e.g., finances, physical space, staff) to provide the same intervention/technique in my setting.

9. The intervention/technique fits in with my agency's values and views about treatment.

The statement is:
3—true
2—somewhat true
1—somewhat untrue
0—untrue

(continued)

Table 4.6. (continued)

Criteria	Items/Descriptions	Rating The statement is: 3—true 2—somewhat true 1—somewhat untrue 0—untrue
Leader	10. The intervention/technique is compatible with my professional values and ethical guidelines.[a]	_____
	11. I have the competence (knowledge, skills, and experience) or appropriate supervision to use the intervention/technique in practice.[a]	_____
	12. There are no other relevant leader differences between me and the authority (or group leader in the report) that might affect my use of the intervention/technique, such as gender, race and ethnicity, language/acculturation, and socioeconomic background.	_____
Group	13. My group members are sufficiently similar to those in the study (or those led by the authority) in terms of sociodemographic variables that the results are likely to apply (consider age, gender, culture, race/ethnicity, language/acculturation, problem/diagnosis, developmental level, and socioeconomic status). (When there are differences in sociodemographic variables, rate this item positively if the differences are not likely to affect how the intervention/technique would likely perform with your group members.)[a]	_____
	14. The intervention/technique fits in with my group members' norms, culture, or values (if possible, involve group members in rating this item).[a]	_____
	15. My group members are likely to support this intervention/technique (if possible, involve group members in rating this item).[a]	_____
Summary	Overall, this intervention/technique is applicable for my situation	_____

Decision: Considering the rigor, impact, and applicability, should I use this evidence in this situation? Circle one: yes / probably / probably not / no lack a formal process for evaluating primary research, a systematic review is a summary that uses strict, explicit, and reproducible methods to systematically search, critically appraise, and synthesize the literature on a topic (Shaughnessy et al., 1994; Straus et al., 2005). Strong reviews also evaluate the methodological rigor of the included studies so the conclusions are not confounded by poorly executed studies. As with controlled studies, the primary intent of a systematic review is to reduce the amount of bias in deriving a conclusion about a topic. The risk of an informal, unstructured descriptive review is that the findings are more subjective: "Buyer beware: unsystematic reviews lead to unsystematic conclusions" (Shaughnessy et al., 1994, p. 4).

A meta-analysis is a rigorous systematic review that quantifies research about a subject, often reporting the results of statistical analyses such as effect sizes to offer numerical weight to findings about a particular intervention. Not all systematic reviews are meta-analyses. Sometimes the body of research is too small to allow researchers to derive statistical conclusions, too heterogeneous for aggregation, or lacking the data for analysis. However, all systematic reviews clearly minimize bias by making the process of selection and review explicit, evenly applied to all studies, and reproducible.

The guide for evaluating literature reviews (systematic and nonsystematic) in Table 4.7 is developed from a number of sources and adapted for group work (Agency for Healthcare Research and Quality, 2002a; Miser, 2000a; Straus et al., 2005). The table includes items that distinguish high- from poor-quality reviews, according to the AHRQ (Agency for Healthcare Research and Quality, 2002a), such as search strategy, the method used to assess study quality and validity, data synthesis and analysis, and sponsorship of the study. These items appear mostly in the "rigor" section of the guide and are further described below. Because the items in the applicability section are the same as those in Table 4.2, they are not discussed here. Some of the criteria in the table, such as items in the section on synthesis and analysis, relate mainly to meta-analyses and would not apply to most narrative systematic reviews (nonrelevant items are rated "N/A"). Similarly, descriptive reviews would not report effect sizes and instead would report narrative conclusions and recommendations based on the review. In these cases, a group worker's assessment of impact would rely on outcomes provided in the author's review. Apart from these examples, the other items should apply to most systematic reviews. Because of their lack of attention to biases, nonsystematic, narrative-style reviews will inevitably be rated "weak" using the guide, either because items are rated low or because many items are not applicable. To help illustrate how to use the guide for evaluating a systematic review, a case example is provided in the chapter (Keisha Smith).

Explanation of Items in Table 4.7

Rigor   *Items 1–3 (Search strategy).* A comprehensive search strategy is important in a literature review. The methods for searching must be documented (Item 1), and clear inclusion and exclusion criteria must be provided (Item 2).

Table 4.7. Guide to Evaluating a Group-Based Literature Review (Systematic and Nonsystematic)

Criteria	Items/Descriptions	Rating The study provided: 3—strong evidence 2—moderate evidence 1—weak evidence 0—no evidence N/A—not applicable
A. Rigor (Did the study use sound research methods?)		
1. Search Strategy	1. The method for searching for group-based studies was clearly described (list of keywords used, dates covered, databases used) in sufficient detail that the search could be reproduced.	
	2. Clear and justified inclusion and exclusion criteria were provided.	
	3. Unpublished (e.g., conference proceedings, theses, grant reports, government sources) as well as non-English studies were included in the search. If not, a clear justification for exclusion was documented.	
2. Study Quality	4. The method of assessing the quality of the individual studies was clearly specified and rigorous.	
	5. At least two independent evaluators were used to evaluate study quality and the extent of rater agreement was evaluated (i.e., interrater reliability).	
	6. Raters were blind to (unaware of) the studies' authors, institutions, and results.	
3. Synthesis & Analysis	7. Separate analyses were undertaken for different research designs (e.g., randomized clinical trials were evaluated separately from nonrandomized studies), accounting for variations in study quality.	
	8. Studies were similar enough in terms of population, group sizes, interventions, and outcome measures to allow combining the results. Differences or similarities may be determined by statistical tests for *heterogeneity* or *homogeneity*, respectively, and *sensitivity analyses* may be used	

146

9. The researchers considered whether the original study used statistical procedures that accounted for the dependence of observations (e.g., multilevel analyses such as Hierarchical Linear Modeling [HLM]).

10. If applicable, potential conflicts of interest were identified and, if present, were dealt with to allay concerns about sponsor influence over the research.

11. The study is in a publication or source with blind peer review.

Summary   Overall, what is the level of evidence for the rigor of the study?

B. Impact (How consistent, powerful, and in what direction were the main findings?)

1. Consistency   The outcomes were generally consistent across all studies included in the review.

2. Strength   The intervention/technique had powerful effects. In a meta-analysis, researchers can demonstrate this with documented interpretations of reported effect sizes (ES), such as the Binomial Effect Size Display (BESD), a report of relative risks (RR), absolute risk reduction (ARR), numbers needed to treat (NNT) with accompanying 95% confidence interval (CI), or odds ratios (ORs).

3. Direction   The intervention/technique had positive outcomes.

Summary   Overall, what is the level of evidence for consistent, powerful, and positive outcomes? (In general, interventions/techniques with damaging outcomes should not be used.)

C. Applicability (Is this intervention/technique relevant to my situation?)
1. Intervention/Technique

Group members   1. The characteristics of group members were identified (age, gender, race/ethnicity, language/acculturation, developmental level, problem/diagnoses, SES).

Group approach(es)   2. The intervention/technique was detailed (e.g., a manual or session outline was provided or available).

(continued)

4. Sponsorship/Support

5. Quality of Source

Table 4.7. *(continued)*

Criteria	Items/Descriptions	Rating The study provided: 3—strong evidence 2—moderate evidence 1—weak evidence 0—no evidence N/A—not applicable
	3. The timing of sessions was detailed (number of sessions, how often, how long each session lasted).	
	4. Group composition was detailed (size, gender, age, race/ethnicity, criteria for membership).	
	5. Group format was identified (closed, open, slow open) and location specified.	
Group leadership	6. Group leadership was adequately described (number of leaders, co-leadership, race/ethnicity, gender, training/education/experience).	
Group components	7. The study included measures of group processes or dynamics (e.g., cohesion, engagement, therapeutic alliance, interaction) to help in replication.	
Summary	Overall, what is the level of evidence that the review included sufficient information about the group intervention/technique?	
2. Situation		The statement is: 3—true 2—somewhat true 1—somewhat untrue 0—untrue
Setting	8. I have adequate resources (e.g., finances, physical space, staff) to provide the same intervention/technique in my setting.	

Leader	9. The intervention/technique fits in with my agency's values and views about treatment. _____
	10. The intervention/technique is compatible with my professional values and ethical guidelines. [a] _____
	11. I have the competence (knowledge, skills, and experience) or appropriate supervision to use the intervention/technique in practice. [a] _____
	12. There are no other relevant differences between me and the group leader in the study that might affect implementation, such as gender, race and ethnicity, language/acculturation, and socioeconomic background. _____
Group	13. My group members are sufficiently similar to those in the study in terms of sociodemographic variables that the results are likely to apply (consider age, gender, culture, race/ethnicity, language/acculturation, problem/diagnosis, developmental level, and socioeconomic status). (When there are differences in sociodemographic variables, rate this item positively if the differences are not likely to affect how the intervention/ technique would likely perform with your group members.) _____
	14. The intervention/technique fits in with my group members' norms, culture, or values (if possible, involve group members in rating this item). [a] _____
	15. My group members are likely to support this intervention/technique (if possible, involve group members in rating this item). [a] _____
Summary	Overall, this intervention/technique is applicable for my situation _____

Decision: Considering the study's rigor, impact, and applicability, should I use this evidence in this situation? Circle one: yes / probably / probably not / no

Material in this table is drawn from a number of sources (Miser, 2000a; Agency for Healthcare Research and Quality, 2002; Straus, Richardson, Glasziou, & Haynes, 2005).

[a] In general, a rating of "untrue" or "somewhat untrue" in these items indicates that the intervention/technique should not be used.

Publication bias (or selection bias) is a significant limitation of some meta-analyses (Miser, 2000a) and occurs when a meta-analysis includes only published studies or only those in the English language (Item 3). The concern about including only published studies is that researchers are more likely to submit (and editors are more likely to publish) reports with statistically significant (positive) results than studies with nonsignificant or negative findings (McAuley, Pham, Tugwell, & Moher, 2000; Miser, 2000a; Straus et al., 2005). This has been called the "file drawer problem," as this is where such reports usually languish (Rosenthal, 1979). Thus researchers should "carry out an extensive search for unpublished data and obtain them if possible" (Miser, 2000a, p. 61). In addition, researchers should search internationally and not restrict results to English-only journals (Miser, 2000a). Researchers can use different methods to detect the file drawer problem, such as reporting "funnel plots," "fail-safe n," and related procedures (for more information about these procedures, see Peters, Sutton, Jones, Abrams, & Rushton, 2006; Vevea & Woods, 2005). It is beyond the scope of this book to discuss the merits of the various procedures, but strong literature reviews should use and identify a method for detecting the presence of selection bias.

Items 4–6 (Study quality). The method the study used to evaluate study quality is also important. The authors of the review should include two independent (i.e., not affiliated with the study) evaluators who will evaluate the quality of the original studies, and the interrater reliability between these raters should be reported (Item 5). In general, reliability estimates should be at least 70%, or 0.70, between raters, depending on the method used (kappa [κ] is one method, and corrects for chance agreement). Ideally, the raters should also be unaware of the study authors or their affiliations (Item 6). For more details about interrater reliability, refer to the discussion below about the Guide to Evaluating Instruments for Group Work (specifically, Item 2 under "Rigor").

Items 7–9 (Synthesis and analysis). One limitation of some systematic reviews, such as meta-analyses, is that they may include dissimilar and poor-quality studies in their analyses (Atkins, Eccles, et al., 2004; Miser, 2000a; Moher et al., 1998) (Item 7). Poor-quality RCTs are more likely to find positive effects than high-quality RCTs (Moher et al., 1998). Studies may aggregate dissimilar samples, interventions, or outcomes. There are several methods for addressing the problem of potentially dissimilar studies (Item 8). Researchers should include tests of heterogeneity to assess for differences related to characteristics of the samples or treatments across studies. As the AHRQ has noted (Agency for Healthcare Research and Quality, 2002a), "Statistical pooling of study results using meta-analytic techniques may not be advisable when substantial heterogeneity is present." Researchers may also include tests of homogeneity (results of individual studies are mathematically compatible with each other) to rule out the possibility that chance differences did not occur (Miser, 2000a). In addition, sensitivity analyses may be used to determine whether the results might be different if particular subgroupings of the data are used (e.g., by diagnostic category, lower methodological quality) (Miser,

2000a). Ideally, these tests should not produce different results. Thus, researchers in a meta-analysis should provide procedures that account for differences across studies, whether the differences are due to sample differences, outcomes, or study quality.

Another concern (Item 9) is whether the researchers considered the potential difference in outcomes if the original studies' methods did not control for the group effect. As discussed previously in the section on RCTs, outcome effects might be different if analyses control for the effects of nonindependence of observation. Strictly speaking, authors of a systematic review should discuss and control for this concern in their review as well.

Impact   Item 1. The first area to evaluate is whether the effects were consistent across all the studies reviewed (Straus et al., 2005). There should be some concern, for example, if some studies report strong beneficial findings and others report strong detrimental findings. In such cases, the authors should test to learn whether the differences in outcomes ("heterogeneity") were due to chance and, if not, explain why the heterogeneous differences might have occurred (Straus et al., 2005).

Item 2. Another important area to evaluate is the reported treatment effect. To determine this, most meta-analyses calculate and report an effect size, which is a method "of examining the magnitude of the effect of an intervention (how large it is) of one study or across a number of studies" (Bloom et al., 2003, p. 358). Effect sizes are useful because as a metric, an effect size can be compared across studies. There are different types of effect sizes and ways of calculating, aggregating, and interpreting effect sizes (Cooper & Hedges, 1994; Hedges & Olkin, 1985). A common form is the standardized mean difference (often symbolized as Cohen's *d* statistic, after its developer) that indicates the difference in standard deviation units between groups (a positive and higher figure is better). Studies may also report an odds ratio (OR), defined as "the odds of an event in a [client] in the experimental group relative to that of a [client] in the control group" (Straus et al., 2005, p. 151). An OR of less than 1.0 is a negative relation, and one that is higher than 1.0 is a positive relation (Vogt, 1999). The researchers should specify and justify (through discussion and references) which method they used. Other methods used in group-based meta-analysis are the ARR, number needed to treat (NNT), and confidence intervals, which were discussed above (see Table 4.2 and explanation of items).

Regardless of which method is used, meta-analyses should give an interpretation of the *magnitude* or meaning of the effect size to indicate the impact of the findings. For example, an effect size of 0.25 has no meaning on its own. There are different methods that researchers may use to translate the effect size statistic into a more meaningful figure. One method is to interpret it as small (0.20), medium (0.50), or large (0.80) (Cohen, 1988). An example of a more "clinically relevant" unit is the Binomial Effect Size Display (BESD) (Prendergast, Podus, & Urada, 2002, p. 63), derived from Rosenthal and Rubin

(Rosenthal & Rubin, 1979, 1982). The BESD is "the percentage of treatment participants and comparison participants who meet a common success criterion, defined arbitrarily as the median of the scores of the combined groups" (Prendergast et al., 2002, p. 63). Similarly, ORs and risk ratios (RRs) ("risk of an event in a patient in the experimental group relative to that of a patient in the control group," Straus et al., 2005, p. 151) are, on their own, of limited clinical value and should be interpreted by the researchers (Straus et al., 2005). ORs and RRs can be converted to NNTs or NNHs, which are more clinically useful. NNTs and NNHs are interpreted the same way as in individual studies, discussed in an earlier guide (Table 4.2).

Guide to Evaluating the Research/Clinical Support of an Intervention/Technique in Group Work

This guide is different from the others in that it evaluates the corporate body of research and clinical support of an intervention (i.e., multiple studies/reports). (For questions about which guide to use, consult Figure 4.2.) After a thorough search, a group worker may acquire a number of studies or reports about a specific intervention or technique. Before the guide is used, the quality of the original studies must be determined. There are good- and bad-quality RCTs, and their quality should be distinguished. Using such a hierarchy without critical review of the original studies may easily produce misleading results (see Gambrill, 2006a, for examples). Thus, after reviewing the rigor, impact, and applicability of each study using the previous guides, the group worker may determine the *collective* rigor, impact, and applicability of an intervention/technique across studies using the guide in Table 4.8. Group workers could also use the guide to evaluate the level of clinical and research support of their own practice. Admittedly, the term *clinical support* supports the false dichotomy between practice and research, but it serves to identify practice without explicit research support, such as group work guided only by authority-based evidence. The guide is valuable in recognizing that although group workers base some of their practices on convention or word of mouth, *best practice* has strong research and clinical support.

The guide is adapted from the Treatment Protocol Classification System, developed for child physical and sexual abuse and designed to classify interventions according to their theoretical, empirical, and clinical support (Saunders, Berliner, & Hanson, 2003, pp. 20–23). It was adapted by adding language applicable to group work and incorporating the standards for empirically "validated" therapies developed by the American Psychological Association's Division 12 Task Force (Chambless et al., 1996; Chambless et al., 1998), which defined "well-established" and "probably efficacious" treatments.[15] These criteria appear in levels A and B of the guide. Although the guide's items are based on respectable research and consensus among researchers, the guide has not been empirically tested for group work.

Table 4.8. Guide to Evaluating the Research/Clinical Support of an Intervention/Technique in Group Work

Criteria	Items/Descriptions	Check[a]
	Part I. Rigor & Impact: Was the intervention/technique responsible for positive change?	
	Interventions/Techniques with Research and Clinical Support	
A. Well-Established, Efficacious Intervention/Technique	1. The treatment/technique has a sound theoretical basis in generally accepted group work principles (e.g., cited across widely used textbooks).	_____
	2. Clinical-anecdotal (i.e., nonresearch) literature suggests the treatment/technique helps group members.	_____
	3. There is no clinical or empirical evidence or theoretical basis indicating that the intervention/technique presents risk of harm to group members compared to its likely benefits.	_____
	4. The treatment/technique has a book, manual, or guide that specifies the components of the intervention/technique and describes how to administer it with attention to group work principles.	_____
	5. a. At least two good between-group design experiments have found the intervention/ technique to be superior (statistically significantly so) to a psychotherapy placebo or to another intervention/technique, and/or equivalent to an already established intervention/technique in studies with adequate statistical power (e.g., sample size of 30 per group, OR	
	b. A large series of single-case design experiments ($n > 9$) demonstrating efficacy. These experiments must have used good experimental designs and compared the intervention to another treatment as in 5a.	

(continued)

Table 4.8. (continued)

Criteria	Items/Descriptions	Check[a]
	Additional criteria for both a and b:	
	c. The experiments must have been conducted with treatment manuals or equivalent clear description of intervention/technique.	___
	d. Characteristics of the client (and group) samples must be specified.	___
	e. Effects must have been demonstrated by at least two different investigators or teams.	___
B. Supported and Probably Efficacious Intervention/Technique	1 to 4 above and:	
	5. a. At least two group studies (controlled) have demonstrated that the intervention/technique is superior (statistically significantly so) to a waiting-list control group OR	
	b. One or more experiments meeting the well-supported criteria 5a, 5c, 5d, but not 5e (listed under level A, above), OR	
	c. A small series of single case design experiments ($n \geq 3$) otherwise meeting well-supported treatment.	___
	6. If multiple treatment outcome studies have been conducted, the overall weight of evidence supports the efficacy of the treatment/technique.	___
C. Promising and Acceptable Intervention/Technique	1 to 4 above and:	
	5. At least one study utilizing some form of control without randomization (e.g., matched wait list, untreated group, placebo group) has demonstrated the intervention/technique's benefits over time, benefits over placebo, or found it to be comparable to or better than an already established intervention/technique.	___

154

Interventions/Techniques with Clinical/Anecdotal Support

Intervention/Technique	Description	
D. Conventional and Acceptable Intervention/Technique	1 to 4 above	
E. Innovative or Novel Intervention/Technique	1. The intervention/technique may have a theoretical basis that is innovative or novel but is based on reasonable application of generally accepted group work principles.	
	2. A relatively small clinical literature exists to suggest the value of the intervention/technique.	
	3. There is no clinical or empirical evidence or theoretical basis suggesting that the intervention/technique constitutes a substantial risk of harm to group members compared to its likely benefits.	
	4. The intervention/technique has a book, manual, or guide that specifies the components of the approach and describes how to administer it with attention to group work principles.	
F. Potentially Harmful Intervention/Technique	1. The theoretical basis for the intervention/technique is (a) unknown, (b) a misapplication of group work principles, or (c) a unique—and potentially risky—application of group work principles.	
	2. Only a small and limited clinical literature suggests the intervention/technique has value.	
	3. There is a reasonable theoretical, clinical, or empirical basis suggesting that, compared to its likely benefits, the intervention/technique constitutes a risk of harm to those receiving it.	

(continued)

155

Part II. Applicability: Is this intervention/technique relevant to my situation?

Criteria	Items/Description	Rating 3—true 2—somewhat true 1—somewhat untrue 0—untrue
Setting	1. I have adequate resources (e.g., finances, physical space, staff) to provide the same intervention/technique in my setting.	_____
	2. The intervention/technique fits in with my agency's values and views about treatment.	_____
Leader	3. The intervention/technique is compatible with my professional values and ethical guidelines.[b]	_____
	4. I have the competence (knowledge, skills, and experience) or appropriate supervision to use the intervention/technique in practice.[b]	
	5. There are no other relevant differences between me and the group leader in the study that might affect implementation, such as gender, race and ethnicity, language/ acculturation, and socioeconomic background.	
Group	6. My group members are sufficiently similar to those in the study in terms of sociodemographic variables that the results are likely to apply (consider age, gender, culture, race/ethnicity, language/acculturation, problem/diagnosis, developmental level, and socioeconomic status). (When there are differences in sociodemographic variables, rate this item positively if the differences are not likely to affect how the intervention/ technique would likely perform with your group members.)	
	7. The intervention/technique fits in with my group members' norms, culture, or values (if possible, involve group members in rating this item).[b]	_____

8. My group members are likely to support this intervention/technique (if possible, involve group members in rating this item).[b]

Summary: _____

Overall, this intervention/technique is relevant and appropriate for my situation

Decision: Considering the study's validity, impact, and relevance, should I use this evidence in this situation? Circle one: yes / probably / probably not / no

---

Material in this table is drawn from a number of sources (Chambless et al., 1996; Chambless et al., 1998; Saunders, Berliner, & Hanson, 2003).

[a] All criteria in a section must apply.

[b] In general, a rating of "untrue" or "somewhat untrue" in these items indicates that the intervention/technique should not be used.

Explanation of Items in Table 4.8

Rigor and Impact   The first part of the table relates to both rigor and impact and asks the question, "Was the intervention/technique responsible for positive change?" The guide is hierarchical; that is, interventions/techniques with more research and clinical evidence are strongest (levels A, B, and C of the guide) and interventions/techniques with only clinical and anecdotal support (i.e., based on authoritative evidence) are weakest (levels D, E, and F). In the author's opinion, evidence-based group workers should strive for practice at a level of C or above—that is, practice based on clinical and research support.

Applicability   The second part of the guide is relevant for situations in which the group worker has evaluated the set of evidence and would like to apply it in practice. Assuming the evidence is rigorous and helpful, the group worker rates its applicability for the group situation. The criteria in Part 2 are the same as those in the other guides, which may be consulted for further information.

Guide to Evaluating Instruments for Group Work

An essential element of evidence-based group work is utilizing instruments for the measurement of change. An instrument is defined as "any means used to measure or otherwise study subjects" (Vogt, 1999, p. 140). Instruments may also be called "measures" and are often found in the "Methods" section of a research paper under a subsection titled "Instruments" or "Measures," or some variation on those titles (e.g., "Instrumentation").

An important reason that evidence-based group workers seek and evaluate instruments is to determine whether an intervention or strategy had its desired effect on practice. The guidelines in this section are for rating instruments designed specifically for group work (such as those that appear in Tables 3.2 and 3.3) and do not include problem-based instruments or those related to diagnosis or clinical risk prediction. There are excellent compendia of instruments for evaluating outcomes (see the list of resources in Chapter 3), and other guidelines are available for evaluating diagnostic and clinical risk prediction (Gibbs, 2003; Straus et al., 2005).

Group-related instruments may be classified by method of assessment, including the following: face-to-face interviews, self-reports, behavior rating scales, sociometric methods, and direct observation. Group workers may sometimes use a face-to-face interview. An example of an interview is the Group Assessment Form (Lynn, 1994), used to screen prospective adolescents for group work.

Self-reports measure clients' feelings, perceptions, and attitudes. They are useful for assessing personal concerns that group workers may not discern or that group members may not readily disclose face to face. However, self-reports are limited by response-bias problems such as social desirability (participants' responding in socially acceptable ways rather than the way they really feel) and acquiescent responding (participants' agreeing or disagreeing with certain responses out of politeness, not based on what they really believe) (Paulhus, 1991). An example of a self-report is the Group Leader Self-Efficacy Instrument (Page, Pietrzak, & Lewis, 2001).

Behavior rating scales are a standardized format for making summative judgments about behavior characteristics, completed by a person other than the one whose behavior is being assessed. Rating scales can capture behavior over time and gather information from people who know the subject well, such as a group leader. However, rating scales are subject to response bias and error variance (Merrell, 1994). An example of a behavior rating scale is the Group Counselor Behavior Rating Form (Corey & Corey, 1987, pp. 36–38; DeLucia & Bowman, 1991).

Sociometric methods such as sociograms have been used in group work for decades as a method for mapping relations among group members. An example of a sociometric method is the Group Therapy Interaction Chronogram (Cox, 1973; Reder, 1978).

Direct observation involves raters who collect data based on watching others. In one type, raters are independent of the clinical situation; this method is generally well regarded because it can minimize biases inherent in the other approaches. A less rigorous type occurs when group leaders, who are not independent of the clinical situation, collect data based on their observations of the group members. These forms of observation may be obtrusive (group members know they are being recorded) or unobtrusive (group members are unaware they are being recorded and are thus less likely to act in a socially desirable way). Examples of direct-observation measures in group work are the Systematic Multiple Level Observation of Groups (SYMLOG, Bales, Cohen, & Williamson, 1979; Polley, Hare, & Stone, 1988), the Directives Scale (Stinchfield & Burlingame, 1991), charts for recording the frequency of group interaction (Rose, 1977, p. 137; Toseland & Rivas, 2005, p. 240), and instruments used to identify prosocial and maladaptive group behavior (Macgowan & Wagner, 2005), such as the Youth's Behavioral Repertoire (Feldman & Caplinger, 1977) and Deviancy Training (Dishion, Poulin, & Burraston, 2001). A number of the instruments in Tables 3.2 and 3.3 may be used as direct observation measures. Rose has described the practical use of several simple within-group observation systems in clinical settings with adolescents, which readers may consult (Rose, 1998, pp. 144–147).

Instruments appropriate for practice must be relatively brief, easy to administer and score, and helpful in improving practice. To be useful for practice, the measure should be completed and scored within a few minutes per group member. The guidelines presented in Table 4.9 relate mostly to selecting and using instruments for practice as opposed to research. For workers to rate the instrument properly, they must have the instrument and a publication about the properties of the instrument. The strongest publication about the reliability and validity of a measure is a peer-reviewed journal, in which

Table 4.9. Guide to Evaluating Instruments for Group Work

Criteria	Items/Descriptions	Rating The study provided: 3—strong evidence 2—moderate evidence 1—weak evidence 0—no evidence N/A—not applicable
A. Rigor (What is the evidence for the rigor of the instrument?)		
Reliability	1. The instrument has acceptable internal consistency (also called "Cronbach's alpha," "coefficient alpha," "alpha," or "α") of *at least* 0.70 (a higher score indicates stronger evidence).	_____
	2. For instruments completed by different raters, the interreliability for agreement was at least 70% or 0.70 (higher levels of agreement indicate stronger evidence).	_____
	3. For instruments intended to evaluate stable traits in groups, there is evidence of temporal stability using test–retest.	_____
	4. The instrument's reliability has been good and consistent across multiple studies involving different samples (more studies = stronger evidence).	_____
	5. The reliability has been good and consistent in at least one study by a researcher unaffiliated with the measure's developer(s).	_____
	6. The instrument's reliability has been reported in a publication(s) with blind peer review.	_____
	In sum, what is the level of evidence for the measure's reliability?	_____
Validity	7. The instrument's validity has been tested in the following areas: face/content, criterion (concurrent, predictive, known groups), and construct (e.g., convergent and divergent validity, factorial validity) (more areas = better).	_____

8. Multiple *sources* (at least two, such as group member, group leader, parent, independent observer) were used in testing the measure's validity. _____

9. Multiple *methods* (at least two, such as observation, self-report, rating by others) were used in testing the instrument's validity. _____

10. Those who completed the validation measures were unaware of (blind to) the study's hypotheses. _____

11. The instrument's validity has been good and consistent across multiple studies involving different samples (more studies = stronger evidence). _____

12. The instrument's validity across cultures has been demonstrated (e.g., it has been tested for cultural biases). _____

13. The validity has been good and consistent in at least one study by a researcher unaffiliated with the measure's developer(s). _____

14. The instrument's validity has been reported in a publication(s) with blind peer review. _____

In sum, what is the level of evidence for the measure's validity?

Summary   Overall, how reliable and valid is the instrument? _____

B. Applicability (Is this instrument relevant and appropriate for my situation?)
1. Instrument Background

Conceptual foundation   1. The conceptual foundation of the instrument was described. _____

Administration/scoring   2. The amount of time to complete and score the measure was specified. _____

3. The source provides clear instructions on how to complete and score the instrument. _____

(continued)

161

Table 4.9. (*continued*)

Criteria	Items/Descriptions	Rating The study provided: 3—strong evidence 2—moderate evidence 1—weak evidence 0—no evidence N/A—not applicable
Group/members	4. The characteristics of group members with which the instrument was developed were identified (age, gender, race/ethnicity, language/acculturation, developmental level, problem/diagnoses, socioeconomic status).	
	5. The groups were clearly identified (i.e., size, length, and timing).	_____
	6. The group format was identified (closed, open, slow open) and location specified.	_____
Group leadership	7. Group leadership was adequately described (number of leaders, co-leadership, race/ethnicity, gender, training/education/experience).	_____
Summary	Overall, what is the level of evidence for describing the instrument?	_____
2. Situation		The statement is: 3—true 2—somewhat true 1—somewhat untrue 0—untrue
Setting	8. I have the time to complete and score the instrument, as specified by the instrument's instructions.	_____
	9. I have the resources needed to complete the instrument (e.g., computer).	_____

162

	10. The instrument is compatible with my agency's values and views.
Leader	11. I have permission to use the instrument.
	12. The instrument is compatible with my professional values and ethical guidelines.[a]
	13. I have the competence (knowledge, skills, and experience) and/or appropriate supervision to use the instrument with my group.[a]
Group	14. My group members are sufficiently similar to those in the reliability/validity studies in terms of sociodemographic variables that the results are likely to apply (consider age, gender, culture, race/ethnicity, language/acculturation, problem/diagnosis, developmental level, and socioeconomic status). (When there are differences in sociodemographic variables, rate this item positively if there is evidence that the differences are not likely to affect how the measure would perform with your group members.)
	15. If the instrument is a self-report, group members are likely to be willing to complete it accurately.
	16. I think this measure will help my group or group members, or it will help improve group services.
Summary	Overall, this instrument is appropriate for my situation.

Decision: Considering the instrument's rigor and applicability, should I use it in this situation? Circle one: yes / probably / probably not / no

Material in this table is drawn from a number of sources (Agency for Healthcare Research and Quality, 2002a; Lewis-Snyder, Stoiber, & Kratochwill, 2002; Pyrczak, 2005; Rubin & Babbie, 2005, pp. 182–192, 510–520).

[a] In general, a rating of "untrue" or "somewhat untrue" in these items indicates that the instrument should not be used.

two or three independent reviewers have determined the quality of the study about the measure. However, a review article about the instrument in which the authors report the psychometric properties of the instrument based on previously published empirical research would also be a good source of information.

The guideline in Table 4.9 is derived from a number of sources (Agency for Healthcare Research and Quality, 2002a; Lewis-Snyder et al., 2002; Pyrczak, 2005; Rubin & Babbie, 2005, pp. 182–192, 510–520) and provides ratings in the areas of rigor (i.e., reliability and validity) and applicability.

Explanation of Items in Table 4.9

Rigor   *Items 1–6 (Reliability).* Reliability is the absence of measurement error (Vogt, 1999) and is "the consistency or stability of a measure or test from one use to the next" (Vogt, 1999, p. 245). Types of reliability include internal consistency, test–retest, and interrater.

Item 1. Internal consistency, usually indicated by Cronbach's alpha, coefficient alpha, alpha, or α, should be high. It has a range of 0.00 to 1.00, with values of 0.70 and higher indicating *adequate* internal consistency (Kratochwill, 2003, p. 26), although 0.80 is indicative of *good* internal consistency (higher internal consistency indicates stronger evidence).

Item 2. Another form of reliability is interrater, or interobserver. If multiple ratings are used, as in direct observation measures, the interrater reliability coefficient should be high, indicating good agreement between raters. Sometimes interobserver reliability is reported as the percentage of agreement between observers. However, this is subject to inflation by chance agreement and by higher frequency behaviors. The kappa [κ] statistic, which corrects for chance agreement, is sometimes reported (Vogt, 1999). A standard of 70% for percentage agreement (Blythe & Tripodi, 1989) or a kappa score (κ) of 0.70 (Fleiss, 1981) may be considered a minimal standard. *Good* agreement is indicated by scores of 0.80, or 80%. Thus instruments must meet the "adequate" standard to be rated as having "minimal" evidence, with higher reliability values indicating stronger evidence.

Item 3. To determine stability, researchers examine an instrument's test–retest reliability. The same person's scores on the same items at two different points in time are compared; high correspondence is desirable. High stability would indicate that scores are relatively unaffected by changes in situations or times. However, an instrument's stability is also affected by the length of time between tests, whether the attitude or behavior being measured is considered a trait or state, and the age of the respondent. Generally, the longer the interval, the lower the temporal stability (Nunnally & Bernstein, 1994). Thus some judgment is needed in evaluating a measure's stability.

Items 4 and 6. The performance standards of instruments should be consistent across peer-reviewed publications.

Item 5. Measures with good psychometric properties should also be consistent across studies not affiliated with the instrument's developer.

Items 7–14 (Validity). In addition to the reliability of an instrument, group workers should also consider its validity, "a term to describe a measurement instrument or test that accurately measures what it is supposed to measure; the extent to which a measure is free of systematic error" (Vogt, 1999, p. 301).

Item 7. Types of validity include face, content, criterion-related, and construct. The simplest, face validity, is determined by examining the items and making a judgment about whether they appear to measure what they are supposed to measure. Sometimes expert judges are involved in a systematic approach to assessing the items. The systematic examination of the content of items is called content validity.

Another form of validity is criterion-related validity, which includes concurrent, predictive, and known-groups. Concurrent validity involves determining how well the measure agrees (correlates) with another measure (criterion) the researcher believes is valid (Vogt, 1999). Predictive validity refers to how well the measure correlates with a measure to be administered in the future. The difference between concurrent and predictive validity is the time at which the criterion is applied. Known-groups validity has to do with how well the measure is able to discriminate between two criterion groups. In assessing criterion validity, the appropriateness of the criterion and the validity coefficient must be considered. Are there theoretical or empirical grounds for using the criterion? If so, the coefficient may then be examined. In measures intended for clinical applications, both concurrent and predictive validity coefficients should be statistically significant, and the correlations should be moderate to high (Fischer & Corcoran, 1994). Typically, however, predictive validity coefficients are much lower and there is no simple standard for interpreting validity coefficients: "How high should a validity coefficient be? No general answer to this question is possible, since the interpretation of a validity coefficient must take into account a number of concomitant circumstances" (Anastasi & Urbina, 1997, p. 143).

Construct validity validates both the instrument and the theory underlying it: "To establish construct validity, the meaning of the construct must be understood, and the propositions the theory makes about the relationships between this and other constructs must be identified" (Grinnell, 1993, p. 186). For construct validity to be supported, the measure should have both convergent and divergent validity (Fischer & Corcoran, 1994). In convergent validity, the construct being tested should be significantly related to a conceptually similar variable. With divergent validity, the measure should not be associated with dissimilar variables. For example, a measure of engagement was expected to be positively related to a measure of cohesion and negatively related to a measure of resistance (Macgowan, 1997). Sometimes construct validity is determined using factor analysis to determine the dimensionality or structure of a measure. If a measure includes subscales, researchers should establish its heterogeneity through statistical procedures such as factor analysis.

Items 8–9. To reduce bias, the instrument should also have used multiple sources (e.g., member, leader) and methods (e.g., observations, self-reports) in establishing its validity (Pyrczak, 2005, p. 86). However, this may not always be applicable, as in the case of measures that were designed only for direct observation (Kratochwill, 2003; Lewis-Snyder et al., 2002).

Item 10. Those who completed the validation instruments should not be aware of the expected direction or scores on the instrument.

Items 11–12. Whether an instrument or measurement procedure is equally valid across diverse groups of people has been referred to as its social validity (Bloom et al., 2003). There might be language or behaviors that are not valid across cultures (Chen & Han, 2001; Chen & Davenport, 2005). For example, although verbal contribution in groups is an important value among Caucasians in North America, nonverbal means of communication may be more relevant to other groups. Discriminatory bias may occur when instruments are administered to people from ethnic or racial groups for which the measure was not developed (Groth-Marnat, 1997). In view of this concern, a compendium of measures for African Americans has been published (Jones, 1996a). In addition to using relevant measures, group workers should collect assessment data in a manner that is culturally competent (Jones, 1996b; Padilla & Medina, 1996). Worker biases or knowledge deficiencies about race or culture may affect the reliability and validity of the information collected (Ridley, 1995).

Applicability *Items 1–7.* Studies about instruments should include sufficient background information to allow readers to determine their suitability for a practice situation. These items assess whether the source included adequate information for application in the group situation in question. Most of the items on applicability have been discussed in other guides, so only the unique item is discussed here at length.

Item 1. Group workers should evaluate the underlying conceptual scheme and expectations of the instrument to make sure it matches what the group worker would like to assess. For example, there are many different conceptualizations of group development, but few have been developed specifically for women (Schiller, 1995). Expectations of performance inherent in an instrument may not be valid with all groups. For example, the Hostility/Support Scale (Beck, 1983) was used in studies to assess boundaries in group development. The scale was designed "to assess whether statements made in the course of group interaction are negative or supportive toward the person being addressed" (Lewis, Beck, Dugo, & Eng, 2000, p. 230). The scale identified changes in periods of tension, criticism, and conflict to periods of support and encouragement (Beck, Dugo, Eng, & Lewis, 1986). An important question is whether this expectation of negative or supportive periods is valid across genders or cultures. Thus, group workers need to evaluate each instrument's conceptual foundation and expectations to determine whether it is appropriate for the target group.

Items 8–17. As in the previous guides, group workers need to evaluate the instrument's applicability to the group situation. It must be appropriate for the setting, leader, and group members.

Conclusion

This chapter presented guidelines for evaluating a range of evidence acquired to answer a practice question. Group workers do not need to master the details of the guidelines or understand the underlying statistical or methodological theory. The guides are to be used in a critical process to determine the research merit (rigor), impact, and clinical applicability of evidence. Examples illustrated the guidelines in use. Once it is decided that evidence is rigorous, helpful, and applicable, it can be applied, as discussed in the next chapter.

5

Apply the Evidence and Evaluate the Achievement of Desired Outcomes

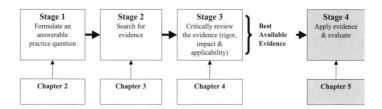

After determining the rigor, impact, and applicability of the evidence, the group worker applies the chosen intervention or technique in the group situation. The clinical-expertise skills of weighing the group situation and context, group member preference and actions, and research evidence described in Chapter 1 are essential in this stage of evidence-based group work (EBGW). The leader must balance the *research* concern of maintaining fidelity to the essential ingredients of the original evidence (to ensure that he or she delivers the intervention or technique to achieve success) and the *clinical* concern of ensuring that the evidence is relevant to the group situation. Once the strategy is applied, the group worker must evaluate the effects of the action to determine whether the desired results have been achieved. This chapter describes these two steps of the process—namely, applying the evidence in practice and evaluating its effects. A final section discusses documenting the application and evaluation.

Application in Practice

In applying evidence in practice, group workers should consider whether their application of the evidence maintains fidelity to the original evidence (i.e., is a replication) or is an adaptation.

Intervention Fidelity and Adaptation

In some cases, an intervention or technique will directly apply to a group situation. However, based on the evaluation of applicability described in

Chapter 4, a group worker may consider adapting it for the group situation. An adaptation may occur in different ways. A group worker may want to alter the intervention/technique itself, apply the intervention/technique to a different population, or use it for a different problem. Whenever possible, group workers should maintain the integrity of the original intervention/technique and not substantially adapt or change it. Although there is debate as to how much intervention fidelity accounts for change and what precisely constitutes fidelity (Gresham, 2005; Perepletchikova & Kazdin, 2005), there is substantial research reporting that fidelity to interventions significantly increases favorable outcomes, and a loss of fidelity reduces program effectiveness (Elliott & Mihalic, 2004; Gresham, Gansle, Noell, Cohen, & Rosenblum, 1993; Gresham, MacMillan, Beebe-Frankenberger, & Bocian, 2000; Henggeler, Melton, Brondino, Scherer, & Hanley, 1997; Henggeler, Pickrel, & Brondino, 1999; Henggeler, Schoenwald, Liao, Letourneau, & Edwards, 2002; Kam, Greenberg, & Walls, 2003; Rosen, 1999).[1] If adherence is important, an important question is, "What constitutes a substantial replication?"

Currently, there are no research-derived standards for determining what a replication is. However, the Task Force on Evidence-Based Interventions in Psychology (Kratochwill, 2003) developed a set of criteria through consensus of experts. The Task Force identified criteria to determine whether two interventions are essentially the same and whether they address the same target problem. These criteria will be used to suggest when a group intervention is substantially the same and addresses a similar target problem and population.

The Task Force noted that a replication of an intervention occurs if (a) the same manual/procedures are used or the original authors affirm that the intervention is essentially the same (this could be done through personal contact) and (b) the intervention duration is the same, a shorter version is at least 75% of the longer version, or a longer intervention is used (Kratochwill, 2003, pp. 77–78). Thus group workers should strive to ensure that the number of group sessions is at least three-quarters of the original and that they follow a treatment manual, practice protocol, or the "essential ingredients" of the intervention. The best manuals are backed by strong research and have a clinical foundation. A shortcoming of many manuals is that they do not include material related to maximizing the full benefits of group work (e.g., tips on effective leadership, how to get group members more involved) and may prescribe a strict cookbook approach without identifying the components essential for replication (see Box 4.2 for further discussion of some of these issues). A number of treatment manuals have been published for group work, and are of varying quality (Bourke & Van Hasselt, 2001; Kalter & Schreier, 1994; Sampl & Kadden, 2001; Siepker & Kandaras, 1985; Webb, Scudder, Kaminer, & Kadden, 2002), but group workers need to be cautious, as treatment manuals may be published without strong research evidence. Group workers need to critically examine the rigor, impact, and applicability of manuals. To do this, they may use one of the appropriate guides from the previous chapter, such as the guide for evaluating literature reviews or the guide for evaluating the research/clinical support of an intervention/technique in group.

Though not mentioned by the Task Force, another way to enhance replication of an intervention is to use an instrument. Studies may provide measures for identifying the essential ingredients of the theoretical model. For example, Kaminer and colleagues developed and tested a 7-item measure of treatment adherence for group treatment of adolescent substance abusers called the Group Session Rating Scale (GSRS) (Cooney, Kadden, Litt, & Getter, 1991; Getter, Litt, Kadden, & Cooney, 1992; Kaminer et al., 1998). The GSRS was developed to monitor and discriminate between cognitive-behavioral group therapy and interactional group therapy. The measure displayed moderate to good reliability and was able to distinguish between the two treatments. The brief instrument may be used to distinguish between these two general approaches to group work.

With respect to whether the intervention addresses the same target problem and population, the Task Force noted that the same target issue/problem and the same age/grade group should be involved in the replication.

> [O]therwise, the new study represents a new test with a new target issue/problem and/or developmental group. When an intervention is tested with a different target issue/problem or with a different age/grade group than in previous research, this is considered evidence of a new application of the intervention, not a replication. (Kratochwill, 2003, p. 78)

For classifying age ranges, the Task Force guidelines suggested the following groupings: infant (birth to 2 years), preschool (2–5 years), elementary (6–11 years), secondary (12–17 years), adult (18–65 years), and geriatric (over 65 years) (Kratochwill, 2003, p. 78).

The guidelines were less clear about what constituted the same problem, except to note that there were obvious differences (e.g., depression and anxiety in children 8 to 11 years) and similarities (e.g., conduct problems and oppositionality in children 8 to 11 years) and that questionable circumstances should be resolved by committee. Group workers rarely work by committee, but they may seek consultation from a colleague or supervisor if they have questions about whether they can consider the problems the same or if the age-group classifications are relevant for the application.

The Task Force offered no guidance as to the relevance of other demographic variables such as gender, race, and ethnicity in determining whether an intervention is a replication or a new application. Although group workers should consider gender, race, and ethnic differences between the original study and the proposed application, as noted in an earlier discussion, there is good research evidence to suggest that the differences will have little effect on the outcome (see the discussion about applicability in Chapter 4). Group workers must use judgment informed by knowledge, values, and skills in determining whether they should consider the findings a novel application with the proposed group members. A clear example of a new application would be if a group worker would like to apply a gender-, race- or culture-based group intervention (i.e., interventions that include variables specifically related to a particular group; see Pack-Brown & Fleming, 2004) with a population not intended by the original study. Group workers must determine whether applying the intervention with a new problem or population would likely be helpful, or at least not be harmful. If necessary, group workers should consult with a colleague, supervisor, or cultural guide (e.g., person, advisory group) who may have been involved in the evaluation of the group work evidence (see Chapter 4 for further discussion). Group workers would use cultural-competence skills in applying the evidence in a cultural setting different from the original setting. There are different models of culturally competent group work in the literature that group workers may consult (Chen & Han, 2001; Comstock, Duffey, & St. George, 2002; DeLucia-Waack & Donigian, 2003; Merchant & Butler, 2002).

In clinical group work, there will not likely be perfect replication, and the circumstances will dictate what and how components or processes of delivery should be modified. There needs to be some room for the flexible adaptation of services, without compromising the essential elements of an intervention or technique. Group workers may use the guidelines above to determine whether what they want to apply is a substantial adaptation of the original intervention or an application with a new population or problem. In these circumstances, group workers should be aware that they might not achieve the original effects of the intervention and should monitor implementation carefully.[2]

Evaluate to Ensure Achievement of Desired Results

Regardless of whether the evidence was adapted, group workers need to evaluate the results to know whether the intended effects were achieved and desirable. As the American Psychological Association has noted, "The application of research evidence to a given patient always involves probabilistic inferences. Therefore, ongoing monitoring of patient progress and adjustment of treatment as needed are essential to EBPP [Evidence-Based Practice in Psychology]" (American Psychological Association, August 2005, p. 3). In addition, transferring empirically supported treatments from one context to another does not invariably improve outcomes over what is currently being done (Weisz et al., 2004).

The type of evaluation that EBGW is concerned with is *practice evaluation*, described in the next section. Later sections highlight two important parts of practice evaluation, namely goal setting and monitoring progress using research tools. These discussions provide an overview of evaluation of group work practice suitable for EBGW and are not exhaustive. Readers may consult general books on practice evaluation (e.g., Bloom et al., 2003; Blythe, Tripodi, & Briar, 1994; Nugent, Sieppert, & Hudson, 2001) and group work texts

(Garvin, 1997, pp. 190–207; Toseland & Rivas, 2005, pp. 389–416) in addition to the specific resources listed below.

Practice Evaluation, not Clinical Research

Evaluation designs actually used by clinicians are not likely to reach the high standard of those in the literature. Frequently, research studies in the literature benefit from controlled circumstances, access to expertise, and funding, which are unavailable to most practitioners. Research studies generally use a model of research—clinical research—whose purpose is different from the model used by practitioners (practice evaluation). "Although practice evaluation uses research methods and procedures, its primary goals are to provide feedback about client change and enhance the client's outcome . . . . [I]n contrast, clinical research uses rigorous research procedures to develop scientific knowledge" (Corcoran, Gingerich, & Briggs, 2001, p. 67). Clinical research intends to control for extraneous factors, maximizing internal validity, to ensure that the effects of the intervention are clear and certain. Practice evaluation puts a smaller emphasis on controlling for rival explanations. The emphasis in practice evaluation is "to reduce uncertainty—for [practitioners] to believe that they probably are helping their clients but cannot control all aspects of their lives with such a degree of tyranny that no other explanations of their behavior are possible" (Briggs, Feyerherm, & Gingerich, 2004, pp. 324–325). Practice evaluation helps group workers to monitor the well-being of group members and the group, and may provide evidence that the intervention or strategy was responsible for change, but "because the methods used in practice evaluation are not as rigorous as those for research purposes, you will be limited in what you can conclude about the effectiveness of your intervention" (Corcoran et al., 2001, p. 67).

Group workers should strive to make practice evaluation as rigorous as possible, including using controls such as those used in strong single-subject designs, but controls typically become second in priority to the clinical goal of providing feedback about group work and enhancing outcomes of the group or group members. Often clinical priorities and organizational constraints require that the group worker loosen or abandon controls. EBGW is concerned primarily with the impact and effectiveness of practice interventions or techniques. Unless they are supported by their organizations or through funded research projects, most practitioners do not have the time, resources, or abilities to mount controlled, clinical research studies. Thus, absent substantial resources and expertise, practice evaluation is the appropriate model of research in EBGW.[3]

Practice evaluation has three attributes (Briggs et al., 2004, p. 325). The first is goal setting, which may include a range of targets based on the group worker's evaluation of the problem, and depending on whether the group worker wishes to include goals related to individual group members (e.g., reducing depression) or to elements of group work (e.g., improved cohesion or group interaction). The second is monitoring or tracking progress toward targets using research tools for tracking progress and outcomes and using measures with good psychometric properties suitable for clinical practice. The third attribute is "a systematic, analytical process of developing insights into the applicability of the specific intervention with the specific client (rather than the generalized program clientele of the evaluator). In this sense, this is a bridge that brings the tools of research and evaluation into the world of practice" (Briggs et al., 2004, p. 325). Two important areas that need further elaboration are goal setting, which involves identifying and measuring outcomes, and tracking progress and outcomes using evaluation design.

Goal Setting: Identifying and Measuring Desired Outcomes

In the discussion about the first stage of EBGW (formulating an answerable practice question), it was pointed out that it is important to identify an outcome for a question. Readers may recall that the outcome is what the group worker would like to see changed. In addition, outcomes (or goals) were distinguished as problem or group related, and as proximal or distal. Distal outcomes may be related to the problem that brought group members to the group service, such as reducing anxiety to a manageable level (problem-related distal outcomes), or to the group, such as member satisfaction with the group service (group-related distal outcomes). Group-related proximal outcomes are what a group worker would like to achieve during the life of the group, such as a level of engagement, cohesion, or interaction, to name a few.

Figure 5.1 depicts how outcomes and goals relate to measurement of group phenomena. It begins with defining the desired outcome in the MAP question, which can be either a problem-related outcome or a group-related outcome (outcomes may include problem reduction but may also include enhancement of protective factors or strengths). Problem-related outcomes may include (a) achievement of a change in diagnostic criteria, problem level, or level of positive functioning; (b) subjective evaluation by significant others; or (c) comparison with norm reference groups (Kratochwill, 2003). Group-related outcomes may include achieving a certain outcome within the group, such as expecting a particular level of engagement as measured by the Group Engagement Measure (Macgowan, 2006b), or it may include achieving an outcome by the end of group, such as a certain level of satisfaction with the group service as measured by a brief session-evaluation instrument (e.g., Rose, 1977, pp. 60–61; Rose, 1984, pp. 34–36). Both group- and problem-related outcomes may be measured during and/or at the end of the group to provide process and outcome evaluations.

There are different methods of measurement (Figure 5.1) and a range of quantitative instruments to choose from, as discussed in Chapter 3. Group workers may also want to include qualitative measures. For example, there are relatively open-ended, lengthy formats such as the classic process recording (Wilson & Ryland, 1949, pp. 76–80), a narrative, verbatim record of the session, including worker reactions and supervisor analysis (Wilson, 1980, pp. 18–26, 89–98), and the Group Process Note (Yalom & Leszcz, 2005, pp. 468– 469). There is also a summary recording format that captures the main events of the session using the Group Recording Form (Toseland & Rivas, 2005, pp. 395–397) and the Group Report Form (MacKenzie, 1990, pp. 262–263, 276). A structured format that is more selective in what it records is a critical incident record, such as William Schwartz's matrix analyzing worker responses in group situations (Berman-Rossi, 1994, pp. 764–767). Finally, there are process-outcome instruments such as the Group Work Recording Form (Garvin, 1997, pp. 199–200), Process Recording Form (Henry, 1992, pp. 243–246), and Record of Service (Berman-Rossi, 1994, pp. 768–769; Shulman, 2006, pp. 226, 387–393, 597–599). These methods are helpful for in-depth information about the impact of an intervention or technique, and group workers may use them to supplement the information provided by quantitative measures.

The subject of measurement (who completes the instrument) may include the individual group member, a dyad, a subgroup, the entire group, or a significant other from outside the group. Group member scores may be summed or averaged to create an aggregated subject rating.

The object of measurement may be the individual, dyad, subgroup, or entire group, with the possibility that ratings of group phenomena may be obtained by summing or averaging individual ratings. However, some phenomena are best measured at the molar level because the whole may have different properties from the individual parts (Lewin, 1951, p. 146). Examples include how a group member would rate the helpfulness of the group experience or would rate the value of group norms. In addition, merely aggregating individual ratings prevents examining individual or subgroup differences and introduces the risk of the ecological fallacy (Patterson & Basham, 2002), which is "an error of reasoning committed by coming to conclusions about individuals based only on data about groups" (Vogt, 1999, p. 92). Thus, aggregating individual scores should be done thoughtfully with an understanding of what data are lost and what conclusions may or may not be made with the aggregated information.

Two examples in Figure 5.1 illustrate the connection between the desired outcome as stated in the MAP question and the various choices in measurement. The example of a problem-related outcome of achieving subclinical stress involves a self-report using the Index of Clinical Stress (Abell, 1991), completed by the individual group member about himself or herself. The example of a group-related proximal outcome is increased verbal contribution and involves direct observation by the group leader using a simple behavior count (number of times each person spoke), completed by the leader about each individual but aggregated to create a subgroup score.

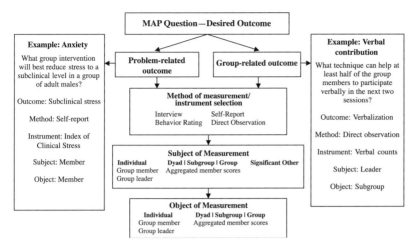

Figure 5.1. Measurement and outcomes in evidence-based group work.

Tracking Progress Toward Outcomes:
Evaluation Design

Evaluation design provides the structure for determining progress and success. The type of question and clinical circumstance would determine the most appropriate type of design to select. There are different approaches to evaluating whether an intervention or technique was successful. Approaches that focus on goal or outcome achievement include Goal Attainment Scaling (GAS), Task Achievement Scaling (TAS), and pre–post designs. Other approaches such as single-subject designs (SSDs) provide data on both progress and outcome. This section presents an overview of these approaches. More detail on the approaches may be found in the sources cited below.

GAS is a system for measuring progress in achieving goals and was originally developed by Kiresuk and Sherman for individual clients (Bloom et al., 2003, pp. 102–105; Kiresuk, Smith, & Cardillo, 1994). However, it is also a viable approach for group work (Garvin, 1985b, 1997; Toseland & Rivas, 2005, pp. 407–408). Goals may be a change in the problems of individual group members (problem-related outcomes) or a change desired within the group itself (group-related outcomes), such as in the level of cohesion or engagement.

In task-centered practice, goals are achieved by accomplishing tasks (Reid, 1992; Reid & Epstein, 1972, 1977; Tolson, Reid, & Garvin, 2003). TAS is used to measure these achievements (examples of the TAS are in Reid, 1992, pp. 66–67; Reid & Epstein, 1972, pp. 239–240; Sheafor & Horejsi, 2003, pp. 482–483). Although GAS and TAS are focused on achieving an outcome, they may also be used to track progress toward achieving the outcome (Magen & Rose, 1994). Charles Garvin and colleagues have written extensively on task-centered group work (Garvin, 1974, 1985b, 1986, 1992; Tolson et al., 2003, pp. 253–345)

An approach that examines only problem-related distal outcomes is to assess change from pretreatment to post-treatment. There are a number of potential designs in this category, from nonrandomized designs, such as the one-group pretest–post-test design, to experimental designs, such as the pretest–post-test control-group design (Blythe et al., 1994, pp. 179–204; Rubin & Babbie, 2005). Outside of well-resourced agency settings or in funded research studies, randomized designs are not feasible for group workers. Though lacking controls, nonrandomized designs are feasible in clinical settings. In one of the simple designs—the one-group pretest–post-test design—a group worker makes one observation of a phenomenon at pretest (before the group begins), implements the intervention or technique, and measures the same phenomenon at the end of service. Sufficient change from pretest to post-test may be determined graphically or statistically. These designs have limitations. In addition to lacking control over rival explanations for change, pretest–post-test designs provide no information about ongoing progress.

An evaluation approach that is effective in examining both outcome and progress toward outcomes is the SSD. The use of repeated measures over time to track progress is an important advantage of using SSD. An overview and discussion of the technical aspects of reviewing the quality of SSDs was presented in the previous chapter, but the value of using SSDs in practice evaluation should be briefly considered. Detailed discussions about the clinical application of SSDs are in the general practice literature (Bloom et al., 2003; Blythe et al., 1994, pp. 165–179; Briggs et al., 2004; Gambrill, 2006b, pp. 600–611; Richards, 1999; Rubin & Babbie, 2005, pp. 364–393; Sheafor & Horejsi, 2003, pp. 486–494; Tripodi, 1994) and in that of group work in particular (Garvin, 1997; Toseland & Rivas, 2005; Zastrow, 2001). Although SSDs have been widely embraced, group workers need to be wary of the following potential limitations of them when applied in clinical settings (adapted from Straus et al., 2005, p. 173):

1. Some problems are self-limited and group members may get better on their own.
2. Extreme clinical signs, if left unresolved and reassessed later, often return to normal.
3. A placebo can lead to substantial improvement in symptoms.
4. Both our own and our group members' expectations about the success or failure of an intervention or technique can bias conclusions as to whether the intervention or technique actually worked.
5. Polite or compliant group members may exaggerate the effects of the intervention or technique.

Straus and colleagues caution that "if a treatment was used during any of the above situations, it would tend to appear efficacious when in fact it was useless" (Straus et al., 2005, p. 173).

There is a range of potential SSDs that group workers may utilize, with different levels of rigor. In general, group workers should utilize the most powerful design to reduce the likelihood of rival explanations for change, such as multiple baseline designs and withdrawal-reversal designs (see previous chapter). Basic designs, though commonly used, lack adequate controls. However, with replication within and across groups over time, and by using the other methods for recording change described above (such as qualitative notes), group workers may discern patterns allowing them to determine the effectiveness of an intervention or a technique. In addition, "even if the therapist and clients are not certain that the intervention was the sole cause of the changes, it still makes it possible to ascertain the degree to which goals are being achieved" (Rose, 1977, p. 67). Without a systematic method of evaluation, the information a group worker would have about the effectiveness of a group intervention or technique would be based on memory, selective inquiry, and unchecked bias (see Chapter 1 for more discussion about the use of critical thinking and systematic inquiry).

Specific examples of SSDs in group work are in Table 5.1. Most of the published examples use relatively simple designs, with a few using multiple baseline designs, such as Edleson and colleagues (1985) and one of the Rose (1977) examples (#7). Three of the studies lack a sufficient baseline (Cetingok & Hirayama, 1983; O'Brien et al., 1999; Patterson & Basham, 2002) and instead track outcomes or treatment response during the intervention. Some of the outcomes were related to the problems that brought the members to the group (e.g., Edleson et al., 1985), and others were related to group functioning (e.g., Hauserman et al., 1972; Johnson et al., 2001; Rose, 1977), although these outcomes are not mutually exclusive. Methods of evaluation include visual to statistical. The Patterson and Basham example utilizes an interesting and informative visual approach to presenting group data by using three-dimensional surface plots created with Microsoft Excel. Readers are encouraged to read these examples for applications of SSDs in group work.

Document the Application and Evaluation

Group workers should document what intervention/technique they applied, how they adapted it, and the results of the application and evaluation. Table 5.2 provides a form with which to document the application and evaluation. A more elaborate method for recording the application of a group intervention/ technique is to create a manualized practice outline. As described by Cournoyer (2004), there are resources that help clinicians develop their own practice outlines, including a series of PracticePlanners by John Wiley and Sons. Examples include the group therapy treatment planner (Paleg & Jongsma, 2005) and the group therapy homework planner (Bevilacqua, 2002). Cournoyer provides other resources, including a framework for developing a practice manual, which group workers may consult in constructing their practice outlines (Cournoyer, 2004, pp. 184–185). Another method, compatible with a practice outline, is to prepare a report on practice effectiveness,

Table 5.1. Examples of Single-Subject Designs in Group Work

Publication (Number of Examples)	(Example #) Problem/ Outcome	(Example #) Population	(Example #) Design	(Example #) Method of Evaluation
(Cetingok & Hirayama, 1983)(1)	Health-care knowledge; health attitudes and behaviors	Elderly with diabetes, heart disease, and hypertension	Simple time series (B only)	t-tests for change differences; t-tests for autocorrelation
(Edleson, Miller, Stone, & Chapman, 1985)(1)	Incidence of partner abuse	Adult males who physically abused female partners	Modified multiple baseline	Celeration line analysis
(Hauserman, Zweback, & Plotkin, 1972)(1)	Member verbalizations	Six male and female adolescents hospitalized for mostly externalizing behaviors	Crossover multiple baseline (concurrent groups): Group 1: ABAB; Group 2: AABB	Descriptive, visual
(Johnson, Beckerman, & Auerbach, 2001)(3)	(1) Attendance (2) Member verbalization (3) Self-expression	(1) Adolescent girls (2) Shelter residents, adult male veterans (3) Children who have experienced loss	(1) AB (2) AB (3) AB	(1) Celeration line analysis (2) Two standard-deviation band test (3) Percent increase from baseline
(O'Brien, Korchynsky, Fabrizio, McGrath, & Swank, 1999)(1)	Positive and negative group processes, satisfaction with group	Adults	Simple time series (B only)	Repeated measures MANOVA for change differences; ANOVA; trends analysis and pairwise comparisons
(Patterson & Basham, 2002)(1)	Satisfaction with group	Graduate students	Simple time series (B only)	Surface plot

(Petry, Martin, & Finocche, 2001)(1)	Group attendance, completing steps to-ward treatment goals	Adults with HIV infection, substance use	AB^{1}B^{2}CA	Descriptive, visual
(Rose, 1977, pp. 66–72)(7)	(1,2) Member-to-member interactions (3) Member praise statements (4) Leader-to-member interactions (5) Leader suggestion giving (6) Positive affectual responses (7) Suggestion-opinion giving response; information-giving response; positive affectual response	(1–5) Adults (6) Divorced women. (7) Hospitalized chronic schizophrenic patients	(1–5) AB (6) ABAB (7) Multiple baseline	(1–7) Visual

This table includes a selection from the literature. Other examples include Rose's edited book (1980) that includes a number of additional case examples.

A = baseline phase; B, C, D = different intervention phases; B^{1}B^2 = small variations in an intervention; ANOVA = analysis of variance; MANOVA = multivariate analysis of variance.

Table 5.2.   Record of Application of Evidence in Practice

MAP Question:

Citation/source of evidence used:

Date(s) of application(s):

Specific intervention/technique:

If applicable, how was the intervention/technique adapted?

Results of application (attach any charts or figures from the results of evaluation):

Next steps:

Additional notes:

---

which emphasizes recording the effects of a practice intervention (Blythe et al., 1994, pp. 218–222).

These notes and evaluations become part of the development of protocols and manuals that group workers may develop for their practice. More discussion about the dissemination of results is in the next chapter.

Case Examples

The following three examples illustrate the two main steps of this chapter: application in practice and the use of evaluation to ensure desired results. The actual results of the evaluation are not included as they are not important for illustrating the principles. In addition, there are good examples in the literature about how to conduct practice evaluation, as cited earlier in the chapter. The first example illustrates application and evaluation for a question involving problem-related outcomes, and the second example illustrates application and evaluation for questions related to group-related proximal outcomes. The third example illustrates application and evaluation for a question involving group-related proximal and distal outcomes.

Keisha Smith: Refreshing an Existing Group Intervention

Keisha reviewed the information about the intervention with her supervisor and was permitted to lead the group, with another co-worker, on a trial basis. In the meantime, the existing group would continue. The intervention is a replication, as Keisha would include essentially the same content and length, and the program would address essentially the same target problem.

To evaluate the group, Keisha had to decide on the desired outcomes, ways to measure them, and a suitable evaluation design for structuring the inquiry. Keisha first needed to decide what outcomes to measure. She noted that although the original study used four instruments, the two main outcome measures were parenting and child behavior. To determine what measure to use, she first consulted the article to see whether the measures used in the study were appropriate and available. If this inquiry did not yield a good instrument, she would consult other sources of measures that evaluated the same constructs, such as those noted in Chapter 3. To measure parenting behaviors, the original article (Bradley et al., 2003) used the Parenting Scale (Arnold, O'Leary, Wolff, & Acker, 1993). Keisha found the Parenting Scale online (after a search using Google) and downloaded it with the scoring key. After she and her supervisor reviewed it, they decided that the measure was appropriate for use with her group. The scale is completed by parents, who rate their parenting practices. Using the same search approach, Keisha easily found the Preschool Behavior Questionnaire (PBQ), which was available from the author's Web site (http://www.lenorebehar.com/preschool.htm). Because the instrument was copyrighted, the author of the instrument was contacted by e-mail, and she readily gave the student permission to use it. Parents complete the PBQ, describing their child's behavior at home. Both instruments were readily available, clinically suitable (i.e., relatively brief and easily scored), and appropriate for Keisha's situation. Thus, Keisha had the necessary instruments to evaluate parenting and child behavior. In addition to these outcome measures, she would also include a measure of satisfaction with the group at the end of each of the four sessions, using a brief post-session questionnaire (Rose, 1984, pp. 34–36).

The evaluation design she used to determine the effectiveness of her group was a single-group pretest–post-test design. She knew this design had limitations, but it would provide her feedback about the intervention within her limited resources. She would administer the pretest before the group began—around intake after parents agreed to participate—and after the last group session. She did not plan follow-up evaluations. To determine whether sufficient change had occurred from pretest to post-test, she would simply graph the results using the function in her word processor, with an expectation that results would be sufficiently clear. In addition, she would examine the group satisfaction ratings session by session and as an aggregate to determine her group members' satisfaction with the overall group service.

Roselia Gomez: Increasing Verbal Contributions

Roselia wanted to use rounds to draw out a few silent group members. Her use of the technique was a replication. With respect to goal setting, Roselia could not readily locate an appropriate measure of verbal contribution, so she created one. She defined "verbal contributions" as any verbal contribution consisting of a word, phrase, or sentence that related to the group topic. She would be the one to rate the contribution. The desired outcome was at least two relevant verbal contributions by the reticent group members in a session.

Her choice of evaluation design was the basic SSD with a single baseline and treatment phase. She created a retrospective baseline using the first five group sessions, which had occurred by the time she found the best available evidence. As described (in more detail) in Chapter 4, Roselia would initially use a designated word or phrase round and would subsequently vary the type of round depending on the circumstances. She would use the rounds as long as needed, until the two target group members contributed spontaneously at least once for two consecutive sessions. To monitor progress, she would map the verbal contributions using the graph function in her word processor. To evaluate change, she would compare the baseline with the treatment phase, expecting a clear difference in the amount of verbal contributions by the group members.

James Herrera: Increasing Attendance

Based on his review of the evidence from his search, James decided that he would use the behavioral, contingency management (CM) approach (Petry et al., 2005) to help increase attendance in an outpatient group of older adolescents with alcohol and other drug problems. James would utilize the strategy with the next group in which he would be the primary group worker.

As outlined in the study (Petry et al., 2005), the CM approach involved a prize bowl, and group members earned draws for attending sessions. For each session attended, members drew one slip of paper from the prize bowl, and the number of draws increased by one for each consecutive session attended. To maximize the approach's applicability for adolescent groups, James wanted to make sure he included developmentally appropriate prizes. To ensure this

James polled the adolescents in the group in which he was currently co-worker and learned that the youths would value electronics and music. A national electronics chain store was willing to donate $100 in gift cards to the program. Given the limited budget, James had to adapt the reward strategy from the original study, which had a much larger prize budget. He thought the adaptation did not meaningfully depart from the original strategy.

He applied the strategy in the following way: The prize bowl for each session included six slips of paper (representing the maximum number of group members), with five containing the words "Good job!" and one containing a $5 gift certificate to the electronics store. Each member attending that session would draw one (if there was no winner, the amount would be added to a separate pot for a final drawing, described below). If an adolescent attended both sessions for that week, he would participate in a drawing for a second $5 gift certificate, in addition to drawing for a $5 certificate for attending that session. Thus, any group member who attended both sessions in a week would be eligible to receive up to $15 in gift certificates per week. In addition, in the last session, a separate drawing would be made for a $10 gift certificate for members who attended all sessions. Attendance was defined as being present in the group before the curriculum content began and remaining until the end, when the draw was made. The CM strategy would be introduced to the group in the first session, as part of the discussion about group purpose and norms, to ensure that expectations were clear and concerns fully addressed.

James's evaluation design for determining progress was a form of Goal Attainment Scaling (GAS). According to the MAP question, James wanted most of the group members to attend each group session. Thus, as long as four (of six) adolescents attended a complete session, the goal was achieved. Attendance was plotted on a chart.

The GAS design was not adequate to determine whether the particular strategy was responsible for the increase in attendance. James had few practical choices among single-case or grouped evaluation designs. Due to the relatively short time frame of the group (6 weeks), he thought it was impractical to include a withdrawal phase. Furthermore, his review of the study (Petry et al., 2005) suggested strong effects, and he felt uneasy about withdrawing the strategy midway through group. Thus, he was committed to using the CM approach throughout the group. In addition, James would not be leading a second group, so there was no possibility that he could involve a comparison group that would have the same leader. Thus, the only source for comparison was the attendance records from the previous group. If the attendance record in the new group clearly improved (at least one more person per session, assuming the same group size) over that of the previous group, this could indicate that the strategy might have contributed. Ideally, he would replicate the experience at least several times to determine consistent effects over that of the previous groups (though this was not possible due to the end of his field experience). Admittedly, this simple evaluation design could not reliably determine effects, but it could provide the basis for a subsequent effort with some controls.

Conclusion

Application and evaluation are not separate endeavors but are intertwined in a circular and iterative process. Group workers apply the best available evidence in practice, remaining as faithful to the original intervention/technique as possible and adapting only where necessary. They monitor the effects of the strategy using valid measures and a research design that structures the evaluation process, record results, and determine how to improve both the evaluation and the practice. Thus, the process does not end with knowing whether the strategy "worked" but continues with a systematic, critical process of improving practice based on the ongoing results of the application in practice and evaluation. Three case examples involving Keisha Smith, Roselia Gomez, and James Herrera illustrated the two main steps of the chapter: application and evaluation to ensure desired results.

PART III

DISSEMINATION OF EVIDENCE-BASED GROUP WORK

6

Advancing Evidence-Based Group Work in Research, Clinical Practice, and Education

In order for evidence-based group work (EBGW) to be sustained and to grow, activity and further development are required in the areas of research, clinical practice, and education.

Advance Evidence-Based Group Work in Research

More research evidence about group work and reports on the application of EBGW in practice are needed, including studies on its effectiveness.

More Research Evidence About Group Work

Good research evidence is a foundation of EBGW. More research studies are needed to guide practice. To facilitate this end, action is needed in five areas.

First, more studies are needed on how groups are effective in achieving problem-related distal outcomes—that is, studies of group work interventions that improve functioning of group members at post-test and beyond. As was suggested by the number of systematic reviews involving groups shown in Table 3.6 (Chapter 3), there are many empirical research studies on the efficacy of group work. Recent reviews suggest an increase in small-group research studies over the years (Brower, Arndt, & Ketterhagen, 2004). An examination of some of that research, however, suggests that there are many qualifications in their conclusions. Group work is known to be generally effective (Burlingame et al., 2003), but much more evidence is needed concerning different problem areas and populations, particularly across cultural groups. To strengthen the quality of the research, there are "very good solutions" for group work design problems

(Brower et al., 2004), and the future of group work research is bright, as researchers can now utilize more sophisticated methods that capture the "iterative, dynamic, and holistic" nature of the group, linking processes and outcomes to bring about an understanding of what makes group work effective (Burlingame, Fuhriman, et al., 2004a, p. 657; Morgan-Lopez & Fals-Stewart, 2006). Within these outcome studies, researchers must provide more details about studies and protocols. Many intervention studies lack sufficient detail for replication in practice. They need to provide practice protocols, treatment manuals,[1] and basic information about the structure of the group (e.g., group size, number of sessions, timing), group composition (e.g., gender, age, ethnicity/race), and leadership (e.g., gender, training and experience, adherence). Assessment of applicability can not be accomplished without these elements (see Chapter 4 for more on applicability). Table 6.1 provides more details on recommended data for the publication of group therapy studies.

Table 6.1.   Recommended Data for the Publication of Group Psychotherapy Studies

Sample/Patients	Sample size
	Demographic (gender, age, ethnicity, and socioeconomic status)
	Diagnostic information (diagnosis and source, e.g., comorbidity and duration, clinical interview or standardized measure)
	Experiences with mental health treatment
	• before entering group
	• subsequent to group therapy (in case of follow-up)
	Recruited patients vs. walk-ins
Therapists/Leaders	Number of therapists
	Gender
	Training and experience
	Adherence
	Co-leadership
Treatment Model/Groups	Theoretical model (manualized, session outline)
	Duration, number, frequency of sessions, and groups
	Group composition (gender, age, diagnoses, criteria for membership)
	Group size
	Group format (closed, slow open, open)
Methodology	Research design
	Sample selection throughout the study (i.e., attrition)
	Measures
	Follow-up
	Information necessary to compute effect sizes (means, standard deviations)
	Both total group and individual group results
	Intraclass correlation coefficients to ascertain dependency

Source: Burlingame, G. M., MacKenzie, K. R., & Strauss, B. (2004). Small group treatment: Evidence for effectiveness and mechanisms of change. In M. J. Lambert (Ed.), *Bergin and Garfield's handbook of psychotherapy and behavior change* (5th ed., pp. 647–696). Hoboken, NJ: Wiley. Used with permission.

Research is also needed on factors outside the group itself. Although the five within-group factors described in Chapter 2 have received the most research attention (i.e., change theory, the individual group member, group structural factors, group processes, and leadership), they are not the only factors that contribute to outcomes. Extra-group factors within the group's social environment, such as the organizational setting (Glasser & Garvin, 1976; Hasenfeld, 1974), and broader factors such as poverty, injustice, and racism also likely affect the benefits of group work. As Meyer once sharply noted, research often leaves out the " 'large blue sky' that everyone wants to avoid because it is formless, nonconceptualized, and so hard to work with" (Meyer, 1972, p. 161). However, because there is scant empirical research on how these factors contribute to outcomes in groups, they are not part of available research findings; even so, they remain an important area of focus for social work research.

Third, although there is a growing amount of literature concerning problem-related distal outcomes, there is a paucity of research on techniques for achieving group-related outcomes. This is the source of many MAP questions. There are many ideas in the group work literature for increasing attendance, communication structures, norms, cohesion, and engagement, but few of the suggestions have been tested in controlled research, and those available are mostly authority-based.[2] Thus there is a pressing need for more research-based solutions to the kinds of problems group workers face daily in their practice.

Fourth, clinical group workers can contribute to the literature by reporting the effectiveness of the techniques and interventions they employ. Use of SSD methodology to test group work techniques, described in the previous chapter, is well within the resources and capabilities of group workers. Group workers in need of expertise or other resources for publication may collaborate with full-time researchers, such as faculty in professional schools. Most practitioners don't have much incentive in their settings to generate evidence, but full-time academics do. This collaboration can promote the publication of the "hidden efforts" of group workers.

Last, rather than one-time, often unidirectional collaborative efforts, the advancement of EBGW research and publication would be significantly expanded by a systemic and systematic collaboration between practitioners and researchers. Traditional approaches have been hierarchical and unidirectional, operating on the principle that knowledge originates only in research and not in practice, as Addis has noted:

> Practitioners are more likely to adopt research products when they find them useful and can contribute creatively to their development and evaluation; at least more likely than if they are simply told they should adopt them because scientific knowledge is inherently better than clinical knowledge. In short, the pragmatic goal of increasing evidence-based practice is hindered by heavy-handed polemics about the inherent superiority of empirical research and the inferiority of clinical experience. (2002, p. 375)

There are good examples in the literature of reciprocal, university–community organization partnerships (Allen-Meares, Hudgins, Engberg, & Lessnau, 2005; Barlow, Levitt, & Bufka, 1999; Borkovec, 2004; Galinsky, Turnbull, Meglin, & Wilner, 1993; Hatgis et al., 2001; Lamb, Greenlick, & McCarty, 1998; Sherrod, 1999; Webster-Stratton, 1997). There is a growing opportunity for developing and testing knowledge within a translational research (TR) model, developed in medicine but expanding into other disciplines, which is essentially the clinical application of scientific research knowledge ("bench to trench" or "bench to bedside") (Hait, 2005; Hudgins & Allen-Meares, 2000). Importantly, the pathway must be *bidirectional*; basic research is applied in the field, and clinical observations are used to provide the impetus for further scientific research ("bench to bedside and bedside to bench") (Marincola, 2003). Translational research has been increasing, along with the number of requests for applications for research from the U.S. federal government. For example, one of the three main initiatives of the National Institutes of Health is titled "Re-engineering the Clinical Research Enterprise," with the largest component dedicated to awards for clinical and translational science (National Institutes of Health, 2006; Zerhouni, 2006). All U.S. government institutes and centers participate in road map initiatives, so this initiative is likely to encourage applications in health-related group work. Group work researchers and practitioners may work together strategically to exploit the opportunities for funding to develop practice-relevant knowledge within the TR model. This collaboration can fuel the development and promulgation of practice-relevant evidence.

More Reports on the Application and Testing of Evidence-Based Group Work

A theme of this book is that models or frameworks for practice must be subject to critical review. EBGW remains a proposition to be tested in research. A review of seven studies evaluated whether evidence-based practice (EBP) training helped practitioners take action based on evidence or whether their clients were helped more than the clients of practitioners who used another approach (Gibbs & Gambrill, 2002). The review reported generally positive results, but none of the studies was a randomized clinical trial comparing the effects of EBP on clients with a different approach to practice. Another recent review that included over a dozen studies in evidence-based medicine (EBM) reported the effects of teaching strategies in improving learners' searching skills, critical appraisal skills, and clinical decision making (Straus et al., 2005, pp. 259–261). The descriptive review reported positive effects of the teaching strategies.

These research findings in EBP and EBM are encouraging. However, specific studies are needed to determine the effectiveness of these approaches (including EBGW) in improving client outcomes on their own or when compared to traditional, non-evidence-based approaches. In creating a plan for testing EBGW, conceptual, measurement, and design issues must be clarified, such as (a) whose outcomes to measure (group workers and/or members), (b) the *essential* educational components of EBGW, and (c) the relevant outcomes (group worker attitudes, behaviors, and/or group members' improvement and satisfaction with service) (adapted from Straus et al., 2005, pp. 257–258). A number of studies that include both group worker and group member outcomes are needed.

Advance Evidence-Based Group Work in Clinical Settings

A number of needs exist related to advancing EBGW in practice settings. Several are outlined here, followed by a separate discussion about how group workers might advance EBGW within their organizations.

One pressing need is for group workers to be able to acquire good, relevant evidence quickly. As mentioned in an earlier chapter, it would be ideal if group workers had access to relevant, preappraised evidence that provides a review and recommendation about the quality of strategies/interventions that seem to answer clinical questions they are facing. There are synoptic journals (so-called because they summarize the best evidence from traditional journals) such as *ACP Journal Club*, *Evidence-Based Mental Health*, and *Evidence-Based Nursing* that include helpful Web sites (see Chapter 3, Table 3.5, for a list of such sites that include preappraised evidence). One of the sites developed in clinical medicine is Patient-Oriented Evidence that Matters (POEMs), which includes two types of electronic information available for download to a personal computer or a personal data assistant (PDA) (http://www.infopoems.com). Daily InfoPOEMs alerts clinicians to the latest developments in clinical medicine research, applying specific criteria for validity and relevance to practice. The second type is InfoRetriever, which provides filtered, synopsized, evidence-based information for practice. Readily accessible, preappraised, *group-relevant* research is needed.

Second, an organized collective effort could greatly facilitate the availability of good, relevant evidence (group workers should be experts at this!). Group work associations at the national or chapter level such as the Association for the Advancement of Social Work with Groups (http://www.aaswg.org/) or the Association for Specialists in Group Work (http://www.asgw.org/) could form collaborative practice-research networks that include group work practitioners and faculty (Borkovec, 2004). These networks could be both physical and virtual. Peers may organize into EBGW journal clubs "that can spread the burden of finding and evaluating new information" (Slawson et al., 1994, p. 5). These clubs essentially would go through the first three EBGW steps but would spend the most time in critical appraisal of the evidence. Journal clubs have been used for a number of years in medicine, and more details about establishing an effective club can be found in the literature (Straus et al., 2005, pp. 227–231). Findings could be posted to a Web site established for the purpose. Such networks would be particularly important for independent group workers who lack the EBGW supports that organizations might have to offer.

Third, evidence should be free or available for a nominal cost. Although a number of sites are free (see Table 3.5), some are fee based. Hospitals or medical settings often have access to databases, and group workers in these settings can request journals related to group work (Table 3.4). One idea for making more evidence freely available is for professional schools to provide field placements access to university libraries, online bibliographic services, and periodical-retrieval services (Howard, McMillan, & Pollio, 2003). Specifically, field instructors could be given adjunct faculty status, which includes the benefit of library privileges.

For the group worker employed in an agency, perhaps the most important need for advancing EBGW is that the organization be supportive of EBP principles, discussed in the next section.

Building Support for Evidence-Based Group Work in an Organization

Individual group workers alone can not sustain EBGW in an organization. Studies of technology transfer, EBP dissemination, and organizational adoption of innovations (henceforth called EBP dissemination) across settings and disciplines suggest that for EBP to be successful, it must be supported at all service levels from clients to policy makers (Fals-Stewart, Logsdon, & Birchler, 2004; Hatgis et al., 2001; Kitson, Harvey, & McCormack, 1998; Proctor, 2004; Ringeisen, Henderson, & Hoagwood, 2003; Rosenheck, 2001; Rycroft-Malone, Kitson, et al., 2002; Simpson, 2002). In particular, the organizational environment (e.g., its climate for change, staff attributes) will affect EBP dissemination. Organizations that have cultures of innovation, clear roles, and transformational leadership are more likely to adopt innovations than those that do not (Kitson et al., 1998; Rosenheck, 2001; Rycroft-Malone, Kitson, et al., 2002; Simpson, 2002). However, organizations provide little support for EBP. An agency-based survey of practitioners reported that most social workers (N = 81) were poorly informed about practice guidelines, rarely used findings in practice, and seldom read the literature; instead they sought direction from supervisors, experienced workers, or consultants (Mullen & Bacon, 2004). In another study, medical practitioners reported feeling overwhelmed by the literature and said they often relied on what they had learned in their formal training (Haynes et al., 1996).

Support and resources are needed in order for EBGW to be viable in organizations. Although some of the models of EBP dissemination require policy change and resources outside the responsibility and reach of many group workers, there are avenues that group workers may pursue to develop initial organizational support for EBGW or for implementing particular evidence-based interventions. The following suggestions for early-stage adoption of EBGW are drawn from several models based mostly on correlational research. Thus there is no direct evidence that they will positively affect an organization's likelihood of adopting an innovation or EBGW.

An important factor in the early stage of innovation adoption in organizations is motivation to change, defined as perceived needs and pressure for change (Simpson, 2002). One way to initiate change in an organization is to build a coalition of group workers and advocates within an organization, "to argue, through both formal and informal channels, for a change in treatment process or for the development of a new program" (Rosenheck, 2001, p. 1610). It is suggested that this coalition include three important components to encourage EBGW and evidence-based interventions. First, group workers must highlight the quality and applicability of the evidence related to the proposed intervention (Kitson et al., 1998; Rycroft-Malone, Kitson, et al., 2002). The evidence is best when (a) it is of highest quality, (b) it fits with adopters' clinical experience, and (c) clients' opinions are involved. Second, the intervention or approach should be linked "to broad organizational agendas that have taken-for-granted legitimacy, such as 'excellence in health care value' . . . and if it can be linked to narrower legitimizing agendas, such as relying on evidence based medicine or addressing the problems of highly publicized target populations such as homeless veterans or Vietnam veterans" (Rosenheck, 2001, p. 1610). Third, the manner in which change is posited— that is, the "facilitation of change"—is important. Rycroft-Malone and colleagues defined facilitation as "a technique by which one person makes things easier for others" (Rycroft-Malone, Kitson, et al., 2002, p. 177). It is most effective when a person flexibly adapts roles, skills, and attributes based on whether the need requires a focused process to achieve a specific task (task orientation) or a holistic process "of enabling teams and individuals to analyze, reflect, and change their own attitudes, [behaviors], and ways of working (Holistic orientation)" (Rycroft-Malone, Kitson, et al., 2002, p. 177). Thus, one approach for the early adoption of EBGW is to build a coalition of partners who communicate a need to innovate that is based on high-quality evidence linked to an organization's agenda and which uses a facilitative process.

When the initial organizational response has been favorable, other steps may be taken involving more personnel and resources. Additional steps and elements about EBP dissemination in various organizations are more fully described in the literature, including drug treatment organizations (Simpson, 2002), schools (Ringeisen et al., 2003), health services (Kitson et al., 1998; Rycroft-Malone, Kitson, et al., 2002), and the Department of Veterans Affairs health-care system (Rosenheck, 2001).

Advance Evidence-Based Group Work in Education

Education and training are essential ingredients for disseminating research into practice (Herschell, McNeil, & McNeil, 2004). EBGW must be supported and sustained by education, which may occur in two contexts: as part of degree-granting programs in higher education or as part of continuing education (CE) in the form of workshops or training sessions. The author's reflections in this section will highlight educational trends and offer his experience teaching EBGW in a graduate program in social work, but the ideas may be applied in other programs and disciplines. Suggestions will also be offered regarding how EBGW might be delivered in CE contexts. It is beyond the scope of this section to discuss in detail the pedagogy of teaching EBP. Readers are directed to other sources for substantial discussions about EBP in education across disciplines such as social work (Howard et al., 2003), psychology (Herschell et al., 2004), psychiatry (Bilsker & Goldner, 2000), nursing (Crawford, Brown, Anthony, & Hicks, 2002; Rycroft-Malone, Harvey, et al., 2002; Stuart, 2001), medicine (Hatala & Guyatt, 2002; Straus et al., 2005, pp. 199–245), and behavioral health (Stuart, Tondora, & Hoge, 2004). What follows are ideas and models of teaching EBGW, which amount to case examples based on the author's experience. The next sections describe EBGW in higher education, EBGW in CE, and the evaluation of EBGW education.

Evidence-Based Group Work in Higher Education

Traditional research methods and clinical practice courses do not teach EBP. A review of popular research methods and clinical practice textbooks in social work reported that none of the books dealt with posing well-structured clinical questions, searching for evidence, and applying standards for evaluating evidence (Gibbs & Gambrill, 2002). However, books dedicated to EBP (Cournoyer, 2004; Gibbs, 2003) and EBM (Straus et al., 2005) are emerging, and these can be used as texts. As far as the author is aware, this book is the first available dedicated to outlining the process of EBGW.

The author has taught EBGW as part of a one-semester introductory graduate course in social-work group work. The following discussion describes the pedagogy underlying the approach and provides specifics about what is taught and how. This is presented as one approach used in one particular organizational context and is based only on limited and subjective observations and feedback from students, field instructors, and the author. At the time of this writing there were no published examples of how to teach EBGW, so the author tentatively offers his limited experience, expecting that others will build on what is presented to make it better. The last part of this section describes how the approach could be improved.

To understand the educational approach, it is important to know about the educational context. The course was titled "Theories and Practice with Groups" and was the only course on group work in the graduate curriculum. Thus, EBGW had to be integrated into a course already full of other material on group work. It was taught in a university generally favorable to research (a research university with high research activity). However, the school of social work did not have a curriculum model that systematically integrated

EBP throughout the courses. All students enrolled in the course were required to have completed introductory courses in micro (clinical) practice, social policy, human behavior in the social environment, and research methods. Thus, students who entered the course had no previous experience in the EBP model, although they would have learned the basics of research methods, which was an important foundation that was built upon in the course. A co-requisite of the course was a field placement, which gave the students the opportunity to apply the stages of EBGW in their groups. Thus, EBGW was taught in an environment that was not optimal for its advancement. The author's experience gives an example of how it could be taught in similar circumstances, but this is not promoted as the best approach.

The underlying pedagogical (or, more appropriately, andragogical) model used combined didactic and problem-based learning/practice-based learning (PBL) approaches. Although some material was taught using passive learning through lectures, most of the teaching of EBGW used PBL that actively involved students in their learning by posing a practice question they were to answer. First developed for the education of physicians (Barrows, 1983; Spencer & Jordan, 1999), PBL "is an instructional method that encourages learners to apply critical thinking, problem-solving skills, and content knowledge to real-world problems and issues" (Levin, 2001, p. 1). PBL helps students achieve the following learning outcomes: (a) think critically and be able to analyze and solve complex, real-world problems; (b) find, evaluate, and use appropriate learning resources; (c) work cooperatively in teams and small groups; (d) demonstrate versatile and effective communication skills, both verbal and written; and (e) use content knowledge and intellectual skills acquired at the university to become continual learners (Duch, Groh, & Allen, 2001a, p. 6). This model is ideally suited for teaching EBGW, as it instructs in the process of critical thinking as students develop evidence-based solutions to real group work problems.

In addition to incorporating PBL, the author's teaching approach included elements from other EBP teaching models. For example, one EBP pedagogical paradigm (Howard, McMillan, & Pollio, 2003, pp. 242–253) includes seven elements, which the author adapted for EBGW. This model expected learners to be able to (a) understand and value EBGW so that they can learn and use it in practice, (b) select the best available evidence, (c) appreciate and know the evidence base of group work interventions and techniques, (d) effectively deliver group interventions or techniques that contribute to positive outcomes, (e) adapt the best available evidence for practice (if necessary), (f) evaluate whether their group intervention or technique was effective, and (g) know how to apply the four stages of EBGW.

The teaching model also incorporated most of the "successes" that Straus and colleagues described in their experience in teaching EBM. Straus and colleagues (2005, pp. 202–210) noted that teaching EBM is best when it (a) centers around real clinical decisions and actions; (b) focuses on learners' actual learning needs; (c) balances passive and active learning; (d) connects new knowledge to what learners already know; (d) involves everyone in the learning team (or dyad); (e) attends to both the feelings and knowing of learning; (f) adapts to the clinical setting, available time, and other circumstances; (g) makes explicit how to make judgments, whether about the evidence itself or about how to integrate evidence with other knowledge, clinical expertise, and client preferences; and (h) builds learners' lifelong learning abilities.

Thus, the author's teaching of EBGW used PBL and incorporated the outcomes and processes described by Howard and by Straus and colleagues. The following discussion presents more details about the EBGW content and how it was incorporated into the group work course.

As noted above, EBGW was built into the existing course and taught along with the other content. As seen in the first column of Figure 6.1, the content or principles of EBGW were delivered as part of four to six classes during the semester. However, the philosophy and practices were taught throughout the semester. Students were encouraged to utilize critical thinking about the quality of all types of evidence they encountered in the course. Thus, EBGW was taught as a commitment to a process carried throughout the semester. The methods of teaching included didactic (i.e., lecture–discussion, factual learning), but mostly nondidactic methods using PBL were employed. Because students were in their practicum, specific examples of group concerns or challenges were solicited from students, and these became examples in class to illustrate the stages of EBGW.

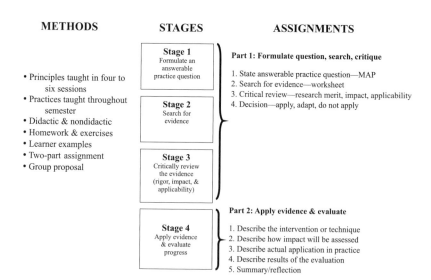

Figure 6.1. An example of teaching evidence-based group work in a foundation group work graduate course.

There were two written assignments. The first required students (who worked in pairs) to find evidence-based approaches to solving challenges they were having in their groups. Thus, it dealt with questions that occur during the life of a group (group-related proximal outcomes). The assignment consisted of two parts, described in the last column of Figure 6.1. The first part related to the first three stages of EBGW and required students to formulate a MAP question, search for evidence, critically review the evidence, and decide if/how the evidence would be adapted for the clinical situation. The assignment was due about a third of the way into the semester. The second part of the assignment was the application of the evidence in practice and the results of the evaluation. This assignment was submitted at the end of the semester.

The second assignment, done in groups of five to seven students, required students to develop a proposal for a treatment or a task group. Unlike the first assignment in which students applied and evaluated the evidence in practice, this assignment required students to follow the first three stages of EBGW to propose a group intervention that was the most rigorous, impactful, and appropriate for the population to be served. Students were not required to implement the proposal but were expected to include sufficient detail in their proposals so that they could be presented to an administrator and be readily implemented.

Collaborative learning was a critical element in the assignments. Students worked in pairs or small groups (learning teams) where they learned to apply the concepts. This was particularly important for students weak in research methods, who were paired with others who had stronger knowledge.[3]

Some impressions can be offered about the experience. Based on student comments and a review of the quality of assignments over the semesters, the concepts of EBGW can be adequately taught in an introductory graduate-level course. However, the process must be taught with learner involvement and not through traditional didactic methods alone. Most students seem to appreciate the linking of research and practice in the EBGW approach. However, some students struggle with the technical aspects of reviewing research evidence (e.g., some of the variables related to rigor in the guides for evaluating RCT and systematic reviews). Encouraging students to work with other students with stronger research knowledge can be helpful as long as there is sharing of learning. In addition, the teacher must be committed to working closely with students as they search for and critically evaluate evidence. Without a commitment to working closely with students in a PBL approach, teaching EBGW in an introductory group work course would be a failure. Students would become frustrated and lose interest, and the quality of their learning and completed assignments would suffer.

Although the author has informally observed preliminary successes, there are ways the experience could be strengthened. Indeed, the approach described above is not meant to be taken as ideal. The generic model of EBP (particularly effective and efficient information acquisition) should be taught in an earlier foundation class, such as Research Methods or Introduction to

Micro Practice. This would allow more time to apply the stages to group work. In places where there is only one group work course, this would ensure that other essential content about groups (theories about group work, group dynamics) is adequately covered. In cases where there are two consecutive group work courses, the material may be placed in the second course. In addition, there should be a strong integration into the field setting, and internship supervisors and agency group work supervisors should be trained in the EBGW model (for a general guide about building EBP in field settings consult Thomlison & Corcoran, 2007). Courses on community and organizational practice could include content on how practitioners can effect change favorable to EBP. In short, a coordinated approach to teaching EBP that is curriculum-wide is needed (for an example, see Howard et al., 2003). An *optimal* approach is systemic and includes establishing a curriculum supportive of EBP and collaborative partnerships between practitioners and researchers, as described earlier in the chapter.

Evidence-Based Group Work in Continuing Education

Because EBP is new and not widely taught in higher education, most employed group workers will receive training in EBGW only through CE. Licensed and certified professionals require CE credits, but in most professions like clinical psychology CE requirements do not specify that training include content about empirically supported therapies (Addis, 2002). Although there are empirically supported training protocols for specific therapies or treatments, such as Multisystemic Therapy (Henggeler et al., 2002) and Multidimensional Treatment Foster Care (Chamberlain & Smith, 2005), the author is not aware of any empirically supported training protocols for EBP.[4] Several training approaches are proposed here that increasingly expose participants to the actual practice of EBGW.

The first approach is an overview of EBGW in a half-day format (i.e., 3 hours), which includes an overview of the four stages of EBGW and an emphasis on developing skill in undertaking the first two stages. In this approach, participants develop a MAP question and identify a strategy for searching. In terms of outcomes, knowledge can be evaluated, as can the skill of formulating a MAP question and identifying several appropriate sources for a potential search. However, in this approach participants do not have the opportunity to apply the evidence and evaluate it in practice.

A variation of the first approach is to offer a full-day format, with learners engaging in a search for the best evidence in the second half of the day. In this approach, learners are paired, oriented to the databases, and then directed to search and find appropriate evidence related to their MAP question. This approach requires more resources (e.g., computer stations connected to potential sources of evidence) and would be best staffed with one or two others with knowledge and experience in completing successful searches. This approach includes the same outcomes as above, except that it also affords the opportunity to evaluate participants' abilities to engage in fully completing the second stage of EBGW (undertaking a search for evidence).

A third approach more fully engages learners in EBGW by providing an opportunity to develop initial skill in all stages of EBGW.[5] This approach may be delivered over five modules that are approximately 3 hours each. The first two sessions include content about the first two stages and could be offered in one day (similar to the variation on the first approach above). Learners would then engage in a search for evidence on their own and return a week later to review their efforts and learn the third stage, evaluating the evidence. This could be offered in one 3-hour session, followed in the afternoon by a detailed presentation of the fourth stage, applying and evaluating the evidence in practice. In teaching about the fourth stage, appropriate research designs and measures would be identified so learners would have a plan to evaluate progress toward achieving desired outcomes in their groups. A fifth and final session would be offered several weeks later, with consultation available between sessions, to allow learners the opportunity to actually apply the evidence and evaluate progress in achieving desired outcomes. In this last 3-hour session, learners would be given the opportunity to report successes and concerns, and a plan would be formulated for maintenance of knowledge and skills.

In any of the above models, follow-up is recommended to help participants retain learning and sustain practices (Herschell et al., 2004). Establishing a peer group after training has been shown to help participants successfully implement learning (Wilkerson & Irby, 1998, as cited in Herschell et al., 2004). These peer networks would be established by local organizers as part of the training. Periodic audits of EBGW practice are also advisable (Stuart et al., 2004). Ongoing training, education, and supervision are essential, as EBP is a lifelong learning commitment (Gibbs, 2003, p. 6; Howard et al., 2003, p. 234).

Evaluating Evidence-Based Group Work Education

Currently, which education format is best is debatable, because there is only anecdotal, case study evidence. The approaches listed above remain educational or training models to be formally evaluated. It is outside the scope of this book to discuss in detail the evaluation of teaching EBGW, and readers are directed to other sources for more information (Straus et al., 2004; Stuart et al., 2004). However, some general comments and direction for further study can be offered.

Straus and colleagues (Straus et al., 2004) described a conceptual model in the evaluation of teaching EBP, which is adapted here for the teaching of EBGW. Their model for evaluating teaching methods includes three domains: the learner (group member, leader, administrator, and their learning styles and needs), the education approach (content and intensity), and the desired outcomes. The education models described above were designed for group workers who needed education about all stages of EBGW (learner), using a range of teaching methods (didactic and experiential, the education approach) to build knowledge, skills, and behavior change (desired outcomes). There are a range of potential outcomes in the evaluation of teaching EBGW. These outcomes include evaluating (a) participants' reactions to the learning experience, (b) changes in participants' attitudes or perceptions, (c) participants' acquisition of knowledge and skills, (d) actual change in participants' behavior in clinical settings, (e) changes in organizational practice attributable to an education program, and (f) actual benefits to group members (Hammick, 2000).[6] The educational approaches described above relate to evaluating all but (e) and (f), although these could also be measured. Formal evaluations should assess participants' attitudes, knowledge, and skills in EBGW.

Conclusion

This chapter has discussed how EBGW could be disseminated. A number of activities in the areas of research, clinical practice, and education were explored, with the conclusion that more research evidence is needed about group work and reports on the application of EBGW in practice, including studies on the effectiveness of EBGW. Although there are exciting developments in making good, appropriate evidence readily available to group workers, more efforts are needed. Some strategies for building support for EBGW in organizations were examined, and suggestions were made regarding how to advance EBGW in higher and continuing education, including models to be tested in research.

The suggestions offered for advancing research, practice, and education could be substantially addressed by a planned and systemic collaboration (such as the Translational Research approach) among researchers, educators, and practitioners. In this model, organizational structures would be supportive of EBGW, research would be practice-relevant and readily available to group workers, and education and consultation would be ongoing. This is certainly not the current practice, but it is a desirable direction and goal.

Review of Book

To review the main elements of the book, in Part I, EBGW was defined as the process of the judicious and skillful application of the best evidence in group work, based on research merit, impact, and applicability, using evaluation to ensure that desired results are achieved. EBGW may be viewed within the historical context of EBM and EBP and the tradition of research and practice in group work. The EBGW framework is important for the advancement of group work as it promotes accountability, is part of ethical practice, and helps to organize and access the growing evidence in group work, incorporate good practices, and avoid harmful ones. Best evidence was identified as the result of an iterative process in assessing the research merit, impact, and applicability of evidence. Ideas for the judicious and skillful application and evaluation of evidence in practice were presented.

Part II examined how EBGW is operationalized through a sequence of four stages in which group workers (1) formulate an answerable practice question; (2) search for evidence; (3) undertake a critical review of the evidence (with respect to research merit, impact, and applicability); and (4) apply the evidence with judgment, skill, and concern for relevance and appropriateness for the group, utilizing evaluation to determine whether desired outcomes are achieved.

In the first stage, strategies were described for formulating MAP questions that include particular components for an effective search. To facilitate the search for evidence, suggestions were made on where and how to look for evidence, with a discussion of the hierarchy of research merit and locations of interventions/techniques and measures of change. Also presented were specific techniques for searching using the COMPASS search strategy. The next chapter included guidelines that group workers can use for critically evaluating the rigor, impact, and clinical applicability of evidence. The last chapter of Part II addressed applying and evaluating the evidence in practice.

Part III began with a discussion of how EBGW could be disseminated. A number of activities were examined in the areas of research, clinical practice, and education; recommendations were made for a planned, systemic collaboration among these three areas to increase the likelihood of successful advancement of EBGW.

In conclusion, EBGW is a growing necessity and requirement for practice. This book has described and provided resources for applying the process of EBP to group work, with the goal of advancing best practices that improve the beneficial effects of group work—and this should be the beginning of a lifelong journey!

Appendix

List of Abbreviations

AHRQ: Agency for Healthcare Research and Quality
AOD: alcohol and other drug
ARR: absolute risk reduction
BESD: Binomial Effect Size Display
CE: continuing education
CG: control group
CI: confidence interval
CM: contingency management
COMPASS: COncepts, Methodology, Publication, And Search String
EB: evidence-based
EBGW: evidence-based group work
EBM: evidence-based medicine
EBP: evidence-based practice
EBPP: evidence-based practice in psychology
ES: effect size
GAS: Goal Attainment Scaling
HLM: Hierarchical Linear Modeling
MAP: Member-relevant, Answerable, and Practical
NIH: National Institutes of Health
NNH: number needed to harm
NNT: number needed to treat
OR: odds ratio
PBL: problem-based learning/practice-based learning
PDA: personal data assistant
PLoS: Public Library of Science
POEMs: Patient-Oriented Evidence that Matters
RCI: reliable change index
RCT: randomized clinical trials

RR: risk ratio
RRR: relative risk reduction
SES: socioeconomic status
SSD: single-subject design
TAS: Task Achievement Scaling
TG: treatment group
TR: translational research

Notes

Chapter 1

1. Some of the material in this chapter is revised from Macgowan, M. J. (2006). Evidence-based group work: A framework for advancing best practice. *Journal of Evidence-Based Social Work*, *3*(1), 1–21.
2. Evidence-based practice also draws from the empirical practice literature published over the last five decades (Blythe & Briar, 1985; Briar, 1973; Goldstein, 1962b; Jayaratne & Levy, 1979; Kirk & Reid, 2002; Reid, 1994; Siegel, 1984; Thyer, 1996; Tripodi & Epstein, 1980; Tripodi, Fellin, & Meyer, 1969). In addition, it incorporates some of the principles from the social design and development literature (Rothman, 1980; Rothman & Thomas, 1994; Thomas, 1984; Thomas, 1992).
3. In this book, the term *intervention* connotes a theoretical model or general approach to group work that guides the worker's actions. Examples include cognitive-behavioral group therapy, interactional group therapy, and mutual aid groups. *Techniques* are discrete and circumscribed and are goal-oriented, planned actions undertaken by the group worker (Sheafor & Horejsi, 2006). Examples include specific actions to increase a group member's participation, such as the use of rounds, or manipulating group conditions to maximize verbal contributions. Techniques may be affiliated with a particular intervention or treatment approach, or they may be atheoretical. In addition, the term *strategy* is used interchangeably with *technique*.

Chapter 2

1. The term *group structural factor* is not to be confused with the term *group structure*, defined as "an identifiable arrangement of elements at a given point in time. In a group, the structure contains elements that are interactive in nature or are products

of interaction" (Rose, 1998, p. 369). Group structures include group norms, status, roles, authority, cohesion, and patterns of communication at a given point in time (Cartwright & Zander, 1968, p. 486; Forsyth, 1990, p. 110; Garvin, 1985a, p. 204). In the model developed by Burlingame et al., these group structures fit better with the term *group processes*, described in the text.

Chapter 3

1. A criticism of classification systems that include systematic reviews at the top of the hierarchy is that such reviews may mix "poor quality studies with inconsistent results with high quality studies with consistent results" (Atkins, Eccles, et al., 2004, p. 5). Only systematic reviews that include high-quality studies with consistent results can be counted at the highest level of research evidence. Similarly, poor-quality randomized clinical trials (RCTs) may not always have strong research merit. The GRADE Working Group asked, "Should a small, poorly designed RCT be considered level I evidence?" (Atkins, Eccles, et al., 2004, p. 2). Should convincing evidence from a nonrandomized trial always be considered inferior? The guides in this book are intended to separate high-quality RCTs and systematic reviews from poor-quality ones so that practitioners may judge whether such studies should be considered stronger in quality than those lower in the hierarchy. Currently, there are no protocols for determining when a poorly designed RCT may be considered lower quality than a nonrandomized study. Thus the hierarchy of research evidence in Figure 3.1 should be considered a general model.

2. Only research merit is being discussed here. As discussed later, there are times when, based on considerations of impact and applicability, authority-based evidence is the best available evidence. For example, a trusted colleague who works with the same population and in the same context as you may offer a particular technique that is assured to have good results (e.g., increase verbal participation or attendance) based on that colleague's extensive group experience. In the absence of any research evidence suggesting potential damaging effects as a result of using the technique, the authority-based evidence would be preferred (assuming the authority-based evidence has rigor, which is discussed in a later chapter) to less applicable techniques. Although there are times when authority-based evidence is appropriate in answering proximal-type outcome questions, group workers should make every effort to base their practice on rigorous, applicable research evidence.

3. The Clinical Outcome Research Evaluation (CORE) Battery, originally developed in 1982 (MacKenzie & Dies, 1982), was revised and recently published but was not available early enough to be expanded upon in this volume. The CORE-R (Burlingame et al., 2006) includes a toolbox of psychometrically sound and clinically appropriate outcome and process measures that have been linked to effective group work. The value of the CORE-R is that the instruments have been preappraised by a panel of group work experts, so their rigor and clinical utility have been tested (although the instruments should still be reviewed for their applicability to one's particular group, as described in Chapter 4). Group workers may consult the instruments in the CORE-R first and then decide if different or other measures may be needed, as outlined in the text.

Chapter 4

1. As its focus is strictly on effective worker actions in group (i.e., interventions/ techniques and how to measure within-group change), this book does not include guides for evaluating epidemiological research, such as survey research and instruments related to diagnosis, prognosis, and risk prediction. Other sources may be consulted for such guidelines (e.g., Gibbs, 2003; Straus et al., 2005).

2. Abbreviated guides for evaluating the quality of research evidence have been around for decades in sociology (Caplow, 1958; Knop, 1967) and social work (Goldstein, 1962a) but are not readily applicable to clinical practice. Perhaps the first example of an expanded guide to evaluating social research literature is the book *Assessment of Social Research* (Tripodi, Fellin, & Meyer, 1969).

3. The biomedical field has been at the forefront of evaluating systems for evaluating research quality (e.g., Agency for Healthcare Research and Quality, 2002b; Moher et al., 1995).

4. An exception to this might be if the group worker clearly and fully addresses the factors that contributed to the damaging outcomes, as identified by the authors of the study, and there is no likelihood of negative outcomes (e.g., a study might indicate that a particular group composition contributed to negative effects, which can be corrected). In addition, the group worker must seek consultation and/or supervision to ensure there is no likelihood of further risk.

5. The exception is the guide for rating group-based instruments, which does not include rating "impact."

6. For example, a leader considering interventions in hospice group work may decide that the item "follow-up" would not be weighed as heavily as the item "randomization." In an example on applicability, an intervention or technique that is contrary to the cultural values of group members and which may not be supported by group members should not be used, regardless of how applicable the setting or leadership is. Similarly, an intervention that a leader is not competent to deliver (without supervision) or that is against the values or ethics of the leader's profession should not be used.

7. Tip for finding terms mentioned in the guidelines: if the evidence is electronic, conduct a search of the document for particular keywords used in the guide, such as "heterogeneity" or "multilevel."

8. Tip for finding information about impact: it is typically in the middle to last part of the document.

9. However, the researchers included a calculation of effect size later in the article to determine clinical significance. To calculate the effect size, they would have included their sample sizes. Thus, although the researchers did not include in the sample section an explicit mention of the adequacy of their sample size, the later analyses of clinical significance (which yielded moderate to large effect sizes) clearly justified their sample size.

10. Readers who wish to evaluate the quality of a publication source in more detail may consult Cournoyer's Source Rating Rubric, which assigns a numerical value (-2 [inferior] to $+2$ [superior]) along five dimensions: author credentials, author authority and expertise, author affiliation, publisher and publication, and currency of source (Cournoyer, 2004, pp. 127–128).

11. Although there is no gold standard for determining clinical significance, the Reliable Change Index is a well-regarded method (Atkins et al., 2005, p. 982). Effect size (ES), widely used to report the magnitude of outcomes, is not a direct indicator of clinical significance: "Although large effect sizes are more likely to be clinically significant than small ones, even large effect sizes are not necessarily clinically significant" (Jacobson & Truax, 1991, p. 12).

12. Some studies may also include relative risk reduction (RRR), but this method does not discriminate between small and large treatment effects and is not considered as meaningful a measure of treatment effects as the ARR (Straus et al., 2005, p. 126).

13. There may be exceptions to this general rule, and clinical judgment must be used. For example, one might find a technique that was not in a study about group work but which may be applicable to an *individual* within the group. In this case, the applicability rating may be mixed; although the evidence was not "tested" within a group context, it has some applicability for working with an individual within the group.

14. The author would like to thank colleagues at Florida International University Stephen E. Wong and Frederick L. Newman for their helpful comments on the guideline and discussion about SSDs.

15. The general term *empirically supported*, as opposed to *empirically validated*, is preferred because the process of "validation" is ongoing rather than final (Chambless & Hollon, 1998). However, the term *validated* is used as it is the term used in the literature to define the criteria incorporated in the table.

Chapter 5

1. Treatment integrity or fidelity includes three elements: treatment adherence, therapist competence, and differentiation of treatment. "Adherence refers to the degree of utilization of specified procedures by the therapist. Competence refers to the level of skill and judgment shown by the therapist in delivering the treatment. Differentiation refers to whether treatments under investigation differ from each other along critical dimensions" (Perepletchikova & Kazdin, 2005, p. 365). Adherence and differentiation are related in that both can be measured using the same instrument, as was done in a study that included a measure of adherence to cognitive-behavioral group therapy and interactional group therapy (Kaminer, Blitz, Burleson, Kadden, & Rounsaville, 1998). In the application of group interventions or techniques, group workers need to ensure that they both adhere to the essential elements of an intervention and deliver those elements with competence.

2. Pollio has described the process of applying positivistic, reductionist evidence from research studies to a unique client system as the *deconstruction–reconstruction* approach, in which "the evidence is deconstructed by the clinician based on EB [evidence-based] thinking and reconstructed through the clinical interaction into the approach with the individual client" (Pollio, 2006, p. 226). Although clinicians should strive for replication at the end of that process, circumstances may dictate an adaptation. Readers should consult Pollio's article for further discussion on the struggles and opportunities of applying evidence in clinical practice.

3. An exception to this occurs if group workers would like to publish the results of their work in research journals. In such a case the goal is to develop research knowledge, and the issue of controlling for rival explanations (i.e., internal validity) becomes prominent. It should also be noted that although the text conveys a dichotomy between practice evaluation and clinical research, the lines between the two may blur or dissolve in situations in which the organizational context provides substantial resources to provide suitable controls and the research design is rigorous but accommodates clinical exigencies. In these rare cases when the lines may dissolve, the two goals of practice evaluation and clinical research become equal: providing feedback and enhancing outcomes, and developing scientific knowledge.

Chapter 6

1. Treatment manuals are one of the four essential ingredients (the others being graduate education, continuing education, and training protocols) for disseminating empirically supported child treatments (Herschell, McNeil, & McNeil, 2004).
2. Examples of research-based studies that have reported the results of application of techniques include some SSDs described earlier in the book (Johnson et al., 2001; O'Brien et al., 1999; Petry et al., 2001; Rose, 1977, pp. 66–72) and a controlled study of the effects of contingency reinforcement on attendance and participation (Petry et al., 2005). There are several good review papers that provide a summary of the state of the science in increasing cohesion and other "common factors" (Burlingame et al., 2001; Burlingame, Fuhriman, & Johnson, 2002; Dies, 2003). In addition, recall that there is empirical support for several group factors; see Table 3.8, Chapter 3. Controlled studies are needed to determine which techniques are the most likely contributors to change in these within-group outcomes.
3. There can be problems in group-based learning, including students who aren't managing their responsibilities or whose contributions are discounted by more assertive group members (Duch, Groh, & Allen, 2001b). The literature provides practical ideas for making learning teams more effective (Allen, Duch, & Groh, 2001; Straus et al., 2005, pp. 233–244).
4. Although there are currently no empirically supported training protocols, there are a number of recognized training approaches for teaching EBP, such as the BEST training on evidence-based practice for agency settings (http://www.columbia.edu/cu/musher/Website/Website/EBP_OnlineTraining.htm).
5. Herschell and colleagues (2004) noted that the best format for CEs in advancing evidence-supported treatments is extended training (e.g., multiple-day courses) that involves experiential activities.
6. For an excellent critical review of instruments for measuring outcomes related to teaching EBP, see Shaneyfelt and colleagues' systematic review of 104 instruments (Shaneyfelt et al., 2006).

References

Abell, N. (1991). The Index of Clinical Stress: A brief measure of subjective stress for practice and research. *Social Work Research & Abstracts, 27*(2), 12–15.

Addis, M. E. (2002). Methods for disseminating research products and increasing evidence-based practice: Promises, obstacles, and future directions. *Clinical Psychology: Science and Practice, 9*(4), 367–378.

Agency for Healthcare Research and Quality. (2002a). *Systems to rate the strength of scientific evidence.* Retrieved June 24, 2007, from http://www.ncbi.nlm.nih.gov/books/bv.fcgi?rid=hstat1.chapter.70996.

Agency for Healthcare Research and Quality. (2002b). *Systems to rate the strength of scientific evidence: Summary.* Retrieved June 24, 2007, from http://www.ahrq.gov/clinic/epcsums/strengthsum.pdf.

Allen-Meares, P., Hudgins, C. A., Engberg, M. E., & Lessnau, B. (2005). Using a collaboratory model to translate social work research into practice and policy. *Research on Social Work Practice, 15*(1), 29–40.

Allen, D. E., Duch, B. J., & Groh, S. E. (2001). Strategies for using groups. In B. J. Duch, S. E. Groh, & D. E. Allen (Eds.), *The power of problem-based learning: A practical "how to" for teaching undergraduate courses in any discipline* (pp. 59–68). Sterling, VA: Stylus.

Allen, J. P., & Wilson, V. B. (2003). *Assessing alcohol problems: A guide for clinicians and researchers* (No. 03-3745). Bethesda, MD: U.S. Deptartment of Health and Human Services, Public Health Service, National Institutes of Health, National Institute on Alcohol Abuse and Alcoholism.

American Psychiatric Association. (2000). *Handbook of psychiatric measures.* Washington, DC: American Psychiatric Association.

American Psychological Association. (2002). Criteria for evaluating treatment guidelines. *American Psychologist, 57*, 1052–1059.

American Psychological Association. (2005a). *Guide to the fields in our database records.* Retrieved August 5, 2005, from http://www.apa.org/psycinfo/about/field guide.html.

American Psychological Association. (2005b). *Thesaurus of psychological index terms* (10th ed.). Washington, DC: American Psychological Association.

American Psychological Association. (2005c). *Policy statement on evidence-based practice in psychology* (pp. 1–3). Washington, DC: American Psychological Association.

Anastasi, A., & Urbina, S. (1997). *Psychological testing* (7th ed.). Upper Saddle River, NJ: Prentice Hall.

Ang, R. P., & Hughes, J. N. (2002). Differential benefits of skills training with antisocial youth based on group composition: A meta-analytic investigation. *School Psychology Review, 31*(2), 164–185.

Arnold, D. S., O'Leary, S. G., Wolff, L. S., & Acker, M. M. (1993). The Parenting Scale: A measure of dysfunctional parenting in discipline situations. *Psychological Assessment, 5*(2), 137–144.

Association for Specialists in Group Work. (1998). *Principles for diversity-competent group workers.* Retrieved March 1, 2006, from http://www.asgw.org/diversity.htm.

Association for Specialists in Group Work. (2000). *Professional standards for the training of group workers.* Retrieved June 2, 2005, from http://www.asgw.org/training_standards.htm.

Association for the Advancement of Social Work with Groups. (2006). *Standards for social work practice with groups* (2nd ed.). Retrieved May 2, 2007, from http://www.aaswg.org/.

Atkins, D., Best, D., Briss, P. A., Eccles, M., Falck-Ytter, Y., Flottorp, S., et al. (2004). Grading quality of evidence and strength of recommendations. *BMJ, 328*(7454), 1490.

Atkins, D., Eccles, M., Flottorp, S., Guyatt, G. H., Henry, D., Hill, S., et al. (2004). Systems for grading the quality of evidence and the strength of recommendations I: Critical appraisal of existing approaches: The GRADE Working Group. *BMC Health Services Research.* Retrieved January 23, 2007, from http://www.biomedcentral.com/1472-6963/4/38.

Atkins, D. C., Bedics, J. D., McGlinchey, J. B., & Beauchaine, T. P. (2005). Assessing clinical significance: Does it matter which method we use? *Journal of Consulting and Clinical Psychology, 73*(5), 982–989.

Avants, S. K., Margolin, A., Usubiaga, M. H., & Doebrick, C. (2004). Targeting HIV-related outcomes with intravenous drug users maintained on methadone: A randomized clinical trial of a harm reduction group therapy. *Journal of Substance Abuse Treatment, 26*(2), 67–78.

Baldwin, S. A., Murray, D. M., & Shadish, W. R. (2005). Empirically supported treatments or type I errors? Problems with the analysis of data from group-administered treatments. *Journal of Consulting and Clinical Psychology, 73*(5), 924–935.

Bales, R. F. (1950). *Interaction process analysis: A method for the study of small groups.* Reading, MA: Addison-Wesley.

Bales, R. F., Cohen, S. P., & Williamson, S. A. (1979). *SYMLOG: A system for the multiple level observation of groups.* New York: Free Press.

Barlow, D. H., & Hersen, M. (1984). *Single case experimental designs: Strategies for studying behavior change* (2nd ed.). New York: Pergamon Press.

Barlow, D. H., Levitt, J. T., & Bufka, L. F. (1999). The dissemination of empirically supported treatments: A view to the future. *Behaviour Research and Therapy, 37*(Suppl 1), S147–S162.

Barlow, J., & Coren, E. (2003). Group-based parent-training programmes for improving emotional and behavioural adjustment in 0–3 year old children. *Campbell Collaboration.* Retrieved July 15, 2007, from http://www.campbellcollaboration.org/doc-pdf/grouppar.pdf.

Barrows, H. S. (1983). Problem-based, self-directed learning. *Journal of the American Medical Association, 250*(22), 3077–3080.

Beck, A. P. (1983). A process analysis of group development. *Group, 7*(1), 19–26.

Beck, A. P., Dugo, J. M., Eng, A. M., & Lewis, C. M. (1986). The search for phases in group development: Designing process analysis measures of group interaction. In L. S. Greenberg & W. M. Pinsof (Eds.), *The psychotherapeutic process: A research handbook* (pp. 615–705). New York: Guilford.

Beck, A. P., & Lewis, C. M. (Eds.). (2000). *The process of group psychotherapy: Systems for analyzing change.* Washington, DC: American Psychological Association.

Berg, A. O. (2000). Dimensions of evidence. In J. P. Geyman, R. A. Deyo, & S. D. Ramsey (Eds.), *Evidence-based clinical practice* (pp. 21–27). Woburn, MA: Butterworth-Heinemann.

Berman-Rossi, T. (Ed.). (1994). *Social work: The collected writings of William Schwartz.* Itasca, IL: F. E. Peacock.

Bevilacqua, L. (2002). *Group therapy homework planner.* New York: Wiley.

Bilsker, D., & Goldner, E. M. (2000). Teaching evidence-based practice in mental health. *Research on Social Work Practice, 10*(5), 664–669.

Bloch, S., Reibstein, J., Crouch, E., Holroyd, P., & Themen, J. (1979). A method for the study of therapeutic factors in group psychotherapy. *British Journal of Psychiatry, 134*, 257–263.

Bloom, M., Fischer, J., & Orme, J. G. (2003). *Evaluating practice: Guidelines for the accountable professional* (4th ed.). Boston: Allyn and Bacon.

Blythe, B. J. (1992). Should undergraduate and graduate social work students be taught to conduct empirically-based practice? Yes! *Journal of Social Work Education, 28*(3), 260–263.

Blythe, B. J., & Briar, S. (1985). Developing empirically based models of practice. *Social Work, 30*(6), 483–488.

Blythe, B. J., & Tripodi, T. (1989). *Measurement in direct social work practice.* Newbury Park, CA: SAGE.

Blythe, B. J., Tripodi, T., & Briar, S. (1994). *Direct practice research in human service agencies.* New York: Columbia University Press.

Bollen, K. A., & Hoyle, R. H. (1990). Perceived cohesion: A conceptual and empirical examination. *Social Forces, 69*(2), 479–504.

Bolman, L. (1971). Some effects of trainers on their T groups. *Journal of Applied Behavioral Science, 7*, 309–325.

Bordia, P., DiFonzo, N., & Chang, A. (1999). Rumor as group problem solving—Development patterns in informal computer-mediated groups. *Small Group Research, 30*(1), 8–28.

Borgatta, E. F. (1963). A new systematic interaction observation system: Behavior scores system (BSS System). *Journal of Psychological Studies, 14*(1), 24–44.

Borgatta, E. F., & Crowther, B. (1965). *A workbook for the study of social interaction processes*. Chicago: Rand McNally.

Borkovec, T. D. (2004). Research in training clinics and practice research networks: A route to the integration of science and practice. *Clinical Psychologist, 11*(2), 211–215.

Bourke, M. L., & Van Hasselt, V. B. (2001). Social problem-solving skills training for incarcerated offenders: A treatment manual. *Behavior Modification, 25*(2), 163–188.

Bradley, S. J., Jadaa, D. A., Brody, J., Landy, S., Tallett, S. E., Watson, W., et al. (2003). Brief psychoeducational parenting program: An evaluation and 1-year follow-up. *Journal of the American Academy of Child and Adolescent Psychiatry, 42*(10), 1171–1178.

Briar, S. (1973). Effective social work intervention in direct practice: Implications for education. In *Facing the challenge: Plenary session papers from the 19th annual program meeting*. New York: Council on Social Work Education.

Briggs, H. E., Feyerherm, W., & Gingerich, W. (2004). Evaluating science-based practice with single-systems. In H. E. Briggs & T. L. Rzepnicki (Eds.), *Using evidence in social work practice: Behavioral perspectives* (pp. 323–342). Chicago, IL: Lyceum Books.

Bright, J. I., Baker, K. D., & Neimeyer, R. A. (1999). Professional and paraprofessional group treatments for depression: A comparison of cognitive-behavioral and mutual support interventions. *Journal of Consulting and Clinical Psychology, 67*(4), 491–501.

Brower, A. M., Arndt, R. G., & Ketterhagen, A. (2004). Very good solutions really do exist for group work research design problems. In C. D. Garvin, L. M. Gutierrez, & M. J. Galinsky (Eds.), *Handbook of social work with groups* (pp. 435–446). New York: Guilford.

Brownlee, K., & Chlebovec, L. (2004). A group for men who abuse their partners: Participant perceptions of what was helpful. *American Journal of Orthopsychiatry, 74*(2), 209–213.

Budman, S. H., Demby, A., Fedstein, M., Redondo, J., Scherz, B., Bennett, M. J., et al. (1987). Preliminary findings on a new instrument to measure cohesion in group psychotherapy. *International Journal of Group Psychotherapy, 37*(1), 75–94.

Budman, S. H., & Gurman, A. S. (1988). Time-limited group psychotherapy. In S. H. Budman & A. S. Gurman (Eds.), *Theory and practice of brief therapy* (pp. 246–282). New York: Guilford Press.

Burchard, E. M. L., Michaels, J. J., & Kotkov, B. (1948). Criteria for the evaluation of group therapy. *Psychosomatic Medicine, 10*, 257–274.

Burlingame, G. M., Fuhriman, A., & Johnson, J. E. (2001). Cohesion in group psychotherapy. *Psychotherapy: Theory, Research, Practice, Training, 38*(4), 373–379.

Burlingame, G. M., Fuhriman, A., & Johnson, J. E. (2002). Cohesion in group psychotherapy. In J. C. Norcross (Ed.), *Psychotherapy relationships that work: Therapist contributions and responsiveness to patients* (pp. 71–87). New York: Oxford University Press.

Burlingame, G. M., Fuhriman, A., & Johnson, J. E. (2004a). Current status and future directions of group therapy research. In J. L. DeLucia-Waack, D. A. Gerrity, C. R. Kalodner, & M. Riva (Eds.), *Handbook of group counseling and psychotherapy* (pp. 651–660). Thousand Oaks, CA: SAGE.

Burlingame, G. M., Fuhriman, A., & Johnson, J. E. (2004b). Process and outcome in group counseling and psychotherapy. In J. L. DeLucia-Waack, D. A. Gerrity,

C. R. Kalodner, & M. Riva (Eds.), *Handbook of group counseling and psychotherapy* (pp. 49–61). Thousand Oaks, CA: SAGE.

Burlingame, G. M., Fuhriman, A., & Mosier, J. (2003). The differential effectiveness of group psychotherapy: A meta-analytic perspective. *Group Dynamics: Theory, Research, and Practice, 7*(1), 3–12.

Burlingame, G. M., Kircher, J. C., & Taylor, S. (1994). Methodological considerations in group psychotherapeutic research: Past, present, and future practices. In A. Fuhriman & G. M. Burlingame (Eds.), *Handbook of group psychotherapy: An empirical and clinical synthesis* (pp. 41–80). New York: Wiley.

Burlingame, G. M., MacKenzie, K. R., & Strauss, B. (2004). Small group treatment: Evidence for effectiveness and mechanisms of change. In M. J. Lambert (Ed.), *Bergin and Garfield's handbook of psychotherapy and behavior change* (5th ed., pp. 647–696). Hoboken, NJ: Wiley.

Burlingame, G. M., Strauss, B., Joyce, A., MacNair-Semands, R., MacKenzie, K., Ogrodniczuk, J., et al. (2006). *CORE Battery—Revised.* New York: American Group Psychotherapy Association.

Callahan, C. D., & Barisa, M. T. (2005). Statistical process control and rehabilitation outcome: The single-subject design reconsidered. *Rehabilitation Psychology, 50*(1), 24–33.

Campbell Collaboration. (2001). *Campbell Collaboration guidelines.* Version 1.0. Retrieved July 8, 2006, from http://www.campbellcollaboration.org/guidelines.asp.

Caplow, T. (1958). Official reports and proceedings, report of the committee on research. *American Sociological Review, 23*(6), 704–711.

Carless, S. A., & De Paola, C. (2000). The measurement of cohesion in work teams. *Small Group Research, 31*, 71–88.

Carter, E. F., Mitchell, S. L., & Krautheim, M. D. (2001). Understanding and addressing clients' resistance to group counseling. *Journal for Specialists in Group Work, 26*(1), 66–80.

Cartwright, D., & Zander, A. F. (Eds.). (1968). *Group dynamics: Research and theory* (3rd ed.). New York: Harper & Row.

Center for Evidence-Based Medicine at Oxford University. (2001). *Levels of evidence.* Retrieved June 29, 2004, from http://www.cebm.net/levels_of_evidence.asp#levels.

Center for Substance Abuse Prevention. (2005). *Substance abuse treatment: Group therapy.* Rockville, MD: Center for Substance Abuse Treatment, Substance Abuse and Mental Health Services Administration.

Centre for Evidence Based Social Services. (2004, October 21). *Appraising research.* Retrieved June 12, 2006, from http://www.cebss.org/appraising_research.html.

Cetingok, M., & Hirayama, H. (1983). Evaluating the effects of group work with the elderly: An experiment using a single-subject design. *Small Group Behavior, 14*(3), 327–335.

Chamberlain, P., & Smith, D. K. (Eds.). (2005). *Multidimensional treatment foster care: A community solution for boys and girls referred from juvenile justice.* Washington, DC: American Psychological Association.

Chambless, D. L., Baker, M. J., Baucom, D. H., Beutler, L. E., Calhoun, K. S., Crits-Christoph, P., et al. (1998). Update on empirically validated therapies, II. *Clinical Psychologist, 51*(1), 3–16.

Chambless, D. L., & Hollon, S. D. (1998). Defining empirically supported therapies. *Journal of Consulting and Clinical Psychology, 66*(1), 7–18.

Chambless, D. L., & Ollendick, T. H. (2001). Empirically supported psychological interventions: Controversies and evidence. *Annual Review of Psychology, 52,* 685–716.

Chambless, D. L., Sanderson, W. C., Shoham, V., Johnson, S. B., Pope, K. S., Crits-Christoph, P., et al. (1996). An update on empirically validated therapies. *Clinical Psychologist, 49*(2), 5–18.

Chau, K. (1990). Social work groups in multicultural contexts. *Groupwork, 3*(1), 8–21.

Chen, M.-W., & Han, Y. S. (2001). Cross-cultural group counseling with Asians: A stage-specific interactive approach. *Journal for Specialists in Group Work, 26*(2), 111–128.

Chen, S. W.-H., & Davenport, D. S. (2005). Cognitive-behavioral therapy with Chinese American clients: Cautions and modifications. *Psychotherapy: Theory, Research, Practice, Training, 42*(1), 101–110.

Chin, W. W., Salisbury, W. D., Pearson, A. W., & Stollak, M. J. (1999). Perceived cohesion in small groups: Adapting and testing the Perceived Cohesion Scale in a small-group setting. *Small Group Research, 30*(6), 751–766.

Cohen, J. (1988). *Statistical power analysis for the behavioral sciences* (2nd ed.). Hillsdale, NJ: Lawrence Erlbaum.

Comstock, D. L., Duffey, T., & St. George, H. (2002). The relational-cultural model: A framework for group process. *Journal for Specialists in Group Work, 27*(3), 254–272.

Cooney, N. L., Kadden, R. M., Litt, M. D., & Getter, H. (1991). Matching alcoholics to coping skills or interactional therapies: Two-year follow-up results. *Journal of Consulting and Clinical Psychology, 59*(4), 598–601.

Cooper, H. M., & Hedges, L. V. (1994). *The handbook of research synthesis.* New York: Russell Sage Foundation.

Corcoran, J. (2003). *Clinical applications of evidence-based family interventions.* New York: Oxford University Press.

Corcoran, K., Gingerich, W. J., & Briggs, H. E. (2001). Practice evaluation: Setting goals and monitoring change. In H. E. Briggs & K. Corcoran (Eds.), *Social work practice: Treating common client problems* (2nd ed., pp. 66–84). Chicago: Lyceum Books.

Cordioli, A. V., Heldt, E., Bochi, D. B., Margis, R., de Sousa, M. B., Tonello, J. F., et al. (2003). Cognitive-behavioral group therapy in obsessive-compulsive disorder: A randomized clinical trial. *Psychotherapy and Psychosomatics, 72*(4), 211–216.

Coren, E., & Barlow, J. (2002). Individual and group based parenting for improving psychosocial outcomes for teenage parents and their children. *Campbell Collaboration.* Retrieved July 14, 2007, from http://www.campbellcollaboration.org/doc-pdf/teenpar.pdf.

Corey, M. S., & Corey, G. (1987). *Groups: Process and practice* (3rd ed.). Monterey, CA: Brooks/Cole.

Cournoyer, B. R. (2004). *The evidence-based social work (EBSW) skills book.* Boston, MA: Allyn and Bacon.

Cournoyer, B. R., & Powers, G. T. (2002). Evidence-based social work: The quiet revolution continues. In A. R. Roberts & G. J. Greene (Eds.), *Social workers' desk reference* (pp. 798–807). New York: Oxford University Press.

Cox, M. (1973). The Group Therapy Interaction Chronogram. *British Journal of Social Work, 3,* 243–256.

Coyle, G. L. (1948). *Group experience and democratic values.* New York: Woman's Press.

Crawford, P., Brown, B., Anthony, P., & Hicks, C. (2002). Reluctant empiricists: Community mental health nurses and the art of evidence-based praxis. *Health & Social Care in the Community, 10*(4), 287–298.

Dahlberg, L. L., Toal, S. B., & Behrens, C. B. (Eds.). (1998). *Measuring violence-related attitudes, beliefs, and behaviors among youths: A compendium of assessment tools.* Atlanta, GA: National Center for Injury Prevention and Control, Centers for Disease Control and Prevention.

Dans, A. L., Dans, L. F., Guyatt, G. H., & Richardson, S. (1998). Users' guides to the medical literature: XIV. How to decide on the applicability of clinical trial results to your patient. *Journal of the American Medical Association, 279*(7), 545–549.

Davis, M. S., Budman, S. H., & Soldz, S. (2000). The Individual Group Member Interpersonal Process Scale. In A. P. Beck & C. M. Lewis (Eds.), *The process of group psychotherapy: Systems for analyzing change.* (pp. 283–308). Washington, DC: American Psychological Association.

Dawes, R. M., Faust, D., & Meehl, P. E. (2002). Clinical versus actuarial judgment. In T. Gilovich & D. Griffin (Eds.), *Heuristics and biases: The psychology of intuitive judgment* (pp. 716–729). New York: Cambridge University Press.

DeLucia-Waack, J. L. (1997). Measuring the effectiveness of group work: A review and analysis of process and outcome measures. *Journal for Specialists in Group Work, 22*(4), 277–292.

DeLucia, J. L., & Bowman, V. E. (1991). Internal consistency and factor structure of the Group Counselor Behavior Rating Form. *Journal for Specialists in Group Work, 16*(2), 109–114.

DeLucia, J. L., & Bridbord, K. H. (2004). Measures of group process, dynamics, climate, leadership behaviors, and therapeutic factors. In J. L. DeLucia-Waack, D. A. Gerrity, C. R. Kalodner & M. Riva (Eds.), *Handbook of group counseling and psychotherapy* (pp. 120–135). Thousand Oaks, CA: SAGE.

DeLucia-Waack, J. L., & Donigian, J. (2003). *The practice of multicultural group work: Visions and perspectives from the field.* Belmont, CA: Brooks/Cole-Thomson Learning.

DeLucia-Waack, J. L., Gerrity, D. A., Kalodner, C. R., & Riva, M. (Eds.). (2004). *Handbook of group counseling and psychotherapy.* Thousand Oaks, CA: SAGE.

Dies, R. R. (2003). Group psychotherapies. In A. S. Gurman & S. B. Messer (Eds.), *Essential psychotherapies: Theory and practice* (2nd ed., pp. 515–550). New York: Guilford Press.

Dies, R. R., & Teleska, P. A. (1985). Negative outcome in group psychotherapy. In D. T. Mays & C. M. Franks (Eds.), *Negative outcome in psychotherapy and what to do about it* (pp. 118–141). New York: Springer.

DiNitto, D. M., Webb, D. K., & Rubin, A. (2002). The effectiveness of an integrated treatment approach for clients with dual diagnoses. *Research on Social Work Practice, 12*(5), 621–641.

Dishion, T. J., Poulin, F., & Burraston, B. (2001). Peer group dynamics associated with iatrogenic effects in group interventions with high-risk young adolescents. In D. W. Nangle & C. A. Erdley (Eds.), *The role of friendship in psychological adjustment* (pp. 79–92). San Francisco: Jossey-Bass.

Ditto, P. H., Munro, G. D., Apanovitch, A. M., Scepansky, J. A., & Lockhart, L. K. (2003). Spontaneous skepticism: The interplay of motivation and expectation in responses to favorable and unfavorable medical diagnoses. *Personality and Social Psychology Bulletin, 29*(9), 1120–1132.

Doel, M. (2004). Difficult behavior in groups. *Groupwork, 14*(1), 80–100.

Duch, B. J., Groh, S. E., & Allen, D. E. (2001a). Why problem-based learning? In B. J. Duch, S. E. Groh, & D. E. Allen (Eds.), *The power of problem-based learning: A practical "how to" for teaching undergraduate courses in any discipline* (pp. 3–11). Sterling, VA: Stylus.

Duch, B. J., Groh, S. E., & Allen, D. E. (Eds.). (2001b). *The power of problem-based learning: A practical "how to" for teaching undergraduate courses in any discipline.* Sterling, VA: Stylus.

Ebell, M. (2000). Information at the point of care: Answering clinical questions. In J. P. Geyman, R. A. Deyo, & S. D. Ramsey (Eds.), *Evidence-based clinical practice* (pp. 153–162). Woburn, MA: Butterworth-Heinemann.

Edleson, J. M., Miller, D. M., Stone, G. W., & Chapman, D. G. (1985). Group treatment for men who batter. *Social Work Research and Abstracts, 21*(3), 18–21.

Eliopoulos, C. (1990). *Health assessment of the older adult* (2nd ed.). Redwood City, CA: Addison-Wesley Nursing.

Elliott, D. S., & Mihalic, S. (2004). Issues in disseminating and replicating effective prevention programs. *Prevention Science, 5*(1), 47–53.

Erickson, D. H. (2003). Group cognitive behavioural therapy for heterogeneous anxiety disorders. *Cognitive Behaviour Therapy, 32*(4), 179–186.

Evans, N. J. (1982). The relationship of psychological type and attraction to group in a growth group setting. *Journal for Specialists in Group Work, 7*(2), 74–79.

Evans, N. J. (1984). The relationship of interpersonal attraction and attraction to group in a growth group setting. *Journal for Specialists in Group Work, 9*(4), 172–178.

Evans, N. J., & Jarvis, P. A. (1986). The Group Attitude Scale: A measure of attraction to group. *Small Group Behavior, 17*(2), 203–216.

Evidence-Based Medicine Working Group. (1992). Evidence-based medicine. A new approach to teaching the practice of medicine. *Journal of the American Medical Association, 268*(17), 2420–2425.

Fals-Stewart, W., Logsdon, T., & Birchler, G. R. (2004). Diffusion of an empirically supported treatment for substance abuse: An organizational autopsy of technology transfer success and failure. *Clinical Psychologist, 11*(2), 177–182.

Feldman, R. A., & Caplinger, T. E. (1977). Social work experience and client behavioral change: Multivariate analysis of process and outcome. *Journal of Social Service Research, 1*(1), 5–33.

Fidler, F., Cumming, G., Thomason, N., Pannuzzo, D., Smith, J., Fyffe, P., et al. (2005). Toward improved statistical reporting in the *Journal of Consulting and Clinical Psychology. Journal of Consulting and Clinical Psychology, 73*(1), 136–143.

Fike, D. F. (1980). Evaluating group intervention. *Social Work with Groups, 3*(2), 41–51.

Fischer, J., & Corcoran, K. (1994). *Measures for clinical practice: A sourcebook (Volume 1: Couples, families, children)* (2nd ed.). New York: Free Press.

Fischer, J., & Corcoran, K. (2007). *Measures for clinical practice and research: A sourcebook* (4th ed. Vols. 1, 2). New York: Oxford University Press.

Fleiss, J. L. (1981). *Statistical methods for rates and proportions* (2nd ed.). New York: Wiley.

Forsyth, D. R. (1990). *Group dynamics* (2nd ed.). Pacific Grove, CA: Brooks/Cole.

Foster, L. H., Watson, T. S., & Young, J. S. (2002). Single-subject research design for school counselors: Becoming an applied researcher. *Professional School Counseling, 6*(2), 146–154.

Fraser, M. W., Nash, J. K., Galinsky, M. J., & Darwin, K. M. (2000). *Making choices: Social problem-solving skills for children.* Washington, DC: NASW Press.

Freud, S. (1922). *Group psychology and the analysis of the ego.* London: International Psychoanalytical Press.

Fuhriman, A., Drescher, S., Hanson, E., Henrie, R., & Rybicki, W. (1986). Refining the measurement of curativeness: An empirical approach. *Small Group Behavior, 17*(2), 186–201.

Galanter, C. A., & Patel, V. L. (2005). Medical decision making: A selective review for child psychiatrists and psychologists. *Journal of Child Psychology and Psychiatry, 46*(7), 675–689.

Galassi, J. P., & Gersh, T. L. (1993). Myths, misconceptions, and missed opportunity: Single-case designs and counseling psychology. *Journal of Counseling Psychology, 40*(4), 525–531.

Galinsky, M. J., & Schopler, J. H. (1977). Warning: Groups may be dangerous. *Social Work, 22*(2), 89–94.

Galinsky, M. J., & Schopler, J. H. (1994). Negative experiences in support groups. *Social Work in Health Care, 20*(1), 77–95.

Galinsky, M. J., Terzian, M. A., & Fraser, M. W. (2006). The art of group work practice with manualized curricula. *Social Work with Groups, 29*(1), 11–26.

Galinsky, M. J., Turnbull, J. E., Meglin, D. E., & Wilner, M. E. (1993). Confronting the reality of collaborative practice research: Issues of practice, design, measurement, and team development. *Social Work, 38*(4), 440–449.

Gambrill, E. (1999). Evidence-based clinical practice: An alternative to authority-based practice. *Families in Society, 80,* 341–350.

Gambrill, E. (2004). Contributions of critical thinking and evidence-based practice to the fulfillment of the ethical obligations of professionals. In H. E. Briggs & T. L. Rzepnicki (Eds.), *Using evidence in social work practice: Behavioral perspectives* (pp. 3–19). Chicago: Lyceum Books.

Gambrill, E. (2006a). Evidence-based practice and policy: Choices ahead. *Research on Social Work Practice, 16*(3), 338–357.

Gambrill, E. (2006b). *Social work practice: A critical thinker's guide* (2nd ed.). New York: Oxford University Press.

Gant, L. M. (2004). Evaluation of group work. In C. D. Garvin, L. M. Gutierrez, & M. J. Galinsky (Eds.), *Handbook of social work with groups* (pp. 461–475). New York: Guilford.

Garvin, C. D. (1974). Task-centered group work. *Social Service Review, 48,* 494–507.

Garvin, C. D. (1985a). Group process: Usage and uses in social work practice. In M. Sundel, P. Glasser, R. Sarri, & R. Vinter (Eds.), *Individual change through small groups* (2nd ed., pp. 203–225). New York: Free Press.

Garvin, C. D. (1985b). Practice with task-centered groups. In A. Fortune (Ed.), *Task-centered practice with families and groups* (pp. 45–77). New York: Springer-Verlag.

Garvin, C. D. (1986). Developmental research for task-centered group work with chronic mental patients. *Social Work with Groups, 9*(3), 31–42.

Garvin, C. D. (1992). A task centered group approach to work with the chronically mentally ill. *Social Work with Groups, 15*(2–3), 67–80.

Garvin, C. D. (1997). *Contemporary group work* (3rd ed.). Boston: Allyn and Bacon.

Gerdes, K. E., Edmonds, R. M., Haslam, D. R., & McCartney, T. L. (1996). Clinical social work use of practice evaluation procedures. *Reseach on Social Work Practice, 6*(1), 27–39.

Getter, H., Litt, M. D., Kadden, R. M., & Cooney, N. L. (1992). Measuring treatment process in coping skills and interactional group therapies for alcoholism. *International Journal of Group Psychotherapy, 42*(3), 419–430.

Gibbard, G. S., & Hartman, J. J. (1973a). The Oedipal paradigm in group development: A clinical and empirical study. *Small Group Behavior, 4*(3), 305.

Gibbard, G. S., & Hartman, J. J. (1973b). Relationship patterns in self-analytic groups: A clinical and empirical study. *Behavioral Science, 18*(5), 335–353.

Gibbs, L. (2003). *Evidence-based practice for the helping professions.* Pacific Grove, CA: Brooks/Cole-Thomson Learning.

Gibbs, L., & Gambrill, E. (1999). *Critical thinking for social workers: Exercises for the helping professions.* Thousand Oaks, CA: Pine Forge Press.

Gibbs, L., & Gambrill, E. (2002). Evidence-based practice: Counterarguments to objections. *Research on Social Work Practice, 12*(3), 452–476.

Gilgun, J. F. (2005). The four cornerstones of evidence-based practice in social work. *Research on Social Work Practice, 15*(1), 52–61.

Gitterman, A. (2004). The mutual aid model. In C. D. Garvin, L. M. Gutierrez, & M. J. Galinsky (Eds.), *Handbook of social work with groups* (pp. 93–110). New York: Guilford.

Glass, G. V., McGaw, B., & Smith, M. L. (1981). *Meta-analysis in social research.* Beverly Hills: SAGE.

Glasser, P. H., & Garvin, C. D. (1976). An organizational model. In R. W. Roberts & H. Northen (Eds.), *Theories of social work with groups* (pp. 75–115). New York: Columbia University Press.

Glisson, C. (1986). The group versus the individual as the unit of analysis in small group research. *Social Work with Groups, 9*, 15–30.

Goldstein, H. K. (1962a). Criteria for evaluating research. *Social Casework, 43*, 474–477.

Goldstein, H. K. (1962b). Making practice more scientific through knowledge of research. *Social Work, 7*, 102–108.

Gray, J. A. M. (1997). *Evidence-based healthcare: How to make health policy and management decisions.* Edinburgh: Churchill Livingston.

Greif, G. L., & Ephross, P. H. (2004). *Group work with populations at risk* (2nd ed.). New York: Oxford University Press.

Gresham, F. M. (2005). Treatment integrity and therapeutic change: Commentary on Perepletchikova and Kazdin. *Clinical Psychology: Science and Practice, 12*(4), 391–394.

Gresham, F. M., Gansle, K. A., Noell, G. H., Cohen, S., & Rosenblum, S. (1993) Treatment integrity of school-based behavioral intervention studies: 1980–1990 *School Psychology Review, 22*(2), 254–272.

Gresham, F. M., MacMillan, D. L., Beebe-Frankenberger, M. E., & Bocian, K. M (2000). Treatment integrity in learning disabilities intervention research: Do we really know how treatments are implemented? *Learning Disabilities Research e Practice, 15*(4), 198–205.

Grinnell, R. M. (1993). *Social work research and evaluation* (4th ed.). Itasca, IL: F. E Peacock.

Groth-Marnat, G. (1997). *Handbook of psychological assessment* (3rd ed.). New York: Wiley.

Grove, W. M., & Meehl, P. E. (1996). Comparative efficiency of informal (subjective, impressionistic) and formal (mechanical, algorithmic) prediction procedures: The clinical–statistical controversy. *Psychology, Public Policy, and Law, 2,* 293–323.

Grove, W. M., Zald, D. H., Lebow, B. S., Snitz, B. E., & Nelson, C. (2000). Clinical versus mechanical prediction: A meta-analysis. *Psychological Assessment, 12*(1), 19–30.

Guyatt, G. H., Keller, J. L., Jaeschke, R., Rosenbloom, D., Adachi, J. D., & Newhouse, M. T. (1990). The n-of-1 randomized controlled trial: Clinical usefulness. Our three-year experience. *Annals of Internal Medicine, 112*(4), 293–299.

Guyatt, G. H., Sackett, D., Adachi, J., Roberts, R., Chong, J., Rosenbloom, D., et al. (1988). A clinician's guide for conducting randomized trials in individual patients. *Canadian Medical Association Journal, 139*(6), 497–503.

Guyatt, G. H., Sackett, D. L., & Cook, D. J. (1994). Users' guides to the medical literature. II. How to use an article about therapy or prevention. B. What were the results and will they help me in caring for my patients? *Journal of the American Medical Association, 271*(1), 59–63.

Guyatt, G. H., Sackett, D. L., Sinclair, J. C., Hayward, R., Cook, D. J., & Cook, R. J. (1995). Users' guides to the medical literature. IX. A method for grading health care recommendations. *Journal of the American Medical Association, 274*(22), 1800–1804.

Hair, J. F., Anderson, R. E., Tatham, R. L., & Black, W. C. (1998). *Multivariate data analysis* (5th ed.). Upper Saddle River, NJ: Prentice Hall.

Hait, W. N. (2005). Translating research into clinical practice: Deliberations from the American Association for Cancer Research. *Clinical Cancer Research, 11*(12), 4275–4277.

Hammick, M. (2000). Interprofessional education: Evidence from the past to guide the future. *Medical Teacher, 22*(5), 461–467.

Hartford, M. E. (1976). Group methods and generic practice. In R. W. Roberts & H. Northen (Eds.), *Theories of social work with groups* (pp. 45–74). New York: Columbia University Press.

Hasenfeld, Y. (1974). Organizational factors in service to groups. In P. H. Glasser, R. C. Sarri, & R. D. Vinter (Eds.), *Individual change through small groups* (pp. 307–322). New York: Free Press.

Hastings-Vertino, K., Getty, C., & Wooldridge, P. (1996). Development of a tool to measure therapeutic factors in group process. *Archives of Psychiatric Nursing, 10*(4), 221–228.

Hatala, R., & Guyatt, G. (2002). Evaluating the teaching of evidence-based medicine. *Journal of the American Medical Association, 288*(9), 1110–1112.

Hatgis, C., Addis, M. E., Krasnow, A. D., Zaslavsky Khazan, I., Jacob, K. L., Chiancola, S., et al. (2001). Cross-fertilization versus transmission: Recommendations for developing a bidirectional approach to psychotherapy dissemination research. *Applied & Preventive Psychology, 10*(1), 37–49.

Hauserman, N., Zweback, S., & Plotkin, A. (1972). Use of concrete reinforcement to facilitate verbal initiations in adolescent group therapy. *Journal of Consulting & Clinical Psychology, 38*(1), 90–96.

Hayes, S. C. (1981). Single case experimental design and empirical clinical practice. *Journal of Consulting and Clinical Psychology, 49*(2), 193–211.

Hayes, S. C. (Ed.). (1992). *Single case experimental design and empirical clinical practice.* Washington, DC: American Psychological Association.

Haynes, R. B., Sackett, D. L., Gray, J. M., Cook, D. J., & Guyatt, G. H. (1996). Transferring evidence from research into practice: 1. The role of clinical care research evidence in clinical decisions. *ACP Journal Club, 125*(3), A14–A16.

Heckel, R. V., Holmes, G. R., & Rosecrans, C. J. (1971). A factor analytic study of process variables in group therapy. *Journal of Clinical Psychology, 27*(1), 146–150.

Heckel, R. V., Holmes, G. R., & Salzberg, H. C. (1967). Emergence of distinct verbal phases in group therapy. *Psychological Reports, 21*(2), 630–632.

Hedges, L. V., & Olkin, I. (1985). *Statistical methods for meta-analysis.* Orlando: Academic Press.

Hemphill, S. A., & Littlefield, L. (2001). Evaluation of a short-term group therapy program for children with behavior problems and their parents. *Behaviour Research and Therapy, 39*(7), 823–841.

Henggeler, S. W., Melton, G. B., Brondino, M. J., Scherer, D. G., & Hanley, J. H. (1997). Multisystemic therapy with violent and chronic juvenile offenders and their families: The role of treatment fidelity in successful dissemination. *Journal of Consulting and Clinical Psychology, 65*(5), 821–833.

Henggeler, S. W., Pickrel, S. G., & Brondino, M. J. (1999). Multisystemic treatment of substance-abusing and dependent delinquents: Outcomes, treatment fidelity, and transportability. *Mental Health Services Research, 1*(3), 171–184.

Henggeler, S. W., Schoenwald, S. K., Liao, J. G., Letourneau, E. J., & Edwards, D. L. (2002). Transporting efficacious treatments to field settings: The link between supervisory practices and therapist fidelity in MST programs. *Journal of Clinical Child and Adolescent Psychology, 31*(2), 155–167.

Henry, S. (1992). *Group skills in social work: A four-dimensional approach* (2nd ed.). Pacific Grove, CA: Brooks/Cole.

Henry, K. B., Arrow, H., & Carini, B. (1999). A tripartite model of group identification: Theory and measurement. *Small Group Research, 30*(5), 558–581.

Hepler, J. B. (1991). Evaluating the clinical significance of a group approach for improving the social skills of children. *Social Work with Groups, 14*(2), 87–104.

Herschell, A. D., McNeil, C. B., & McNeil, D. W. (2004). Clinical child psychology's progress in disseminating empirically supported treatments. *Clinical Psychology: Science and Practice, 11*(3), 267–288.

Higgins, J. P. T., & Green, S. (2005). *Cochrane Handbook for systematic reviews of interventions 4.2.5* (updated May 2005). Retrieved November 28, 2005, from http://www.cochrane.org/resources/handbook/hbook.htm.

Hill, C. E. (1986). An overview of the Hill Counselor and Client Verbal Response modes Category Systems. In L. S. Greenberg & W. M. Pinsof (Eds.), *The psychotherapeutic process* (pp. 131–160). New York: Guilford Press.

Hill, W. F. (1965). *Hill Interaction Matrix manual and supplement, revised edition.* Los Angeles: Youth Studies Center, University of Southern California.

Hill, W. F. (1971). The Hill Interaction Matrix. *Personnel & Guidance Journal, 49*(8), 619–623.

Hill, W. F. (1977). Hill Interaction Matrix (HIM): The conceptual framework, derived rating scales, and an updated bibliography. *Small Group Behavior, 8*, 251–268.

Hoag, M. J., & Burlingame, G. M. (1997). Evaluating the effectiveness of child and adolescent group treatment: A meta-analytic review. *Journal of Clinical Child Psychology, 26*(3), 234–246.

Horner, R. H., Carr, E. G., Halle, J., McGee, G., Odom, S., & Wolery, M. (2005). The use of single-subject research to identify evidence-based practice in special education. *Exceptional Children, 71*(2), 165–179.

Horvath, A. O., & Bedi, R. P. (2004). The alliance. In M. J. Lambert (Ed.), *Bergin and Garfield's handbook of psychotherapy and behavior change* (5th ed., pp. 37–69). Hoboken, NJ: Wiley.

Howard, M. O., McMillan, C. J., & Pollio, D. E. (2003). Teaching evidence-based practice: Toward a new paradigm for social work education. *Research on Social Work Practice, 13*(2), 234–259.

Hudgins, C. A., & Allen-Meares, P. (2000). Translational research: A new solution to an old problem? *Journal of Social Work Education, 36*(1), 2–4.

Hudson, W. W. (1982). *The Clinical Measurement Package: A field manual.* Homewood, IL: Dorsey Press.

Hugh, H. (2006). Tests and measures in the social sciences: Tests available in compilation volumes (August 2006 edition). Retrieved August 17, 2006, from http://libraries.uta.edu/helen/Test&meas/testmainframe.htm#Collections.

Hulse-Killacky, D., Orr, J. J., & Paradise, L. V. (2006). The Corrective Feedback Instrument-Revised. *Journal for Specialists in Group Work, 31*(3), 263–281.

Hyde, P. S., Falls, K., Morris, J. A., & Schoenwald, S. K. (2003). *Turning knowledge into practice—A manual for behavioral health administrators and practitioners about understanding and implementing evidence-based practices.* Boston, MA: Technical Assistance Collaborative.

Institute of Medicine. (2001). *Crossing the quality chasm: A new health system for the 21st century.* Washington, DC: National Academies Press.

Jacobs, E. E., Masson, R. L., & Harvill, R. L. (2002). *Group counseling: Strategies and skills* (4th ed.). Pacific Grove, CA: Brooks/Cole-Thomson Learning.

Jacobson, N. S., & Truax, P. (1991). Clinical significance: A statistical approach to defining meaningful change in psychotherapy research. *Journal of Consulting and Clinical Psychology, 59*(1), 12–19.

Jayaratne, S., & Levy, R. L. (1979). *Empirical clinical practice.* New York: Columbia University.

Johnson, J. E., Burlingame, G. M., Olsen, J. A., Davies, D. R., & Gleave, R. L. (2005). Group climate, cohesion, alliance, and empathy in group psychotherapy: Multilevel structural equation models. *Journal of Counseling Psychology, 52*(3), 310–321.

Johnson, P., Beckerman, A., & Auerbach, C. (2001). Researching our own practice: Single system design for groupwork. *Groupwork, 13*(1), 57–72.

Jones, L. V., & Hodges, V. G. (2001). Enhancing psychosocial competence among Black women: A psycho-educational group model approach. *Social Work with Groups, 24*(3–4), 33–52.

Jones, R. L. (1996a). *Handbook of tests and measurements for black populations.* Hampton, VA: Cobb & Henry.

Jones, R. L. (1996b). Introduction and overview. In R. L. Jones (Ed.), *Handbook of tests and measurements for Black populations* (Vol. 1, pp. 3–15). Hampton, VA: Cobb & Henry.

Kalter, N., & Schreier, S. (1994). Developmental facilitation groups for children of divorce. In C. LeCroy (Ed.), *Handbook of child and adolescent treatment manuals.* New York: Lexington.

Kam, C. M., Greenberg, M. T., & Walls, C. T. (2003). Examining the role of implementation quality in school-based prevention using the PATHS curriculum. Promoting Alternative THinking Skills Curriculum. *Prevention Science, 4*(1), 55–63.

Kaminer, Y., Blitz, C., Burleson, J. A., Kadden, R. M., & Rounsaville, B. J. (1998). Measuring treatment process in cognitive-behavioral and interactional group therapies for adolescent substance abusers. *Journal of Nervous and Mental Disease, 186*(7), 407–413.

Karterud, S. W. (2000). The group emotionality rating. In A. P. Beck & C. M. Lewis (Eds.), *The process of group psychotherapy: Systems for analyzing change.* (pp. 113–134). Washington, DC: American Psychological Association.

Karterud, S. W., & Foss, T. (1989). The group emotionality rating system: A modification of Thelen's method of assessing emotionality in groups. *Small Group Behavior, 20*(2), 131–150.

Kazdin, A. E. (1977). Assessing the clinical or applied significance of behavior change through social validation. *Behavior Modification, 1,* 427–452.

Kazdin, A. E. (1999). The meanings and measurement of clinical significance. *Journal of Consulting and Clinical Psychology, 67*(3), 332–339.

Kazdin, A. E. (2001). Almost clinically significant (p < .10): Current measures may only approach clinical significance. *Clinical Psychology: Science and Practice, 8*(4), 455–462.

Kazdin, A. E. (2006). Arbitrary metrics: Implications for identifying evidence-based treatments. *American Psychologist, 61*(1), 42–49.

Kelley, M. L., Noell, G., & Reitman, D. (2003). *Practitioner's guide to empirically based measures of school behavior.* New York: Kluwer Academic/Plenum.

Kendall, P. C., & Flannery-Schroeder, E. C. (1998). Methodological issues in treatment research for anxiety disorders in youth. *Journal of Abnormal Child Psychology, 26*(1), 27–38.

Kerlinger, F. N. (1986). *Foundations of behavioral research* (3rd ed.). New York: Holt, Rinehart and Winston.

Kew, C. E. (1968). A pilot study of an evaluating scale for group psychotherapy patients. *Pastoral Counselor, 6*(2), 9–24.

Kiresuk, T. J., Smith, A., & Cardillo, J. E. (1994). *Goal attainment scaling: Applications, theory, and measurement.* Hillsdale, NJ: Lawrence Erlbaum.

Kirk, S. A., & Reid, W. J. (2002). *Science and social work: A critical appraisal.* New York: Columbia University Press.

Kitson, A., Harvey, G., & McCormack, B. (1998). Enabling the implementation of evidence based practice: A conceptual framework. *Quality in Health Care, 7*(3), 149–158.

Kivlighan, D. M., & Jauquet, C. A. (1990). Quality of group member agendas and group session climate. *Small Group Research, 21*(2), 205–219.

Kivlighan, D. M., Jauquet, C. A., Hardie, A. W., & Francis, A. M. (1993). Training group members to set session agendas: Effects on in-session behavior and member outcome. *Journal of Counseling Psychology, 40*(2), 182–187.

Kivlighan, D. M., Multon, K. D., & Brossart, D. F. (1996). Helpful impacts in group counseling: Development of a multidimensional rating system. *Journal of Counseling Psychology, 43*(3), 347–355.

Kivlighan, D. M., & Tarrant, J. M. (2001). Does group climate mediate the group leadership–group member outcome relationship? A test of Yalom's hypotheses about leadership priorities. *Group Dynamics, 5*(4), 220–234.

Klein, M. H., Mathieu-Coughlan, P., & Kiesler, D. J. (1986). The Experiencing Scales. In L. S. Greenberg & W. M. Pinsof (Eds.), *The psychotherapeutic process: A research handbook* (pp. 21–71). New York: Guilford Press.

Klein, M. H., Mathieu, P. L., Gendlin, E. T., & Kiesler, D. J. (1969). *The Experiencing Scale: A research and training manual* (Vols. 1 and 2). Madison, WI: Wisconsin Psychiatric Institute.

Klein, W. C., & Bloom, M. (1995). Practice wisdom. *Social Work, 40*(6), 799–807.

Knop, E. (1967). Suggestions to aid the student in systematic interpretation and analysis of empirical sociological journal presentations. *American Sociologist, 2*(2), 90–92.

Kösters, M., Burlingame, G. M., Nachtigall, C., & Strauss, B. (2006). A meta-analytic review of the effectiveness of inpatient group psychotherapy. *Group Dynamics: Theory, Research, and Practice, 10*(2), 146–163.

Kratochwill, T. R. (2002). Evidence-based interventions in school psychology: Thoughts on thoughtful commentary. *School Psychology Quarterly, 17*(4), 518–532.

Kratochwill, T. R. (2003). Task force on evidence-based interventions in school psychology. Retrieved August 6, 2006, from http://www.sp-ebi.org/documents/_workingfiles/EBImanua11.pdf.

Kunda, Z. (1990). The case for motivated reasoning. *Psychological Bulletin, 108*(3), 480–498.

Kurtz, L. F. (1997). *Self-help and support groups: A handbook for practitioners.* Thousand Oaks, CA: SAGE.

Lamb, S. J., Greenlick, M. R., & McCarty, D. (1998). *Bridging the gap between practice and research: Forging partnerships with community-based drug and alcohol treatment.* Washington, DC: National Academies Press.

Lambert, M. J., & Barley, D. E. (2002). Research summary on the therapeutic relationship and psychotherapy outcome. In J. C. Norcross (Ed.), *Psychotherapy relationships that work: Therapist contributions and responsiveness to patients* (pp. 17–32). New York: Oxford University Press.

Lambert, M. J., & Ogles, B. M. (2004). The efficacy and effectiveness of psychotherapy. In M. J. Lambert (Ed.), *Bergin and Garfield's handbook of psychotherapy and behavior change* (5th ed., pp. 139–226). Hoboken, NJ: Wiley.

Lese, K. P., & MacNair-Semands, R. R. (2000). The therapeutic factors inventory: Development of a scale. *Group, 24*(4), 303–317.

Levant, R. F. (2004). The empirically validated treatments movement: A practitioner/educator perspective. *Clinical Psychologist, 11*, 219–224.

Levin, B. B. (2001). *Energizing teacher education and professional development with problem-based learning.* Alexandria, VA: Association for Supervision and Curriculum Development.

Lewin, K. (1951). *Field theory in social science: Selected theoretical papers.* New York: Harper.

Lewin, K. (1975). *Field theory in social science: Selected theoretical papers.* Westport, CT: Greenwood Press.

Lewin, K., Lippitt, R., & White, R. K. (1939). Patterns of aggressive behavior in experimentally created "social climates." *Journal of Social Psychology, 10*, 271–299.

Lewis-Snyder, G., Stoiber, K. C., & Kratochwill, T. R. (2002). Evidence-based interventions in school psychology: An illustration of task force coding criteria using group-based research design. *School Psychology Quarterly, 17*(4), 423–465.

Lewis, C. M., Beck, A. P., Dugo, J. M., & Eng, A. M. (2000). The group development process analysis measures. In A. P. Beck & C. M. Lewis (Eds.), *The process of group psychotherapy: Systems for analyzing change* (pp. 221–261). Washington, DC: American Psychological Association.

Lieberman, M. A., Yalom, I. D., & Miles, M. B. (1973). *Encounter groups: First facts.* New York: Basic Books.

Linton, J. M., & Hedstrom, S. M. (2006). An exploratory qualitative investigation of group processes in group supervision: Perceptions of masters-level practicum students. *Journal of Specialists in Group Work, 31*(1), 51–72.

Lundervold, D. A., & Belwood, M. F. (2000). The best kept secret in counseling: Single-case (N=1) experimental designs. *Journal of Counseling & Development, 78*(1), 92–102.

Lynn, G. L. (1994). The GAF: The Group Assessment Form: A screening instrument for adolescent group therapy. *Journal of Child & Adolescent Group Therapy, 4*(3), 135–146.

Macgowan, M. J. (1997). A measure of engagement for social group work: The Groupwork Engagement Measure (GEM). *Journal of Social Service Research, 23*(2), 17–37.

Macgowan, M. J. (2000). Evaluation of a measure of engagement for group work. *Research on Social Work Practice, 10*(3), 348–361.

Macgowan, M. J. (2003). Increasing engagement in groups: A measurement based approach. *Social Work with Groups, 26*(1), 5–28.

Macgowan, M. J. (2006a). Evidence-based group work: A framework for advancing best practice. *Journal of Evidence-Based Social Work, 3*(1), 1–21.

Macgowan, M. J. (2006b). The Group Engagement Measure: A review of its conceptual and empirical properties. *Journal of Groups in Addiction and Recovery, 1*(2), 33–52.

Macgowan, M. J., & Levenson, J. S. (2003). Psychometrics of the Group Engagement Measure with male sex offenders. *Small Group Research, 34*(2), 155–169.

Macgowan, M. J., & Newman, F. L. (2005). The factor structure of the Group Engagement Measure. *Social Work Research, 29*(2), 107–118.

Macgowan, M. J., & Wagner, E. F. (2005). Iatrogenic effects of group treatment on adolescents with conduct and substance use problems: A review of the literature and a presentation of a model. *Journal of Evidence-Based Social Work, 2*(1/2), 79–90.

MacKenzie, K. R. (1981). Measurement of group climate. *International Journal of Group Psychotherapy, 31*(3), 287–295.

MacKenzie, K. R. (1983). The clinical application of a group climate measure. In R. R. Dies & K. R. MacKenzie (Eds.), *Advances in group psychotherapy: Integrating research and practice* (pp. 159–170). New York: International Universities Press.

MacKenzie, K. R. (1990). *Introduction to time-limited group psychotherapy.* Washington, DC: American Psychiatric Press.

MacKenzie, K. R., & Dies, R. R. (1982). *The CORE Battery: Clinical outcome results.* New York: American Group Psychotherapy Association.

MacKenzie, K. R., Dies, R. R., Coche, E., Rutan, J. S., & Stone, W. N. (1987). An analysis of AGPA Institute groups. *International Journal of Group Psychotherapy, 37*(1), 55–74.

MacNair-Semands, R. (2002). Predicting Attendance and Expectations for Group Therapy. *Group Dynamics: Theory, Research, and Practice, 6*(3), 219–228.

MacNair-Semands, R. (2004). *Manual for Group Therapy Questionnaire—Revised.* Charlotte, NC: University of North Carolina at Charlotte.

MacNair-Semands, R. R., & Lese, K. P. (2000). Interpersonal problems and the perception of therapeutic factors in group therapy. *Small Group Research, 31*, 158–174.

Magen, R. H., & Rose, S. D. (1994). Parents in groups: Problem solving versus behavioral skills training. *Research on Social Work Practice, 4*(2), 172–191.

Mann, R. D., Gibbard, G. S., & Hartman, J. J. (1967). *Interpersonal styles and group development.* New York: Wiley.

Manusov, V. L. (2005). *The sourcebook of nonverbal measures: Going beyond words.* Mahwah, NJ: Lawrence Erlbaum.

Marincola, F. M. (2003). Translational medicine: A two-way road. *Journal of Translational Medicine, 1*(1), 1.

Martin, D. J., Garske, J. P., & Davis, M. K. (2000). Relation of the therapeutic alliance with outcome and other variables: A meta-analytic review. *Journal of Consulting and Clinical Psychology, 68*(3), 438–450.

Marziali, E., Munroe-Blum, H., & McCleary, L. (1999). The effects of the therapeutic alliance on the outcomes of individual and group psychotherapy with borderline personality disorder. *Psychotherapy Research, 9*(4), 424–436.

Mays, N., & Pope, C. (1995). Rigour and qualitative research. *British Medical Journal, 311*(6997), 109–112.

McAuley, L., Pham, B., Tugwell, P., & Moher, D. (2000). Does the inclusion of grey literature influence estimates of intervention effectiveness reported in meta-analyses? *The Lancet, 356*(9237), 1228–1231.

McCullagh, J. G. (1982). Assertion training for boys in junior high school. *Social Work in Education, 5*(1), 41–51.

McDowell, I., & Newell, C. (1996). *Measuring health: A guide to rating scales and questionnaires* (2nd ed.). New York: Oxford University Press.

McGuire, J. M., Taylor, D. R., Broome, D. H., Blau, B. I., & Abbott, D. W. (1986). Group structuring techniques and their influence on process involvement in a group counseling training program. *Journal of Counseling Psychology, 33*, 270–275.

McKenzie, B., & Morrissette, L. (1993). Cultural empowerment and healing for aboriginal youth in Winnipeg. In A. M. Mawhiney (Ed.), *Rebirth: Political, economic, and social development in First Nations* (pp. 117–130). Toronto, Ontario, Canada: Dundurn Press.

McKibbon, K. A. (1998). Evidence-based practice. *Bulletin of the Medical Library Association, 86*(3), 396–401.

McLean, P. D., Whittal, M. L., Thordarson, D. S., Taylor, S., Soechting, I., Koch, W. J., et al. (2001). Cognitive versus behavior therapy in the group treatment of obsessive-compulsive disorder. *Journal of Consulting and Clinical Psychology, 69*(2), 205–214.

Merchant, N. M., & Butler, M. K. (2002). A psychoeducational group for ethnic minority adolescents in a predominantly White treatment setting. *Journal for Specialists in Group Work, 27*(3), 314–332.

Merrell, K. W. (1994). *Assessment of behavioral, social & emotional problems: Direct and objective methods for use with children and adolescents.* New York: Longman.

Meyer, C. H. (1972). Practice on microsystem level. In E. J. Mullen & J. R. Dumpson (Eds.), *Evaluation of social intervention* (pp. 158–190). San Francisco, CA: Jossey-Bass.

Mezey, M. D., Rauckhorst, L. H., & Stokes, S. A. (1993). *Health assessment of the older individual* (2nd ed.). New York: Springer.

Miser, W. F. (2000a). Applying a meta-analysis to daily clinical practice. In J. P. Geyman, R. A. Deyo, & S. D. Ramsey (Eds.), *Evidence-based clinical practice* (pp. 57–64). Woburn, MA: Butterworth-Heinemann.

Miser, W. F. (2000b). Critical appraisal of the literature: How to assess an article and still enjoy life. In J. P. Geyman, R. A. Deyo, & S. D. Ramsey (Eds.), *Evidence-based clinical practice* (pp. 41–56). Woburn, MA: Butterworth-Heinemann.

Moher, D., Jadad, A. R., Nichol, G., Penman, M., Tugwell, P., & Walsh, S. (1995). Assessing the quality of randomized controlled trials: An annotated bibliography of scales and checklists. *Controlled Clinical Trials, 16*(1), 62–73.

Moher, D., Pham, B., Jones, A., Cook, D. J., Jadad, A. R., Moher, M., et al. (1998). Does quality of reports of randomised trials affect estimates of intervention efficacy reported in meta-analyses? *The Lancet, 352*(9128), 609–613.

Moos, R. H. (1974). *Evaluating treatment environments: A social ecological approach.* New York: Wiley.

Moos, R. H. (1996). *Group environment scale manual* (2nd ed.). Palo Alto, CA: Consulting Psychologists Press.

Morgan-Lopez, A. A., & Fals-Stewart, W. (2006). Analytic complexities associated with group therapy in substance abuse treatment research: Problems, recommendations, and future directions. *Experimental and Clinical Psychopharmacology, 14*(2), 265–273.

Mullen, E. J., & Bacon, W. (2004). Implementation of practice guidelines and evidence-based treatment: A survey of psychiatrists, psychologists, and social workers. In A. R. Roberts & K. Yeager (Eds.), *Evidence-based practice manual: Research and outcome measures in health and human services* (pp. 210–218). New York: Oxford University Press.

Naar-King, S., Ellis, D. A., & Frey, M. A. (2004). *Assessing children's well-being: A handbook of measures.* Mahwah, NJ: Lawrence Erlbaum.

National Association of Social Workers. (1999). *Code of ethics of the National Association of Social Workers.* Retrieved June 20, 2004, from http://naswdc.org/pubs/code/code.asp.

National Institutes of Health. (2006). *NIH roadmap for medical research: Re-engineering the clinical research enterprise.* Retrieved September 7, 2006, from http://nihroadmap.nih.gov/clinicalresearch/overview-translational.asp.

Newman, F. L., & Wong, S. E. (2004). Progress and outcome assessment of individual patient data: Selecting single subject design and statistical procedures. In M. E. Maruish (Ed.), *Use of psychological testing for treatment planning & outcome assessment* (3rd ed., Vol. 1, pp. 273–289). Mahwah, NJ: Lawrence Erlbaum.

Newstetter, W. I., & Feldstein, M. J. (1930). *Wawokiye camp: A research project in group work.* Cleveland, OH: School of Applied Social Sciences, Western Reserve University.

Nezu, A. M. (2000). *Practitioner's guide to empirically based measures of depression.* New York: Kluwer Academic/Plenum.

Noble, F., Ohlsen, M., & Proff, F. (1961). A method for the quantification of psychotherapeutic interaction in counseling groups. *Journal of Counseling Psychology, 8,* 54.

Nugent, W. R., Sieppert, J. D., & Hudson, W. W. (2001). *Practice evaluation for the 21st century.* Belmont, CA: Brooks/Cole-Thomson Learning.

Nuijens, K. L., Teglasi, H., Simcox, A. G., Kivlighan, D. M., Jr., & Rothman, L. (2006). The development and validation of the Group Leader Intervention System. *Group Dynamics: Theory, Research, and Practice, 10*(2), 116–135.

Nunnally, J. C., & Bernstein, I. H. (1994). *Psychometric theory* (3rd ed.). New York: McGraw-Hill.

O'Brien, W. H., Korchynsky, R., Fabrizio, J., McGrath, J., & Swank, A. (1999). Evaluating group process in a stress management intervention: Relationships between perceived process and cardiovascular reactivity to stress. *Research on Social Work Practice, 9*(5), 608–630.

Oktay, J. S. (2002). Standards for qualitative research with exemplars. In A. R. Roberts & G. J. Greene (Eds.), *Social workers' desk reference* (pp. 781–786). New York: Oxford University Press.

Openshaw, C., Waller, G., & Sperlinger, D. (2004). Group cognitive-behavior therapy for bulimia nervosa: Statistical versus clinical significance of changes in symptoms across treatment. *International Journal of Eating Disorders, 36*(4), 363–375.

Orme, J. G., & Cox, M. E. (2001). Analyzing single-subject design data using statistical process control charts. *Social Work Research, 25*(2), 115–127.

Oxman, A. D., Cook, D. J., & Guyatt, G. H. (1994). Users' guides to the medical literature. VI. How to use an overview. Evidence-Based Medicine Working Group. *Journal of the American Medical Association, 272*(17), 1367–1371.

Oxman, A. D., & Guyatt, G. H. (1988). Guidelines for reading literature reviews. *Canadian Medical Association Journal, 138*(8), 697–703.

Pack-Brown, S. P., & Fleming, A. (2004). An Afrocentric approach to counseling groups with African Americans. In J. L. DeLucia-Waack, D. A. Gerrity, C. R. Kalodner, & M. Riva (Eds.), *Handbook of group counseling and psychotherapy* (pp. 183–199). Thousand Oaks, CA: SAGE.

Padilla, A. M., & Medina, A. (1996). Cross-cultural sensitivity in assessment: Using tests in culturally appropriate ways. In L. A. Suzuki, P. J. Meller, & J. G. Ponterotto (Eds.), *Handbook of multicultural assessment: Clinical, psychological, and educational applications* (pp. 3–28). San Francisco: Jossey-Bass.

Page, B. J., & Hulse-Killacky, D. (1999). Development and validation of the corrective feedback self-efficacy instrument. *Journal for Specialists in Group Work, 24*(1), 37–54.

Page, B. J., Pietrzak, D. R., & Lewis, T. F. (2001). Development of the group leader self-efficacy instrument. *Journal for Specialists in Group Work, 26*(2), 168–184.

Paleg, K., & Jongsma, A. E. (2005). *The group therapy treatment planner* (2nd ed.). New York: Wiley.

Parsons, T., & Shils, E. (1951). *Toward a general theory of action.* Cambridge, MA: Harvard University Press.

Patterson, D. A., & Basham, R. E. (2002). A data visualization procedure for the evaluation of group treatment outcomes across units of analysis. *Small Group Research, 33*(2), 209–232.

Paulhus, D. L. (1991). Measurement and control of response bias. In J. P. Robinson, P. R. Shaver, & L. S. Wrightsman (Eds.), *Measures of personality and social psychological attitudes: Volume 1 of measures of social psychological attitudes* (pp. 17–59). San Diego, CA: Academic Press.

Pedhazur, E. J., & Schmelkin, L. P. (1991). *Measurement, design, and analysis: An integrated approach.* Hillsdale, NJ: Lawrence Erlbaum.

Perepletchikova, F., & Kazdin, A. E. (2005). Treatment integrity and therapeutic change: Issues and research recommendations. *Clinical Psychology: Science and Practice, 12*(4), 365–383.

Perkinson, R. R. (2002). *Chemical dependency counseling: A practical guide* (2nd ed.). Thousand Oaks, CA: SAGE.

Perri, M. G., Nezu, A. M., McKelvey, W. F., Shermer, R. L., Renjilian, D. A., & Viegener, B. J. (2001). Relapse prevention training and problem-solving therapy in the long-term management of obesity. *Journal of Consulting and Clinical Psychology, 69*(4), 722–726.

Peters, J. L., Sutton, A. J., Jones, D. R., Abrams, K. R., & Rushton, L. (2006). Comparison of two methods to detect publication bias in meta-analysis. *Journal of the American Medical Association, 295*(6), 676–680.

Petrocelli, J. V. (2002). Effectiveness of group cognitive-behavioral therapy for general symptomatology: A meta-analysis. *Journal of Specialists in Group Work, 27*(1), 92–115.

Petry, N. M., Martin, B., & Finocche, C. (2001). Contingency management in group treatment: A demonstration project in an HIV drop-in center. *Journal of Substance Abuse Treatment, 21*(2), 89–96.

Petry, N. M., Martin, B., & Simcic, F., Jr. (2005). Prize reinforcement contingency management for cocaine dependence: Integration with group therapy in a methadone clinic. *Journal of Consulting and Clinical Psychology, 73*(2), 354–359.

Pino, C. J., & Cohen, H. (1971). Trainer style and trainee self-disclosure. *International Journal of Group Psychotherapy, 21*(2), 202–213.

Pinsof, W. M., & Catherall, D. R. (1986). The integrative psychotherapy alliance: Family, couple and individual therapy scales. *Journal of Marital & Family Therapy, 12*(2), 137–151.

Piper, W. E., Marrache, M., Lacroix, R., Richardsen, A. M., & Jones, B. D. (1983). Cohesion as a basic bond in groups. *Human Relations, 36*(2), 93–108.

Piper, W. E., McCallum, M., & Azim, H. F. A. (1992). *Adaptation to loss through short-term group psychotherapy.* New York: Guilford Press.

Piper, W. E., & McCallum, W. E. (2000). The Psychodynamic Work and Object Rating System. In A. P. Beck & C. M. Lewis (Eds.), *The process of group psychotherapy: Systems for analyzing change.* (pp. 263–281). Washington, DC: American Psychological Association.

Polley, R. B., Hare, A. P., & Stone, P. J. (1988). *The SYMLOG practitioner: Applications of small group research.* New York: Praeger.

Pollio, D. E. (2002). The evidence-based group worker. *Social Work with Groups, 25*(4), 57–70.

Pollio, D. E. (2006). The art of evidence-based practice. *Research on Social Work Practice, 16*(2), 224–232.

Pratt, J. H. (1922). The principles of class treatment and their application to various chronic diseases. *Hospital Social Services, 6*, 401–417.

Prendergast, M. L., Podus, D., Chang, E., & Urada, D. (2002). The effectiveness of drug abuse treatment: A meta-analysis of comparison group studies. *Drug and Alcohol Dependence, 67*(1), 53–72.

Proctor, E. K. (2004). Leverage points for the implementation of evidence-based practice. *Brief Treatment and Crisis Intervention, 4*(3), 227–242.

Proctor, E. K., & Rosen, A. (2003). The structure and function of social work practice guidelines. In A. Rosen & E. K. Proctor (Eds.), *Developing practice guidelines for social work intervention* (pp. 108–127). New York: Columbia University Press.

Proctor, E. K., & Rosen, A. (2004). Concise standards for developing evidence-based practice guidelines. In A. R. Roberts & K. Yeager (Eds.), *Evidence-based practice manual: Research and outcome measures in health and human services* (pp. 193–199). New York: Oxford University Press.

Pyrczak, F. (2005). *Evaluating research in academic journals: A realistic guide to realistic evaluation* (3rd ed.). Glendale, CA: Pyrczak Publishing.

Reder, P. (1978). An assessment of the group therapy interaction chronogram. *International Journal of Group Psychotherapy, 28*(2), 185–194.

Redl, F. (1942). Group emotion and leadership. *Psychiatry, 5*, 573–596.

Redl, F. (1944). Diagnostic group work. *American Journal of Orthopsychiatry, 14*(1), 53–67.

Reid, K. E. (1997). *Social work practice with groups: A clinical perspective* (2nd ed.). Pacific Grove, CA: Brooks/Cole.

Reid, W. J. (1992). *Task strategies: An empirical approach to clinical social work.* New York: Columbia University Press.

Reid, W. J. (1994). The empirical practice movement. *Social Service Review, 68*(2), 165–184.

Reid, W. J., & Epstein, L. (1972). *Task-centered casework.* New York: Columbia University Press.

Reid, W. J., & Epstein, L. (1977). *Task-centered practice.* New York: Columbia University Press.

Richards, S. (1999). *Single subject research: Applications in educational and clinical settings.* San Diego: Singular Publication Group.

Ridley, C. R. (1995). *Overcoming unintentional racism in counseling and therapy: A practitioner's guide to intentional intervention.* Thousand Oaks, CA: SAGE.

Ringeisen, H., Henderson, K., & Hoagwood, K. (2003). Context matters: Schools and the "research to practice gap" in children's mental health. *School Psychology Review, 32*(2), 153–168.

Rose, S. D. (1969). A behavioral approach to the group treatment of parents. *Social Work, 14*, 21–29.

Rose, S. D. (1977). *Group therapy: A behavioral approach.* Englewood Cliffs, NJ: Prentice Hall.

Rose, S. D. (1980). *A casebook in group therapy: A behavioral-cognitive approach.* Englewood Cliffs, NJ: Prentice Hall.

Rose, S. D. (1984). Use of data in identifying and resolving group problems in goal oriented treatment groups. *Social Work with Groups, 7*(2), 23–36.

Rose, S. D. (1992). Utilization of research in group work practice: An example. In A. J. Grasso & I. Epstein (Eds.), *Research utilization in the social services: Innovations for practice and administration* (pp. 133–147). New York: Haworth Press.

Rose, S. D. (1998). *Group therapy with troubled youth: A cognitive behavioral interactive approach.* Thousand Oaks: SAGE.

Rose, S. D. (2004). Cognitive-behavioral group work. In C. D. Garvin, L. M. Gutierrez, & M. J. Galinsky (Eds.), *Handbook of social work with groups* (pp. 111–135). New York: Guilford.

Rosen, G. M. (1999). Treatment fidelity and research on eye movement desensitization and reprocessing (EMDR). *Journal of Anxiety Disorders, 13*(1–2), 173–184.

Rosenblum, A., Magura, S., Kayman, D. J., & Fong, C. (2005). Motivationally enhanced group counseling for substance users in a soup kitchen: A randomized clinical trial. *Drug and Alcohol Dependence, 80*(1), 91–103.

Rosenheck, R. A. (2001). Organizational process: A missing link between research and practice. *Psychiatric Services, 52*(12), 1607–1612.

Rosenthal, R. (1979). The file drawer problem and tolerance for null results. *Psychological Bulletin, 86*(3), 638–641.

Rosenthal, R., & Rubin, D. B. (1979). A note on percent variance explained as a measure of the importance of effects. *Journal of Applied Social Psychology, 9*(5), 395–396.

Rosenthal, R., & Rubin, D. B. (1982). Comparing effect sizes of independent studies. *Psychological Bulletin, 92*(2), 500–504.

Rosenthal, R. N. (2004). Overview of evidence-based practice. In A. R. Roberts & K. Yeager (Eds.), *Evidence-based practice manual: Research and outcome measures in health and human services* (pp. 20–29). New York: Oxford University Press.

Rothman, J. (1980). *Social R & D: Research and development in the human services.* Englewood Cliffs, NJ: Prentice Hall.

Rothman, J., & Thomas, E. J. (1994). *Intervention research: Design and development for human service.* New York: Haworth Press.

Rubin, A., & Babbie, E. R. (2005). *Research methods for social work* (5th ed.). Belmont, CA: Thomson Brooks/Cole.

Rycroft-Malone, J., Harvey, G., Kitson, A., McCormack, B., Seers, K., & Titchen, A. (2002). Getting evidence into practice: Ingredients for change. *Nursing Standard, 16*(37), 38–43.

Rycroft-Malone, J., Kitson, A., Harvey, G., McCormack, B., Seers, K., Titchen, A., et al. (2002). Ingredients for change: Revisiting a conceptual framework. *Quality and Safety in Health Care, 11*(2), 174–180.

Sackett, D. L., Rosenberg, W. M., Gray, J. A., Haynes, R. B., & Richardson, W. S. (1996). Evidence based medicine: What it is and what it isn't. *BMJ, 312*(7023), 71–72.

Sampl, S., & Kadden, R. (2001). *Motivational enhancement therapy and cognitive behavioral therapy (MET-CBT-5) for adolescent cannabis users, Cannabis Youth Treatment (CYT) Manual Series, Vol. 1.* (No. DHHS Publication No. [SMA] 01–3486). Rockville, MD: Center for Substance Abuse Treatment, Substance Abuse and Mental Health Services Administration.

Saunders, B. E., Berliner, L., & Hanson, R. F. (Eds.). (2003). *Child physical and sexual abuse: Guidelines for treatment (Final Report: January 15, 2003).* Charleston, SC: National Crime Victims Research and Treatment Center.

Schiller, L. Y. (1995). Stages of development in women's groups: A relational model. In R. Kurland & R. Salmon (Eds.), *Group work practice in a troubled society: Problems and opportunities* (pp. 117–138). New York: Haworth Press.

Schnurr, P. P., Friedman, M. J., Foy, D. W., Shea, M. T., Hsieh, F. Y., Lavori, P. W., et al. (2003). Randomized trial of trauma-focused group therapy for posttraumatic stress disorder: Results from a Department of Veterans Affairs cooperative study. *Archives of General Psychiatry, 60*(5), 481–489.

Schopler, J. H., & Galinsky, M. J. (1981). When groups go wrong. *Social Work, 26,* 424–429.

Schutz, W. (1992). Beyond FIRO-B: Three new theory-derived measures - Element B: Behavior, Element F: Feelings, Element S: Self. *Psychological Reports, 70*(3), 915–937.

Shaneyfelt, T., Baum, K. D., Bell, D., Feldstein, D., Houston, T. K., Kaatz, S., et al. (2006). Instruments for evaluating education in evidence-based practice: A systematic review. *Journal of the American Medical Association, 296*(9), 1116–1127.

Shaughnessy, A. F., Slawson, D. C., & Bennett, J. H. (1994). Becoming an information master: A guidebook to the medical information jungle. *Journal of Family Practice, 39*(5), 489–499.

Sheafor, B. W., & Horejsi, C. R. (2003). *Techniques and guidelines for social work practice* (6th ed.). Boston: Allyn and Bacon.

Sheafor, B. W., & Horejsi, C. R. (2006). *Techniques and guidelines for social work practice* (7th ed.). Boston: Allyn and Bacon.

Shechtman, Z. (2003). Therapeutic factors and outcomes in group and individual therapy of aggressive boys. *Group Dynamics, 7*(3), 225–237.

Sheldon, T. A., Guyatt, G. H., & Haines, A. (1998). Getting research findings into practice: When to act on the evidence. *BMJ, 317*(7151), 139–142.

Sherrod, L. R. (1999). "Giving child development knowledge away": Using university-community partnerships to disseminate research on children, youth, and families. *Applied Developmental Science, 3*(4), 228–234.

Shulman, L. (2006). *The skills of helping individuals, families, groups and communities* (5th ed.). Belmont, CA: Thomson Higher Education.

Siegel, D. H. (1984). Defining empirically based practice. *Social Work, 29*(4), 325–329.

Siepker, B. B., & Kandaras, C. S. (1985). *Group therapy with children and adolescents: A treatment manual.* New York: Human Sciences Press.

Silbergeld, S., Koenig, H. G., Manderscheid, R. W., Meeker, B. F., & Hornung, C. A. (1975). Assessment of environment-therapy systems: the Group Atmosphere Scale. *Journal of Consulting and Clinical Psychology, 43*(4), 460–469.

Simpson, D. D. (2002). A conceptual framework for transferring research to practice. *Journal of Substance Abuse Treatment, 22*(4), 171–182.

Sims, G. K., & Sims, J. M. (1973). Does face-to-face contact reduce counselee responsiveness with emotionally insecure youth? *Psychotherapy: Theory, Research & Practice, 10*(4), 348–351.

Slawson, D. C., & Shaughnessy, A. F. (2000). Becoming an information master: Using POEMs to change practice with confidence. Patient-Oriented Evidence that Matters. *Journal of Family Practice, 49*(1), 63–67.

Slawson, D. C., Shaughnessy, A. F., & Bennett, J. H. (1994). Becoming a medical information master: Feeling good about not knowing everything. *Journal of Family Practice, 38*(5), 505–513.

Slocum, Y. S. (1987). A survey of expectations about group therapy among clinical and nonclinical populations. *International Journal of Group Psychotherapy, 37*(1), 39–54.

Smaby, M. H., Maddux, C. D., Torres-Rivera, E., & Zimmick, R. (1999). A study of the effects of a skills-based versus a conventional group counseling training program. *Journal for Specialists in Group Work, 24,* 152–163.

Smokowski, P. R., Rose, S. D., & Bacallao, M. (2001). Damaging experiences in therapeutic groups: How vulnerable consumers become group casualties. *Small Group Research, 28*(1), 9–22.

Soanes, C. (2003). *Compact Oxford English dictionary* (2nd ed.). New York: Oxford University Press.

Soldz, S., Budman, S., Davis, M., & Demby, A. (1993). Beyond the interpersonal circumplex in group psychotherapy: The structure and relationship to outcome of the Individual Group Member Interpersonal Process Scale. *Journal of Clinical Psychology, 49*(4), 551–563.

Spencer, J. A., & Jordan, R. K. (1999). Learner centered approaches in medical education. *British Medical Journal, 318*(7193), 1280–1283.

Spodick, D. H. (1975). On experts and expertise: The effect of variability in observer performance. *American Journal of Cardiology, 36*(5), 592–596.

Steering Committee. (2002). Empirically supported therapy relationships: Conclusions and recommendations of the Division 29 Task Force. In J. C. Norcross (Ed.), *Psychotherapy relationships that work: Therapist contributions and responsiveness to patients* (pp. 441–443). New York: Oxford University Press.

Steinbrook, R. (2005). Public access to NIH-funded research. *New England Journal of Medicine, 352*(17), 1739–1741.

Stiles, W. B., Startup, M., Hardy, G. E., Barkham, M., Rees, A., Shapiro, D. A., et al. (1996). Therapist session intentions in cognitive-behavioral and psychodynamic-interpersonal psychotherapy. *Journal of Counseling Psychology, 43*(4), 402–414.

Stinchfield, R. D., & Burlingame, G. M. (1991). Development and use of the Directives Rating System in group therapy. *Journal of Counseling Psychology, 38*(3), 251–257.

Stinchfield, R., Owen, P. L., & Winters, K. C. (1994). Group therapy for substance abuse: A review of the empirical literature. In A. Fuhriman & G. M. Burlingame (Eds.), *Handbook of group psychotherapy: An empirical and clinical synthesis* (pp. 458–488). New York: Wiley.

Stinchfield, R. D., & Burlingame, G. M. (1991). Development and use of the Directives Rating System in group therapy. *Journal of Counseling Psychology, 38*(3), 251–257.

Stone, M. H., Lewis, C. M., & Beck, A. P. (1994). The structure of Yalom's Curative Factors Scale. *International Journal of Group Psychotherapy, 44*(2), 239–245.

Straus, S. E., Green, M. L., Bell, D. S., Badgett, R., Davis, D., Gerrity, M., et al. (2004). Evaluating the teaching of evidence based medicine: A conceptual framework. *British Medical Journal, 329*(7473), 1029–1032.

Straus, S. E., Richardson, W. S., Glasziou, P., & Haynes, R. B. (2005). *Evidence-based medicine: How to practice and teach EBM* (3rd ed.). Edinburgh: Churchill Livingstone.

Strauss, A. L., & Corbin, J. M. (1990). *Basics of qualitative research: Grounded theory procedures and techniques.* Newbury Park, CA: SAGE.

Stuart, G. W. (2001). Evidence-based psychiatric nursing practice: Rhetoric or reality. *Journal of the American Psychiatric Nurses Association, 7*(4), 103–111.

Stuart, G. W., Tondora, J., & Hoge, M. A. (2004). Evidence-based teaching practice: Implications for behavioral health. *Administration and Policy in Mental Health, 32*(2), 107–130.

Thibaut, J. W., & Kelley, H. H. (1959). *The social psychology of groups.* New York: Wiley.

Thomas, E. J. (1984). *Designing interventions for the helping professions.* Beverly Hills, CA: SAGE.

Thomas, E. J. (1992). The design and development model of practice research. In A. J. Grasso & I. Epstein (Eds.), *Research utilization in the social services: Innovations for practice and administration* (pp. 71–92). New York: Haworth Press.

Thomas, G. W. (1943). Group psychotherapy: A review of the recent literature. *Psychosomatic Medicine, 5,* 166–180.

Thomlison, B., & Corcoran, K. (2007). *The evidence-based internship: A field manual for social work and criminal justice.* New York: Oxford University Press.

Thyer, B. (1996). Forty years of progress toward empirical clinical practice? *Social Work Research, 20*(2), 77–81.

Tillitski, C. J. (1990). A meta-analysis of estimated effect sizes for group versus individual versus control treatments. *International Journal of Group Psychotherapy, 40*(2), 215–224.

Tinsley, H. E., Roth, J. A., & Lease, S. H. (1989). Dimensions of leadership and leadership style among group intervention specialists. *Journal of Counseling Psychology, 36*(1), 48–53.

Tolman, R. M., & Molidor, C. E. (1994). A decade of social group work research: Trends in methodology, theory, and program development. *Research on Social Work Practice, 4*(2), 142–159.

Tolson, E. R., Reid, W. J., & Garvin, C. D. (2003). *Generalist practice: A task-centered approach* (2nd ed.). New York: Columbia University Press.

Toseland, R. W., Jones, L. V., & Gellis, Z. D. (2004). Group dynamics. In C. D. Garvin, M. J. Galinsky, & P. M. Gutierrez (Eds.), *Handbook of social work with groups* (pp. 13–31). New York: Guilford.

Toseland, R. W., & Rivas, R. F. (2005). *An introduction to group work practice* (5th ed.). Boston: Pearson/Allyn and Bacon.

Treadwell, T., Lavertue, N., Kumar, V. K., & Veeraraghavan, V. (2001). The Group Cohesion Scale-Revised: Reliability and validity. *International Journal of Action Methods: Psychodrama, Skill Training, and Role Playing, 54*(1), 3–12.

Trijsburg, R. W., Frederiks, G. C. F. J., Gorlee, M., Klouwer, E., den Hollander, A. M., & Duivenvoorden, H. J. (2002). Development of the Comprehensive Psychotherapeutic Interventions Rating Scale (CPIRS). *Psychotherapy Research, 12*(3), 287–317.

Tripodi, T. (1994). *A primer on single-subject design for clinical social workers.* Washington, DC: NASW Press.

Tripodi, T., & Epstein, I. (1980). *Research techniques for clinical social workers.* New York: Columbia University Press.

Tripodi, T., Fellin, P., & Meyer, H. J. (1969). *The assessment of social research: Guidelines for the use of research in social work and social science.* Itasca, IL: F. E. Peacock.

Tzeng, O. C. S. (1993). *Measurement of love and intimate relations: Theories, scales, and applications for love development, maintenance, and dissolution.* Westport, CN: Praeger.

van Andel, P., Erdman, R. A. M., Karsdorp, P. A., Appels, A., & Trijsburg, R. W. (2003). Group cohesion and working alliance: Prediction of treatment outcome in cardiac patients receiving cognitive behavioral group psychotherapy. *Psychotherapy & Psychosomatics, 72*(3), 141–149.

Vandiver, V. L. (2002). Step-by-step practice guidelines for using evidence-based practice and expert consensus in mental health settings. In A. R. Roberts &

G. J. Greene (Eds.), *Social workers' desk reference*. New York: Oxford University Press.

Vevea, J. L., & Woods, C. M. (2005). Publication bias in research synthesis: Sensitivity analysis using a priori weight functions. *Psychological Methods, 10*(4), 428–443.

Vogt, W. P. (1999). *Dictionary of statistics and methodology: A nontechnical guide for the social sciences* (2nd ed.). Thousand Oaks, CA: SAGE.

Waites, C., Macgowan, M. J., Pennell, J., Carlton-LaNey, I., & Weil, M. (2004). Increasing the cultural responsiveness of family group conferencing. *Social Work, 49*(2), 291–300.

Waltz, C. F., Jenkins, L. S., & Strickland, O. (2001). *Measurement of nursing outcomes* (2nd ed.). New York: Springer.

Webb, C., Scudder, M., Kaminer, Y., & Kadden, R. (2002). *The motivational enhancement therapy and cognitive behavioral therapy supplement: 7 sessions of cognitive behavioral therapy for adolescent cannabis users, Cannabis Youth Treatment (CYT) Series, Vol. 2* (No. DHHS Pub. No. [SMA] 02-3659). Rockville, MD: Center for Substance Abuse Treatment, Substance Abuse and Mental Health Services Administration.

Webster-Stratton, C. (1997). From parent training to community building. *Families in Society, 78*(2), 156–171.

Weisz, J. R., Chu, B. C., & Polo, A. J. (2004). Treatment dissemination and evidence-based practice: Strengthening intervention through clinician-researcher collaboration. *Clinical Psychology: Science and Practice, 11*(3), 300–307.

Westen, D., & Weinberger, J. (2004). When clinical description becomes statistical prediction. *American Psychologist, 59*(7), 595–613.

Wheelan, S. A., Buzaglo, G., & Tsumura, E. (1998). Developing assessment tools for cross-cultural group research. *Small Group Research, 29*(3), 359–370.

Wheelan, S. A., & Hochberger, J. M. (1996). Validation studies of the Group Development Questionnaire. *Small Group Research, 27*(1), 143–170.

Wheelan, S. A., Verdi, A. F., & McKeage, R. (1994). *The Group Development Observation System: Origins and applications*. Philadelphia: PEP Press.

Whipple, J. L., Lambert, M. J., Vermeersch, D. A., Smart, D. W., Nielsen, S. L., & Hawkins, E. J. (2003). Improving the effects of psychotherapy: The use of early identification of treatment and problem-solving strategies in routine practice. *Journal of Counseling Psychology, 50*(1), 59–68.

Wilson, G. (1976). From practice to theory: A personalized history. In R. W. Roberts & H. Northen (Eds.), *Theories of social work with groups* (pp. 1–44). New York: Columbia University Press.

Wilson, G., & Ryland, G. (1949). *Social group work practice: The creative use of the social process*. Boston, MA: Houghton Mifflin.

Wilson, S. J. (1980). *Recording guidelines for social workers*. New York: Free Press.

Wood, D., Kumar, V. K., Treadwell, T. W., & Leach, E. (1998). Perceived cohesiveness and sociometric choice in ongoing groups. *International Journal of Action Methods, 51*(3), 122–137.

Yalom, I. D. (1995). *The theory and practice of group psychotherapy* (4th ed.). New York: Basic Books.

Yalom, I. D., & Leszcz, M. (2005). *The theory and practice of group psychotherapy* (5th ed.). New York: Basic Books.

Zaidi, L. Y., & Gutierrez-Kovner, V. M. (1995). Group treatment of sexually abused latency-age girls. *Journal of Interpersonal Violence, 10*(2), 215–227.

Zastrow, C. (2001). *Social work with groups: Using the class as a group leadership laboratory* (5th ed.). Pacific Grove, CA: Brooks Cole/Thomson Learning.

Zerhouni, E. A. (2006). Translational and clinical science: Time for a new vision. *New England Journal of Medicine, 353*(15), 1621–1623.

Index

A GUIDE TO

EVIDENCE-BASED

GROUP WORK

MARK J. MACGOWAN